VALUE-ADDED
PUBLIC RELATIONS

VALUE-ADDED PUBLIC RELATIONS

The Secret Weapon of Integrated Marketing

THOMAS L. HARRIS

Foreword by Philip Kotler

NTC Business Books

NTC/Contemporary Publishing Group

Library of Congress Cataloging-in-Publication Data.

Harris, Thomas L., 1931–
    Value-added public relations: the secret weapon of integrated
marketing / Thomas L. Harris; foreword by Philip Kotler.
      p.   cm.
    Includes bibliographical references and index.
    ISBN 0-8442-3411-7.—ISBN 0-8442-3412-5 (pbk.)
    1. Communication in marketing.   I. Title.
HF5415.123.H37   1998
659.2—dc21   97-37323
                                    CIP

Cover design by Scott Rattray
Interior design by City Desktop Productions, Inc.

Published by NTC Business Books
An imprint of NTC/Contemporary Publishing Group, Inc.
4255 West Touhy Avenue, Lincolnwood (Chicago), Illinois 60646-1975 U.S.A.
Copyright © 1998 by Thomas L. Harris
Printed in the United States of America
International Standard Book Number: 0-8442-3411-7 (cloth)
                                        0-8442-3412-5 (paper)
15   14   13   12   11   10   9   8   7   6   5   4   3   2

" This book is dedicated to the memory of my friend and colleague, Ron Kaatz, visionary professional, gifted teacher, and altogether extraordinary human being. His positive spirit touched all who knew him. "

Contents

Part II How to Write an Integrated Marketing Public Relations Plan

Foreword

Businesses operating in today's marketplace must feel like they are walking through a minefield. Markets are splintering into niches, customers are forsaking their brand loyalties, competitors are proliferating, and communication and information channels are exploding. Very few companies feel that they face a secure future.

In the midst of these upheavals, companies are desperately searching for new answers to age-old questions. The questions haven't changed: How do we win new customers? How do we keep our current customers? How do we develop a sustainable competitive advantage that differentiates us from our competitors and wins the continuing loyalty of our customers?

The old answers—to spend megabucks on mass advertising, roll out endless promotions, dispatch a battle-weary sales force—no longer work. A growing number of companies are turning to one promising new answer called *integrated marketing communications (IMC)*. IMC is not simply a call for integrating the various and proliferating means of communication so that they work together and deliver one message. Yes, it is true that company planning of advertising, sales force strategy, sales promotions, direct marketing, and public relations needs to be coordinated. But IMC goes beyond a call for consistent and comprehensive communication planning. IMC is rooted in the notion that consumers do the integration! Consumers put together all their information and experiences and come out with favorable or unfavorable perceptions of companies, products, and brands.

IMC assumes that consumers base their decisions on their perceptions of reality, rather than on reality itself. Consumers buy a Sony if they think it is better than a Panasonic. They don't really know. They don't take apart the Sony and Panasonic TV sets and examine them from an engineering point of view.

They choose the Sony because of a multitude of favorable impressions, experiences, and conversations that they have had about different brands.

All planned communication must start with a rich understanding of all the ways that consumers receive and process information. Marketers must strive to deliver a consistent picture of their brand positions and company position through all the channels that reach consumers. For example, it doesn't help to advertise that Progresso soup has superior quality if the soup cans occupy only a few facings on the lowest supermarket shelves and the cans look dusty and undistinguished. It doesn't help to promote the image that a hotel is friendly if many guests experience surly desk clerks.

Marketers, of course, can only control a fraction of the impressions that consumers receive about companies, products, and brands. Yet the fraction they control, if handled well, can make a major difference in consumer perceptions and company success. And handling these communication tools well means working them in tandem, creating a consistent and distinctive brand-building message stream.

Of the five major communication tools—advertising, personal selling, sales promotion, direct marketing, and marketing public relations—it is the last two that are receiving the most attention and recording the most growth. Direct marketing can account for its growth in being able to customize its messages to segments of one, carry on dialogue and not just monologue, and obtain a pretty good measure of response and therefore communication effectiveness. Public relations can account for its growth by its great versatility, its aptitude for drama, and its capacity to break through the information clutter and capture attention and interest.

It is the science and art of marketing public relations (MPR) that Tom Harris has addressed through *The Marketer's Guide to Public Relations*; he now offers a sequel whose plot and story lines are as absorbing as those in his previous book. This time Tom Harris embeds public relations in the larger marketing paradigm of integrated marketing communications. He relates MPR to all the other communication tools and also shows the role that MPR is playing in the emerging electronic media. He shows how Microsoft, Chrysler, General Motors, and numerous other companies have used MPR to establish such powerful brands as Windows 95, Neon, Saturn, and many others. When you are finished reading this book, you will appreciate, as never before, the power of creative MPR to develop and nourish great companies, products, and brands.

Philip Kotler
S. C. Johnson Distinguished Professor of
 International Marketing
J. L. Kellogg Graduate School of Management,
 Northwestern University

Preface

The Marketer's Guide to Public Relations, published in 1991, was the first book devoted exclusively to the role of public relations in marketing. During the past half dozen years, that role has been dramatically enhanced. Marketers are far more aware of the value that public relations adds to marketing, thus the title of this book.

In my earlier book, I devoted the grand total of one page to the subject of integrated marketing. Since that time, integration has become the most important new marketing concept of the times. Integrated marketing communications (IMC) has been defined many times and in many ways. Some academics and practitioners alike have appropriated the label to support their pet theories. Despite all these theoretical constructs and at the risk of oversimplification, I believe that IMC is simply the strategic coordination of all the elements of a marketing campaign. The primary elements are advertising, sales promotion, direct marketing, and marketing public relations. Few could deny the value that is added to marketing programs when all the pieces are working together.

This is the first book to specifically examine the many ways that public relations is used to add value to integrated marketing. I have cited dozens of case histories that document the successful application of MPR to integrated programs by the nation's most successful marketers. In each case, I have provided readers with a list of "Lessons Learned" that they can apply to their own marketing programs. You don't have to be Coca-Cola, McDonald's, or Microsoft to add value to your integrated marketing through the strategic use of public relations.

The Marketer's Guide only tangentially refers to the massive changes that technology has brought to the way we live, work, play, learn, and communicate. Technology has affected every aspect of our lives and has greatly expanded the boundaries of marketing and public relations. It has added a number of new tools that have quickly become incorporated into standard public relations practice. You will find numerous references to Web sites, satellite conferences, e-mail, online forums, and more throughout the book. Of even greater significance in the future will be the shifting emphasis from directing one-way communications to "publics" to communicating interactively with people one-on-one.

In assembling the material for this book, I have included only those programs that reached me as a reader, listener, viewer, and consumer. If I didn't clip it or tape it myself, it's not here, no matter how many industry accolades it might have earned.

That said, I am grateful to the marketing, advertising, and particularly the public relations trade press for letting me in on the thinking and planning behind these programs that attracted my attention. You will find references to and quotes from *Advertising Age, Adweek, Brandweek, Inside PR, Reputation Management, Jack O'Dwyer's Newsletter, O'Dwyer's PR Services Report, Public Relations News, PR Reporter, PR Tactics,* and *The Public Relations Strategist.*

Also invaluable has been the background information and campaign materials provided by companies including Ben & Jerry's, Binney & Smith, Campbell's, Coca-Cola, Chrysler, Walt Disney, Eastman Kodak, Frito-Lay, Gillette, Harley-Davidson, McDonald's, Miller Brewing Company, Nintendo of America, Nissan Motor Corporation USA, Ocean Spray, Pillsbury, Pepsi-Cola, Procter & Gamble, Saturn, Taco Bell, and the U.S. Postal Service. I also want to thank the leading public relations firms whose work is reported in these pages. They include Bozell Public Relations, Burson-Marsteller, Cohn & Wolfe, Cone Communications, Creamer Dickson Basford, The Dilenschneider Group, Edelman Public Relations Worldwide, Fleishman-Hillard, Flowers Communications Group, Golin/Harris Communications, Hill & Knowlton, Ketchum Public Relations, Laughlin Constable, Manning, Selvage & Lee, Marina Maher Communications, Porter-Novelli, Ruder-Finn, Shandwick USA, Patrice Tanaka & Co., and Warner, Bicking, Morris & Partners. Their work is giving new dimension to the practice of marketing public relations.

Some material in this book has appeared in other forms in *The Handbook of Strategic Public Relations & Integrated Marketing* (McGraw-Hill) and in these periodicals, *Direct Marketing, Public Relations Quarterly,* and *The Public Relations Strategist.* There are a number of references to updated material that first appeared in *The Marketer's Guide to Public Relations* (John Wiley & Son).

I also want to thank my colleagues at the Medill School of Journalism at Northwestern University for the opportunity to teach what I believe to be the first graduate course in marketing public relations. Much of what is in this book first saw the light of day in my classroom.

I want to make it very clear that while the purview of this book is marketing public relations, the function of public relations as practiced by corporations and other institutions, and in their behalf by public relations firms, far exceeds its marketing support function. The principal role of the corporate communications departments and public relations firms cited here and their counterparts throughout the country and the world remains and, in my view, will continue to remain, to counsel management on relationships with all the stakeholders on whose understanding and support corporate health and indeed survival depends—in the current lexicon, to manage the corporate reputation. Those stakeholders include employees, investors, legislators, regulators, and communities, as well as consumers and those that influence them. While marketing may not be everything and everything not marketing, it should be noted that employee jobs and shareholder equity largely depend on marketing success. No top line. No bottom line.

I hope that the documented MPR-driven marketing success stories cited in the first part of this book will inspire more marketers to give public relations the opportunity to add value to their integrated programs, and that the second part of the book will help both marketers and public relations people to plan MPR programs that work.

Thomas L. Harris
Highland Park, Illinois
February 1997

VALUE-ADDED
PUBLIC RELATIONS

.

PART I

How Public Relations Adds Value to Integrated Marketing

The integrated marketing communications process begins with a business problem, does not assume an advertising solution, takes the time necessary to research and develop an integrated strategy that puts all elements in place before pulling the trigger.[1]

—Don Schultz

CHAPTER 1

The Secret Weapon of
Integrated Marketing

INTEGRATED MARKETING COMMUNICATIONS (IMC) IS THE MARKETING *concept* of the 1990s. It will be the marketing *practice* necessary for survival in the 21st century.

The advent of integration is causing marketers, weaned on media advertising as the solution to all marketing problems, to take a fresh look at all the components of marketing and specifically to consider the unique dimension that public relations brings to the marketing mix. Public relations people in turn are seizing the opportunity that integration offers them to make a difference where it counts most to their companies and clients—on the bottom line.

Integrated marketing communications is the culmination of the shift that began in the post–World War II period, from selling what we make to making what consumers want. IMC is focused on what customers want to know about products and services, not what marketers want to tell them in order to sell them.

IMC may be news but it's not new. Thirty or so years ago, as a young public relations executive, I attended my first meeting of the American Marketing Association (AMA). The association's president that year was the top marketing executive of RCA. His speech made a lasting impression on me because it made so much sense. He said that marketers were wasting too much time and money on advertising, public relations, and promotion programs that were poorly, if at all, coordinated. He said that these disparate efforts were

3

counterproductive and confusing to consumers. And he said that it was high time for marketers to get their acts together by coordinating all their marketing programs.

While the proposition was hard to disagree with, there was in those days no compelling reason to get serious about integration—especially if it meant shaking up the organization. Those were the glory days of marketing. Everything was going so well for so many American companies. Americans were rebounding from wartime shortages. They had money and were in the mood to spend it. They were buying new cars and TV sets and all manner of merchandise they saw advertised on the three TV networks or read about in the big general-interest magazines such as *Life, Look,* and the *Saturday Evening Post.* These mass media effectively delivered sales messages about mass-appeal products to a receptive mass audience.

Advertising was king. Promotion was underdeveloped, direct marketing was in its infancy, and, as I discovered early on, public relations was largely an afterthought.

How times have changed!

The mass market has fragmented. As consumers we are better educated, more skeptical, and less vulnerable to a slick sales pitch. We are bombarded with an endless stream of sales messages not just in our homes and cars but wherever we go, whatever we do. They follow us to the movies, the ballpark, the store.

Our TV sets typically receive not three but fifty stations loaded with commercials of varying length from the fifteen-second spots we used to call IDs to half-hour "infomercials," and we are told that a 500-channel assault is on the way. Teens, tweens, boomers, busters, and whatever they now call people my age all watch different shows at different times.

Some of the time we used to spend viewing commercial television is now spent watching videos and playing commercial-free video games. And more and more, our computers have become the venue of entertainment and information as well as work. That is, when we are not reading a book, eating out, working out, playing sports, shopping, taking in a movie, going to a play, a museum, a sports event or a concert, or taking the kids out to play.

Crunch Time for Marketers

If you think we, as consumers, have too many choices, think about the marketer whose job it is to sell us stuff. These are times that try marketing men's and women's souls. They are expected to meet short-term goals while building long-term brand equity. They must work their way through an infinitely more complex marketplace than could have been imagined in the good old days of even a decade ago. People as well as numbers are being crunched.

Network television advertising, the principal medium of mass marketing for nearly a half century, is no longer able to deliver mass numbers of undifferentiated consumers at an affordable cost per thousand (CPM) for all but the most universally consumed products. Then, too, the price of admission, the cost of TV commercial production, is rapidly rising as advertising seeks more innovative, often more expensive ways to grab the consumer's attention.

Change is, of course, the law of business life today. Virtually every company is being forced to reexamine every function of its business operations.

The facts of marketing life today demand that, in order to survive, much less prosper, in an increasingly competitive global marketplace, marketers need to find new ways to get more bang for their marketing bucks. They are beginning to recognize that TV advertising is not the answer to every marketing question and they are examining a variety of options once considered peripheral to marketing campaigns.

A Deceptively Simple Idea

Integrated marketing communications is a deceptively simple idea. It is, in a word, synergy.

> In marketing, synergy means that when all product and corporate messages are strategically coordinated, the effect is greater than when advertising, sales promotion, public relations, etc., are planned and executed independently, with each competing for budgets and power and in some cases sending out conflicting messages, according to Tom Duncan, director of the integrated communications graduate program at the University of Colorado.[2]

Advertising Age sees IMC as "the process of combining a variety of functions that may include advertising, sales promotion, direct response, database marketing, public relations, or direct marketing into a program that has clarity, consistency, and maximum impact."[3]

The Pivotal Role of Public Relations

These definitions make it clear that public relations is a critical element in integrated marketing.

Recent surveys of marketing executives found not only near universal acceptance of the integrated marketing concept but also near unanimous agreement that public relations plays an integral role in its success.

Marketing executives surveyed for *Advertising Age* by OmniTech Consulting Group, Chicago, in 1993, reported that integrated marketing was already very important to their organization's success and said that its importance would be even greater in the next five years. Nine out of ten respondents claimed current participation in an IMC effort.

The survey reveals that while advertising is the most universally applied component of IMC programs, public relations and sales promotion were named as components nine times out of ten.

While respondents felt strongly that IMC improves marketing effectiveness and efficiency, only four in ten felt strongly that clients benefit from one-stop shopping. OmniTech consultant Michael Krauss concluded that clients are looking for "best solutions," adding that "few agencies can claim best-of-breed coverage across the spectrum of integrated communications."[4]

A 1996 survey conducted by The Cantor Concern, an executive recruiting firm specializing in the communications field, confirms the trend toward integrating the public relations function in the marketing mix.

How Public Relations Closes the Credibility Gap

Years ago, Harvard marketing expert Theodore Levitt, author of the classic *Marketing Myopia* and father of global marketing, pointed out the distinction between the public relations message and the advertising message. He labeled public relations "the credible source," pointing out that when the message is delivered by an objective third party, such as a journalist or broadcaster, the message is delivered more persuasively.

This view is every bit as relevant today as it was then. In his influential book *Relationship Marketing*, Silicon Valley marketing guru Regis McKenna writes that while "advertising and public relations can perform many of the same functions, information coming from the press is usually more credible. Articles in the media are perceived as being more objective than advertisements. If a company can win favorable press coverage, its message is more likely to be absorbed and believed."[5]

What IMC Is

Northwestern University's Medill School of Journalism, where I teach, defines IMC as "the process of managing all sources of information about a product/service to which a customer or prospect is exposed which behaviorally moves the customer toward a sale and maintains customer loyalty."[6]

According to studies conducted by both Northwestern and Colorado, integrated marketing has found overwhelming support among marketing decision makers because they believe it provides greater consistency, it reduces waste, and it gives the company a competitive advantage.

IMC is about speaking with one voice. It's about better management of the marketing process so that all messages about a product or service to which a customer is exposed are coordinated and controlled. It's about assuring consistency of messages at every contact point where company meets consumer. It's about integrating the organization with its customers. It's about building relationships, not just making sales. It's about looking at business from the consumer's point of view.

What IMC Is Not

IMC is not about one-stop shopping.

Clients surveyed by Northwestern for the American Association of Advertising Agencies (AAAA) said that they believed the job of integrating is too big and too important to be delegated to their advertising agency, that they didn't want a single agency for advertising, direct marketing, sales promotion, and public relations, and that they themselves must take responsibility for the coordination of their integrated programs. They want to do the integrating themselves and they want to pick the best sources, regardless of parentage.

Marketers are no longer looking to their advertising agencies as the source from which all good ideas must spring. Smart clients are looking for brilliant strategic thinking, creative tactical options, and executional ability from any and all sources, internal and external. Their advertising agencies may be able to do it all. But clients aren't counting on it. Many have had bad experiences with agencies that have confused one voice with one invoice.

IMC isn't a new way for advertising agencies to package their services. There is a world of difference between integration that is in the client's best interests and cross-selling that is in the agency's best interests.

Clients are becoming aware of the pecking-order problems of so-called full-service advertising agencies that often prevent the best ideas from the agency's public relations, promotion, or direct marketing units from seeing the light of day, especially if it means taking dollars from the media budget.

The new-style communications conglomerates that have acquired many of the largest public relations firms in recent years have abandoned the "whole egg" approach. When Omnicom acquired Fleishman-Hillard, one of the largest independent public relations firms, Omnicom President and CEO John Wren said, "You have to be pretty arrogant to think that just because an advertising group wants to reorganize its assets, that's a compelling reason for clients to change the way they buy marketing services. It's even more absurd to think that a good public relations professional is going to make himself subservient to an advertising account director just because the agency said that's the way it should be."

IMC is not about marketing taking over all the communications functions of an organization. Marketing is the vital core of the business. Most marketers are totally focused on the profitable marketing of goods and services. They have neither the capacity nor the inclination to be deterred from that mission. Neither do they have the experience nor the perspective to assume responsibility for communications with other critical corporate stakeholders such as employees, investors, community organizations, and government officials.

Finally, IMC isn't, in my view, another name for database marketing. IMC is an "outside-in" process that begins with an understanding of the individual consumer. But that doesn't mean that in our integrated future, all marketing messages will be delivered to consumers one at a time. Target marketing and even mass marketing aren't going away. The mass media are alive and well. Television continues to be sold out because mass marketers believe it remains the most efficient way to reach masses of consumers. At least ten million and as many as fifteen million viewers watch the top-rated network programs. Despite the dent that online time has made in viewing time, Americans still watch TV three hours a day. Those viewers are exposed not only to advertising but also to public relations messages. I cannot foresee the time when what we now call "traditional media" will be replaced entirely by direct marketing, telemarketing, and interactive media. Rather, these media will take their place with media advertising, promotion, and public relations, as important integrated marketing options.

The Consumer as Integrator

The IMC process begins with the consumer. It requires that marketers radically shift from thinking "inside out" (what we have to sell, what we have to say) to "outside in" (what consumers tell us about themselves, their needs, wants, and lifestyles). Northwestern's Don Schultz says that integration doesn't occur at the agency or at the media level or even with the client. He believes that integration takes place with consumers "because the consumer is the only one who puts together the stuff we create and disseminate. They are the only people and the only place where all of our activities come together at one point and at one time."[7]

He's right. Consumers are, in fact, way ahead of us. It's just that we have become so enamored of our particular specialty that we have failed to recognize that consumers don't distinguish an advertising message from a public relations message. They don't know and don't care. And neither should we as long as we have made contact and it's working. Schultz says the critical dimension is "not what we think we delivered but what the customers or prospects believe they received."[8]

Integration works best when consumers draw on a bank of favorable information from a variety of sources to make a decision to try or buy our product.

The Keys to IMC Success

Integration requires a zero-based communications planning. That means starting from scratch without preconceived notions of what was done in the past. That frees marketers to choose the disciplines that will best fit the strategy.

From the outset, all marketing disciplines are created equal. Public relations has the opportunity to be heard. IMC success demands that all the key players—advertising, public relations, promotion, direct marketing, event marketing, etc.—collaborate as equal partners on the development of the best strategy to achieve the marketing objectives. This strategy incorporates the best thinking of all disciplines. The result may be a marketing program in which each plays a role, or it may be mutually determined that one discipline or the other is more or less essential for success. The resulting program may be driven by advertising or public relations or promotion, with the other disciplines playing supporting roles.

Barriers Versus Benefits

While there is near universal support for the concept of integrated marketing, studies conducted by Northwestern and Colorado identified a number of internal and external barriers to integration. Internally, they include turf battles, fear of departmental budget reductions, and fear of losing expertise in each communications area. External barriers to IMC are agency egos, fear of budget reductions, lack of knowledge about more than one communications area, and loss of motivation.

Despite these very real obstacles, the benefits far outweigh the difficulties:

- IMC delivers a clear consistent message that is both more efficient and more effective.
- It cuts through the increasingly cluttered commercial landscape.
- It fosters a two-way dialogue between consumers and companies.
- This interaction builds bonds that, in turn, lead to long-term consumer-to-brand relationships.

Critically important for the process is the fact that when cumulative messages are more consistent they become more credible.

Closing the Marketing Credibility Gap

Credibility is the key. And of all the components of integrated marketing, public relations alone possesses a priceless ingredient that is essential to every IMC program—its ability to lend credibility to the product message.

Advertising and promotion are about salesmanship. Consumers know it and are on the defensive against being sold something they don't want or need. Public relations, on the other hand, is about information. By providing information to consumers directly or through trusted third parties, public relations makes advertising more believable and promotion more actionable.

That is why public relations is the secret weapon of integrated marketing. Public relations is uniquely able to close the marketing credibility gap.

This book will tell you how to close the gap and unleash the power of positive public relations to make integrated marketing work harder and better. It draws on the experience of dozens of leading companies who have strategically applied the tools and techniques of public relations to achieve marketing success.

CHAPTER 2

Public Relations: The Credibility Quotient

THE SUCCESSFUL INTRODUCTION OF THE INFINITI J-30 WAS THE RESULT OF a two-year integrated marketing plan. Every discipline—marketing, public relations, and advertising—played a role and had a voice in determining the positioning of the vehicle. Brainstorming sessions for the project included people from Nissan's advertising agency, public relations firm, and training consultants, together with Nissan's advertising, public relations, and marketing team.

The integration team went to Japan to confer with their counterparts there. The program was fine-tuned to make sure the positioning in the United States and Japan was similar, while recognizing that consumers in the two countries have different sets of values and priorities. The integrated team began planning two years prior to the introduction, meeting at first monthly and accelerating to biweekly and weekly in the final stages. The result was an extraordinarily successful product introduction.

As a consumer, I know how well it worked. When I leased the brand new J-30, the salesman asked me what brought me in to see the car. No, it wasn't the television commercials starring Michael Douglas. Somehow I had missed them. But I didn't miss the rave reviews the car received in virtually every publication I picked up. Headlines such as "The Infiniti J-30 luxury sedan drives like a sports coupe in Jaguar clothing" worked on me.

Apparently, I'm not alone. The company's surveys show that consumers rank magazine articles as more influential than advertising on their vehicle-buying decisions.

A Peculiar Reality of Marketing

The effect of editorial endorsement has been documented in industry after industry. Take the case of red wine. In 1992, the CBS newsmagazine *60 Minutes*, one of the highest-rated shows on network television, reported that people in France whose diet is rich in butter and cream but who consume red wine with meals suffer far fewer heart attacks than Americans do. It suggested that drinking a moderate amount of red wine could prevent heart attacks by lowering cholesterol. The effect was so astonishing that red wine sales in the United States increased 50 percent after the broadcast. *60 Minutes* was so impressed with its own influence on wine sales that it proudly pointed it out on the program's twenty-fifth anniversary special.

Two years later the advertising column of the *Wall Street Journal* made this belated discovery about the power of the press:

> Wine executives say that the last time there was a favorable link between red wine consumption and health benefits, red wine sales increased. The fact that sales increased after only a news report underscores a peculiar reality of marketing: No matter how many millions of dollars are spent on ads, nothing sells a product as well as free publicity, especially something that discusses health claims.[1]

Third-party endorsements of trusted media personalities can drive up sales of products in every category.

The *New York Times* reported that when Martha Stewart talked about hydrangeas in her magazine *Martha Stewart Living* and then featured them on her syndicated television show, "nurseries could not keep them in stock." A California nurseryman who grows hydrangeas told the *Times* that "within ten days of the magazine hitting the East Coast, about every wholesale hydrangea grower sold out for the whole year."[2]

The *Wall Street Journal* reported in 1997:

> In a testament to the marketing muscle of television, Drake's Bakeries' sales are rising. But not because the snack-cake maker has unveiled an ad campaign or orchestrated a promotional push. No

one has done more to foster the media buzz than Rosie O'Donnell, host of the popular daytime talk show. Since her program began, O'Donnell has eaten Drake's Cakes on the air, interviewed Drake's President Jack Gallagher, and cajoled supermodel Cindy Crawford into eating a Ring-Ding—a chocolate cake with a chocolate coating—on the show. In addition, all the members of the studio audience get Drake's Cakes and a small carton of milk on their seats when they arrive. According to Drake's, sales from all outlets rose 5 percent for 1996. But sales at some points in the second half when O'Donnell's show started airing were as much as 11 percent ahead of a year earlier.[3]

In 1996 Oprah Winfrey caused a huge stir in the publishing industry by initiating Oprah's Book Club. When she recommended a book to her huge viewing audience, as *Time* magazine reported, "Bingo!—her viewers turn it into an instant bestseller."

Her endorsement not only sold literally millions of copies of new titles but made the paperback edition of *Song of Solomon,* a 19-year-old novel by Nobel Prize-winning author Toni Morrison, an overnight bestseller. The *New York Times* reported "that is an extraordinary use of a television star's power. . . . As Morrison said of *Song of Solomon* on the show, 'To give it a new life that is larger than its original life is a revolution.'"

The first three books picked by Oprah's Book Club, including *Song of Solomon*, sold an astonishing 2.3 million copies, more than three times their pre-Oprah sales.

The power of third-party endorsement was expressed this way by Marilyn Ducksworth, associate publisher of Putnam: "You can't buy an hour with Oprah Winfrey. Oprah is the E. F. Hutton of our business. When she speaks, people listen."[4]

The power of publicity is by no means limited to television. A 1994 study conducted by the Wirthlin Group for the Allen Communications Group asked more than 1,000 male and female adults eighteen and over, "If you were thinking about buying a particular product or service, which of the following sources of information would impact your buying decision the most?" The respondents mentioned newspaper articles (35 percent) and magazine features (28 percent) ahead of a variety of other options including television commercials (24 percent). Newspaper articles (95 percent) and magazine articles (89 percent) were also regarded as most believable by those surveyed.

That master marketer of our times, Nike Chairman Phil Knight, likes to point out that while an ad page in *Sports Illustrated* costs $150,000, no amount of money can buy the front cover where swoosh-bearing athletes appear with great frequency. The omnipresent swoosh has 90 percent-plus awareness among consumers, enabling it to stand alone. The Nike name in addition to the symbol has become a redundant intrusion.

The Need for Credibility

The importance of the credibility factor is underscored by a survey of marketing directors and brand managers surveyed in 1994 by my former firm, Golin/Harris Communications. Two-thirds of the respondents said that they believed that public relations is as important or more important than advertising in building brand awareness. But four-fifths of them believed that public relations is more important than advertising in building brand credibility.

Rich Jernstedt, Golin/Harris CEO, said that "the increasing fragmentation of traditional mass media, the rising cost of advertising, and growing consumer sophistication have made public relations a key part of the marketing mix."[5]

The credibility of public relations is needed to reach today's increasingly skeptical consumers because they are finding advertising messages less credible. Seven out of ten respondents of a recent survey conducted by Video Storyboard Tests said they believe few, if any, of the ads they see on TV or in print.

According to the Roper Organization, "Most demographic groups share a suspicion of marketers, and the skepticism is strongest among the most desirable customers."

The situation is especially acute among the consumers of the future. A 1994 study of high school students in 26 countries conducted by DDB Needham found more than half agreed with the statement "most advertising can't be believed."[6]

In his foreword to my 1991 book *The Marketer's Guide to Public Relations*, Philip Kotler of Northwestern's Kellogg School of Management, one of the world's foremost marketing authorities, offers this explanation for the increasing importance of public relations in marketing:

> " In an overcommunicated society, consumers develop communication-avoidance routines. They don't notice print ads; they 'tune out' commercial messages. Message senders are finding it increasingly difficult to reach the minds and hearts of target customers.
>
> As mass advertising and even target advertising lose some of their cost-effectiveness, message senders are driven to other media. They discover, or rediscover, the power of news, events, community programs, atmospheres, and other powerful communication modalities. Sooner or later they discover marketing public relations.[7] "

Don E. Schultz, Stanley Tannenbaum, and Robert R. Lauterborn, authors of *Integrated Marketing Communications,* state that "you cannot depend on the product alone to build consumer confidence. It's the rapport, the empathy, the dialogue, the relationship, the communications you establish with the consumer that makes the difference. They separate you from the pack."[8]

That further underscores the critical role of public relations in integrated marketing success. After all, building relationships is what public relations is all about.

In 1996, *Advertising Age* reported that marketers were seeking to create a brand experience with customers on a personal level by "mixing up a cocktail of paid advertising, public relations, sampling, direct marketing, and more. The aim: to bring customers not just an awareness of a brand but an actual- or virtual-experience of it." *Advertising Age* labeled this hybrid of established disciplines "the PR experience."[9]

Other mainstream media are acknowledging the increasing use of public relations in marketing. A 1997 front-page *Wall Street Journal* story quoted me on the value of third-party endorsement and reported that old-fashioned public relations "that is practically free can be more valuable than paid commercials." The new media recognition of marketing could be seen in a CNN segment on "The World Today." The lead was "consider it a law of human nature. Get their attention and you may get their business as well." The story pointed out that "the explosion of media outlets has led to a PR explosion."

Public Relations Provides the "Glue"

Prominent public relations counselor Robert Dilenschneider, editor of *Dartnell's Public Relations Handbook,* is convinced that the new marketing mix puts to work jointly the tools of marketing and of public relations and that public relations "is the glue that holds the whole thing together." He cites four reasons why marketers are increasingly turning to public relations to promote products and services:

1. *Need to reduce costs.* Global competition has put pricing pressure on American business. This means that costs have to be cut. Marketing departments were motivated to search for less-expensive ways to get results.

2. *Fragmentation of the media.* The mass market has been replaced by marketing niches. To reach as many people now as they did in the 1950s and 1960s, marketers have to use a variety of tools.

3. *Clutter of commercial messages.* The challenge to break through the clutter and have your message noticed has left the door wide open for creative public relations.

4. *Increased competition.* Public relations can get consumers to your company and not your competition by paving the way for the introduction, consumption, or repositioning of a product or service.[10]

Susan Henderson, Director of Marketing Relations at Miller Brewing Company, says, "As the marketplace for products becomes more competitive, more cluttered, more fragmented, and more expensive to compete in, companies are demanding that their marketing departments make the most of all their resources.

"With the ability to build goodwill through credible third-party sources, raise consumer awareness, educate key audiences, and directly involve audiences with a company's product, public relations can give a marketer an extra edge in achieving objectives."

She says this value-added discipline can play several roles in the marketer's toolbox. "Marketing public relations can leverage marketing investments, making advertising and promotion dollars work harder. It can help build trademark and brand equities with consumers. It can help a company define its place in the marketplace and strategically position the company with key audiences. Finally, it can help facilitate communications with and gain acceptance for a company's marketing strategy from customers who sell your products to the end consumer."[11]

The public relations function has survived the reorganization changes that have swept most of our major industries because management recognizes the need to win the support and understanding not only of customers but of all key stakeholders.

When Public Relations Takes the Lead

Despite the fear in some quarters that marketing will assume greater responsibility for corporate communications functions, the fact is that in an increasing number of corporations, public relations is leading the total corporate communications function, including marketing communications. This is especially true with technology, health-care, business-to-business, and financial-services companies.

A 1997 survey of the senior-most communications officials of 700 public companies conducted by Opinion Research Corporation and Northwestern University for Edelman Public Relations Worldwide revealed that 43 percent of corporate communicators maintain oversight for marketing, advertising, and promotions.

The probable reason is that public relations operates from a broader perspective than product marketing. Corporate communications (public relations) departments are concerned with managing the corporation's relations with all those "stakeholders" whose support is needed for the company to achieve its business goals. The achievement of marketing goals is impacted not only by consumers but by other key "stakeholders" who have a "stake" in the success of a company or organization. These stakeholders importantly include employees, shareholders, legislators, regulators, and the communities where the companies do business. Messages to these and other important publics must be consistent with those communicated to consumers.

What an industry analyst or security analyst, for example, says about a product and the company behind it can significantly impact the marketplace. The enthusiastic support of the employee force can have a dramatic impact on sales. The ability of public relations to identify issues that impact marketing, to handle crisis situations and to counsel top management, can exert enormous influence on marketing success or failure. These functions are exclusively the province of public relations and argue for public relations leadership in the development of integrated communications including marketing communications and corporate strategy that encompasses integrated marketing.

CHAPTER 3

Marketing and Corporate Brand Building

THE RELATIONSHIP BETWEEN PUBLIC RELATIONS AND MARKETING IS GROWING stronger as marketers recognize the importance of building relationships between brands and consumers. Public relations is particularly effective in building brand equity because of its power to positively enhance the assets that add value to the brand. These assets include brand awareness, brand loyalty, perceived quality, and other brand associations that identify and differentiate the brand from other market choices.

The long-term brand-building benefits of public relations are cited by the American Association of Advertising Agencies (AAAA) in its 1996 publication *Your Brand Is Your Future*. It cites a study on brand-building versus nonbrand-building activities conducted by Bob Prentice, a former senior marketing executive at both Procter & Gamble and Lever Brothers. He found that brand-building activities such as trade shows, demonstrations, product literature, advertising, and public relations are likely to influence a consumer four times longer than such promotions as coupons, sweepstakes, refunds, price promotions, and trade allowances. While these promotional activities influence sales for less than a year, brand-building activities such as public relations were found to influence sales for four years, to enhance the effect of nonbrand-building activities, and to produce higher profits when the investment is greater than 50 percent of the total marketing budget.[1]

Building brand loyalty has become the guiding principle of integrated marketing and with good reason. Recent studies have confirmed what marketers have long felt—that the longer you can keep a customer, the deeper will be his or her loyalty. A 1993 study by Fred Reichheld of Bain & Company reports that the deeper the loyalty, the more—and more frequently—the customer buys. That means that the cost of sales and marketing can be spread over a greater number of transactions. As the years go by, repeat customers become more and more loyal and ultimately emerge as the brand's most persuasive advocates.[2]

David Drobis, Chairman and CEO of Ketchum Public Relations, identifies five unique benefits that public relations brings to the practice of building brand loyalty and brand equity:

1. *Timeliness.* Public relations can be tied to real-time news coverage. Thanks to satellite technology, grand openings, press conferences, and other special events can be covered and broadcast live, integrating a tremendous sense of urgency into a campaign.

2. *Adaptability.* A public relations campaign can work in concert with advertising, direct mail, or sales promotion.

3. *Credibility.* A unique feature of public relations is "third-person endorsement" or "the halo effect." When a reporter talks about your product, there is implied endorsement. Consumers tend to find messages delivered by a trusted journalist more believable than purchased messages.

4. *Cost-efficiency.* The cost of a public relations effort is typically much lower than it would be for advertising.

5. *Mobility.* You can conduct public relations anywhere your imagination will take you—locally or nationally.[3]

Building Brands Through MPR

The Chrysler Corporation has made a conscious effort in recent years to build personalities for its brands and use its product launches to strengthen brand equity. Terri Houtman, Manager of Corporate Image/Brand Public Relations for Chrysler, listed these five rules for building brand through public relations for *Public Relations News:*

1. Know what the product, and the campaign that surrounds it, stands for.

2. Target those buyers who have a passion for your product.

3. Understand how the industry that your product is part of has evolved.

4. Integrate timeless qualities that have helped make the brand successful.

5. Reduce cross considerations (you don't want to compete with yourself; you want to compete with other manufacturers) by targeting an exclusive market and audience.[4]

Marketing Public Relations Redefined

In my 1991 book, *The Marketer's Guide to Public Relations*, I suggested that marketing public relations had evolved into a distinct discipline. I gave it a convenient acronym, MPR, and suggested a working definition:

> 66 Marketing public relations is the process of planning, executing, and evaluating programs that encourage purchase and consumer satisfaction through credible communication of information and impressions that identify companies and their products with the needs, wants, concerns, and interests of consumers.[5] 99

Another definition appears in the instructive how-to book, *Marketing Public Relations: The How That Makes It Work*, by Rene A. Henry Jr.:

> 66 A comprehensive, all-encompassing public awareness and information program or campaign directed to mass or specialty audiences to influence increased sales or use of an organization's products or services. Marketing public relations is the successful combination of a variety of communications techniques, which when skillfully and professionally used, will help a company achieve its sales and marketing objectives.[6] 99

In his *Webster's New World Dictionary of Media and Communications*, lexicographer Richard Weiner defines marketing public relations as "the use of special events, publicity, and other public relations techniques to promote products and services (term popularized by Thomas L. Harris of Highland Park, Illinois)."[7]

It has become clear that public relations is now widely viewed as a key element in integrated marketing rather than as an isolated function.

From this perspective, I have revised my definition of MPR as follows:

> 66 Marketing public relations is the use of public relations strategies and techniques to achieve marketing objectives. The purpose of MPR is to gain awareness, stimulate sales, facilitate communication, and build relationships between consumers and companies and brands.
>
> The principal functions of MPR are the communication of credible information, the sponsorship of relevant events, and the support of causes that benefit society. 99

Marketing Brands and Corporate Brands

While corporate public relations supports corporate objectives in the broader sense, marketing public relations specifically supports marketing objectives. Marketing public relations also serves corporate public relations objectives because the effective communication of consumer benefits of products and services enhances corporate reputation. Favorable corporate reputation, in turn, fosters positive perceptions of the company's products and services.

In her influential 1991 book, *The Popcorn Report,* trendspotter Faith Popcorn declared, "It used to be enough to make a fairly decent product and market it, but not anymore. In the 1990s, the consumer will want to know who you are before buying what you sell." She says that corporations must form relationships with their customers based on trust and that "companies that do good and are good will inspire trust." She calls it "Marketing the Corporate Soul."[8]

The late Thomas Mosser of Burson-Marsteller, the world's largest public relations firm, defined the interdependence of corporate brands and branded products this way: "Every institution or corporation has two assets on which success and survival are based—its Brand (capital 'B'—the image, reputation of the corporation or institution itself, including its financial assets, performance, and people) and its brands (lower case 'b'—the products or services it sells or provides). The interrelationship between these two assets is critical to survival and success. That is not to say that efforts against either of them must be reduced, with one taking precedence over the other. In fact, it is likely that breakthrough ideas against one or the other will make a significant difference to the organization. But more than ever before, the efforts against each must be considered relative to the impact of the other. And at different phases of recovery or success, the emphasis will move from one to the other."

He concludes, "Well into the next century, we will see the best marketers integrating not only the way they employ their communications resources, but also how the corporation's reputation impacts on the various brands in the marketplace and vice versa."[9]

The 1996 AAAA publication *Your Brand Is Your Future: A Client's Guide* states, "In daily practice, the word *brand* stands as a surrogate for the word *reputation.* In fact, your brand acts just like a person. When you know a person's reputation, you can predict his or her behavior. You know what that person is likely to do or say—or not do or say—in any given situation. Your brand works the same way."[10]

The interrelationship is described this way by Harlan Teller, Executive Managing Director of Hill & Knowlton:

> 66 Corporate reputation provides a "halo" for brand marketing efforts.
> Brand equity enhances the corporation's appeal as an employer

and a neighbor and an investment. Investors want to feel good about the company behind the brand. Likewise, consumers want to feel good about the company behind the brand.

Teller concludes that corporate positioning and product positioning must work together. "Marketing communications gives consumers a reason to buy. Corporate communications gives them permission to buy."

One of the most important roles that public relations can play in marketing is to sensitize the company to the concerns and interests of all the company's stakeholders. Public relations is uniquely capable of identifying issues and interpreting changes in the social and cultural environment that can significantly impact the marketplace. It can lead the company to support causes that consumers care about and help it avoid pitfalls of making marketing mistakes that can lead to consumer backlash.

"Best products and services" stands out as the key driver behind public perceptions of the most highly evaluated companies according to corporate reputation research conducted by the Wirthlin Group, one of the country's leading survey research companies. The April 1996 "Wirthlin Report" states that "Best Products/Services" exert more than a third of the total influence of the six major attributes of corporate reputation, an influence one-and-a-half times stronger than the next most important factor.

This realistic assessment of the value of corporate reputation to product marketing comes from Alvin Golin, Chairman of Golin/Harris Communications and my former partner:

The quality of a product, like the success of a public policy, counts more in the consumer's mind than the ethics of the manufacturer or politician. It is in cases of a tie when products fail that the great value of reputation comes into play.

When that happens, consumers give good guys a break but turn on the bad ones like a pack of wolves. In head-to-head races where everything else is equal, ethics and morality become the tiebreaker.

Make no mistake: character is critical to long-term success. It represents a trust bank from which you can draw when things go wrong. A bad reputation is like a snake waiting to bite the wrongdoer the moment he or she stumbles. Because whether it's choosing a politician, a car, or a hamburger, customers making purchase decisions are, in a very real sense, deciding to buy two things: the product and the company.[11]

In his 1996 book, *Building Your Company's Good Name,* Davis Young states that the first rule corporations must practice in creating and protecting their reputation is "People do business with organizations they trust." He says that "Customers today are a fickle lot. On the one hand, they demand that companies behave like good neighbors; on the other hand, they're disillusioned and mistrustful of most business. A corporation's reputation, then, is one of its key assets. You need to manage your company's good name or get ready to lose it."[12]

There is now a respected public relations trade publication devoted to this updated view of public relations. Paul A. Holmes, the visionary editor and publisher of *Reputation Management,* defines reputation management as:

> 66 (a) a counseling discipline that recognizes the importance of reputation as an organizational asset and seeks to ensure that management decisions are taken in an environment in which reputational implications are fully understood, evaluated, and considered, so that an organization's behavior earns it a strategically appropriate reputation with important stakeholders, and (b) a results-oriented management function that seeks to leverage reputation as an asset, enlisting important stakeholder groups, including employees, consumers, communities, and investors, to assist the organization in the achievement of its strategic design, and seeking to minimize the resistance of those groups to legitimate management objectives. 99

The closer that the corporate brand relates to the product, the better the opportunity to leverage the corporate reputation when problems afflict the product brand. Hill & Knowlton's Teller points out that the relationship between the corporate brand and product brands may take one of four forms. The corporate brand might be: (1) "a silent partner" such as Procter & Gamble whose brands do not incorporate the company name; (2) an "endorser" of the product brand, for example, Microsoft Windows 95; (3) both a product and an umbrella brand, such as Ford, which markets cars under its name as well as under other brand names; and (4) a corporate name that is also the brand name.

There is no better example of the corporate brand as product brand than McDonald's Corporation. It is one of the best-known brands in the world. It stands for customer satisfaction and consumer trust, memorably expressed as "Q. S. C. and V." That is shorthand for Quality food, fast friendly Service, restaurants known for Cleanliness, and a menu that provides Value.

McDonald's is dedicated to earning its customers' trust. The trust factor is so endemic to the way McDonald's Corporation does business that the company has institutionalized and trademarked what it calls its "trust bank."

McDonald's community involvement programs span the country and the globe. Wherever McDonald's does business, its practices reflect founder Ray Kroc's dedication of giving something back to the society from which the company derives its profits, and specifically giving something back to the local communities where it does business. Kroc believed if you take money out of a community, you have a responsibility to give something back. He knew instinctively that good citizenship is good public relations and that good public relations is good for business.

There is no more dramatic evidence of the dividends paid by the trust-bank philosophy than the story of what happened in Los Angeles in 1992 after a jury exonerated police officers who beat motorist Rodney King in an incident captured on videotape and seen by millions on television. The ensuing riots left fifty-two people dead, destroyed more than 2,000 buildings, and caused nearly $1 billion in property damage. While other stores and restaurants went up in flames, not a single one of the thirty McDonald's restaurants in the riot area was touched. The reason: McDonald's had long been a committed, involved, and visible community citizen in these Los Angeles neighborhoods.

In the aftermath of the riot, in an article called "America's Hamburger Helper," *Time* magazine commented, "McDonald's stands out not only as one of the more socially responsible companies in America but also as one of the nation's few truly effective social engineers."

Edward Rensi, President and CEO of McDonald's U.S.A., told *Time* reporter Edwin Reingold, "Our businesses there are owned by African-American entrepreneurs who hired African-American managers who hired African-American employees who served everybody in the community, be they Korean, African-American, or Caucasian."[13]

Equally important is the fact that McDonald's underwrites and its people personally participate in dozens of inner-city programs ranging from support of neighborhood educational and athletic programs to Gospelfest to Spanish Heritage art contests. The people of south central Los Angeles know that McDonald's cares.

Los Angeles McDonald's Owner-Operator Harold Patrick said, "If anyone wants to place a dollar value on the real value of public relations and communications to McDonald's, take what it would cost to rebuild every McDonald's had it been burned in the recent rebellion and then add to it the loss of sales that we would have sustained while we were closed. That really is the value of what we have done in the community. That was the real difference. That was why McDonald's was not burned when others were."

CHAPTER 4

Positioning Your Brand

POSITIONING IS AT THE HEART OF EVERY SUCCESSFUL INTEGRATED MARKETING communications program. It is the guidepost for the development of IMC programs in which advertising, promotion, and public relations messages are cohesive, cumulative, and mutually reinforcing.

Positioning is the way companies and brands are perceived by consumers relative to the competition.

In his *Webster's New World Dictionary of Media and Communications,* Richard Weiner defines positioning as "the creation of a distinct identity, image, or concept for a product or service via advertising, public relations, or other techniques. The arrangement of a product, service, or other entity in its marketplace or other arena in relation to the audience can determine how well it will sell."[1]

Positioning has become so central to business success that in his influential book *The Competitive Advantage of Nations,* Harvard Business School Professor Michael Porter states: "A firm in a highly attractive industry may still not earn satisfactory profits if it has chosen a poor competitive positioning."

The positioning concept was introduced by Al Ries and Jack Trout in a series of 1972 articles in *Advertising Age* they called "The Positioning Era" and popularized in their 1981 breakthrough book, *Positioning: The Battle for Your Mind.* They said that positioning is not what you do to a product. It is what you do to the mind of the prospect. That is, you position the product in the mind of the prospect. They declared that "positioning is an organized system for finding a window in the mind."[2]

Marketing public relations that exists to build relationships between consumers, companies, and brands is a key element in the positioning process.

Product and Corporate Positioning:
An Interlocking Process

Regis McKenna believes that positioning should involve three interlocking stages: product positioning, market positioning, and corporate positioning.

In the first stage, product positioning, a company must determine how it wants to fit into the competitive market. In the second stage, market positioning, the product must gain recognition in the market. In corporate positioning, the final stage of the process, companies must position not their products but themselves.

McKenna says that companies must project their position to the market through education and by establishing relationships with members of the infrastructure.

He says that the first task of positioning a product is to prepare the infrastructure. "Rather than present their own analysis of a situation, most journalists simply quote what other people say. Most often these other people are members of the industry infrastructure—customers, financial analysts, consultants, distributors, and resellers. The infrastructure serves as a filtering mechanism, helping journalists separate fact from fiction. Companies should take advantage of this filtering mechanism. They should educate and win over members of the infrastructure before going to the press."[3]

The Positioning Statement

James Harris, who heads the marketing consulting practice at Thomas L. Harris & Company, calls positioning "the marketing mission statement." It defines the brand's target audience, frame of reference, user benefit, and logical and/or emotional support with reasons why.

The positioning statement is made of up these four elements:

To: target audience
Brand is the: frame of reference
That: user benefit/point of difference
Because: support/reason(s) why

Let's look at how this would apply to the Gillette Company's razors and blades division.

To: men who shave
Gillette: is the brand of shaving products
That: delivers the best shave possible
Because: of its commitment to research and technology

This commitment was expressed by the company's founder, King Gillette, who said, "If there's a better way to shave, we'll find it." That promise is expressed in advertising as "the best a man can get."

The way that public relations supports this positioning was dramatically demonstrated when ABC's *Good Morning America* initiated a new series called "Looking Good/Feeling Great." The popular morning show ran a six-minute segment on "a problem millions of men face every day—how to get a perfect shave." Reporter Bill Ritter began his report with a visit to "a place where they have shaving down to a science," Gillette's research lab. The lab's director took Ritter past a display of Gillette products to an area where men shave daily in ongoing tests of new razors, blades, and shaving creams. When the director explained how Gillette's patented twin-blade razor gives a closer shave by pulling the hair and then cutting it, viewers watched company-produced animation of how it works. Back in the studio, Ritter was shaved by a master barber from New York's Pierre Hotel with a Gillette double-edged razor instead of a straight razor traditionally used by barbers. The barber pronounced the twin-track razor "a revolution in shaving." The message was loud and clear. Gillette is all you need to know about shaving.

Postscript: A few months later, *Good Morning America* once again visited the shaving subject and the Gillette shaving lab, this time to explore the question "Is there a difference between men's and women's razors?" Gillette employees were interviewed while shaving with Sensor Excel Razors for men and women. Gillette's vice presidents of men's and women's shaving were also interviewed. The answer: The blade's the same, but there are meaningful engineering differences in the handles. That is because women shave mostly in the shower or bath and need a handle that works in one continuous motion over a surface area that is nine times greater than a man's face. Men who shave in front of a mirror need a handle that can move over lots of shapes and turns.

So revise that positioning statement target audience from "men who shave" to "people who shave." And credit Gillette with being the only brand discussed, displayed, and demonstrated in both segments.

Repositioning Time

The first step in positioning is to identify current consumer perceptions of your product and other products in the category.

To do this, marketers employ such research methodologies as consumer surveys, in-depth interviews, and focus groups. Some have gone beyond these traditional research methods and are employing a sophisticated technique called perceptual or brand mapping. Consumers are asked to rate your product and competitive products on a number of key attributes. Two of the most important attributes (for example, quality and style) are then mapped on a two-dimensional matrix, creating a picture of how your products are seen compared to other products in the category. Mapping helps marketers determine if consumers' perceptions match what they would like them to think about their products. It is a way to evaluate the effectiveness of their marketing communications programs. The map is especially important because it focuses on the features and benefits consumers are most likely to consider when making a purchase decision. It tells marketers if their positioning is working and how it can be reinforced and strengthened. On the other hand, perceptual mapping may indicate that communications is not working. If so, it may be time for the product to be repositioned.

Product positioning must be reexamined regularly to determine if the niche it occupies remains relevant to consumers.

Today it is hard to remember that both Marlboro cigarettes and Lite beer were once positioned as women's products. They only became category leaders after they were successfully repositioned as products for a man's man. Marlboro's Western imagery has been successfully perpetuated for decades, propelling the brand to commanding category leadership worldwide.

Here is how Lite beer was positioned before it was repositioned by Miller:

To: women who like to drink beer
Lite: is the brand
That: will help you stay slim
Because: it has fewer calories

The product took off when it was repositioned this way:

To: men who like to drink beer
Lite: is the beer
That: enables you to drink more
Because: it tastes good and is less filling.

By repositioning its product, Miller not only created its most successful brand but literally invented the most important new category in the beer business.

The News Factor in Positioning

Jack Trout emphasizes the importance of the news factor in positioning. He says that "one way of overcoming the mind's natural stinginess when it comes to accepting new information is to work hard at presenting your message as news." He says that too many advertisements try to entertain or be clever and often overlook the news factor in their story, pointing to Starch research that shows headlines containing news score better than those that don't.

Because public relations is news-based, it plays a unique role in positioning products and companies.

Trout describes the experience of Samuel Adams beer, a small business that couldn't afford advertising but effectively used public relations to position itself as a high-quality local brew. It won taste tests in Boston, then graduated to win the National Beer Taste-Off in Denver, getting major publicity all the way. "Those credentials and third-party endorsements have paid off. Today Sam Adams has a multimillion advertising budget and it all started with PR." C. James Koch, the company's CEO, became an effective spokesman for the brand in an integrated campaign that included both commercials and media interviews.

Sam Adams is just one example of a local business that gained a national reputation based on a quality product positioning platform communicated through effective media relations. Pepperidge Farm gained national attention when the legendary publicist Ben Sonnenberg landed stories about the goodness of the breads baked by his Connecticut neighbor Margaret Rudkin in *The Reader's Digest* and other national media.[4]

In the 1980s Ben & Jerry's and The Body Shop effectively used public relations rather than advertising to position themselves as the kind of socially responsible companies that sell high-quality products made with the finest natural ingredients. In the 1990s, Starbucks established itself as a national brand by using public relations at the grass-roots level to position their coffeehouses as the places to be to meet friends and enjoy great coffee.

Positioning in a Word

Jack Trout says that "positioning is simply concentrating on an idea—or even a word—that defines the company in the minds of consumers."

He offers the example of Lotus Development Corporation. Trout describes how Lotus repositioned itself from a spreadsheet company by preempting the word *groupware* to describe software for network applications. Through a well-planned and well-managed media relations program, Lotus effectively communicated the concept of groupware as an important development in the business media. *Business Week* described Lotus Notes as the first successful groupware program in a story headlined "Lotus Notes Gets a Lot of Notice. Users Praise 'Groupware' and Rivals Scramble to Catch Up." Other influential stories in the *Wall Street Journal, Information Week,* and *Fortune* successfully repositioned the company in the minds of software consumers. *Fortune* reported "in groupware,

Lotus Development rules. Its product, Lotus Notes, is fast becoming for computer networks what Lotus 1-2-3 was for PCs."

He points out that the advertising for Notes did not start until two years after the start of the PR. "The PR lit the fire and started the repositioning process," Trout says.[5]

Lotus was still identified with groupware long after it had been acquired by IBM. In 1996, *Time* reported that "Lotus Notes, the collaborative 'groupware' product that made Lotus a cash cow, seemed to be threatened by the Internet's ability to link teams of workers across networks for free. Lotus responded with Domino, a net-based system that makes it simple to move Notes applications on the Web. Analysts predict that the easy-to-use software will attract thousands of new customers to Lotus."[6]

CHAPTER 5

Creating Marketplace Excitement

BECAUSE OF ITS UNIQUE ABILITY TO DOMINATE THE NATION'S NEW AGENDA, THE impact of marketing public relations has alone driven some of the most successful marketing campaigns of recent years.

A Letter from the Postman

Moving with the times, the once staid U.S. Postal Service (USPS) discovered the joys and rewards of MPR when it issued the Elvis Presley twenty-nine-cent commemorative stamp in 1992. What might have well been a one-day news story was extended into a well-orchestrated campaign that built public excitement over a period of more than a year. In April, the USPS first captured the imagination of the nation's news media by offering Americans a chance to vote for the Elvis design of their choice to appear on the new stamp, the young rock and roller or the older, beefier, glitzier Elvis.

Declaring that Elvis was certifiably dead, a requirement for stamp honorees, Postmaster General Anthony Frank and a company of celebrities unveiled the designs at a March news conference in, of all places, Las Vegas, at the Hilton where Elvis gave 839 sold-out performances. Flanked by Vegas headliners such as Milton Berle and Barbara Eden, Frank announced that the Postal Service was printing up five million postcard ballots to be distributed free at post

33

offices throughout the United States and urged his fellow citizens to "vote early, vote often."

The event was beamed via satellite to television networks and stations with remarkable results. Anchormen Tom Brokaw of NBC, Dan Rather of CBS, and Peter Jennings of ABC appeared to be enjoying themselves enormously and their news departments dug into their archives for vintage Elvis footage and unleashed their best wordsmiths to have fun with the story. CNN carried the story repeatedly to viewers in the United States and abroad. The story made headlines in newspapers and newsmagazines. Even the *New York Times* indulged itself with a story titled "The Elvis Wars: Two Kings Compete for a Stamp," which described the first public vote on a stamp design as "a fit of derring-do and marketing ingenuity."[1]

Local TV and radio stations picked up the story and involved their listeners and viewers for weeks by conducting their own polls.

The second big event was the announcement in June of the winning design by Priscilla Presley at the family homestead in Memphis. In all, more than one million Americans cast their ballots. The winner, by a wide margin, was the younger Elvis. A five-column *New York Times* headline proclaimed, "People Say Don't Be Cruel to Image: They Like Younger Elvis."[2]

The third and final event on January 8 found more than a thousand fans lined up in a driving rain at Graceland at midnight to celebrate what would have been Elvis's fifty-eighth birthday and be part of history by buying their Elvis stamps on the first day of issue. More than 100 news organizations from around the world were there, transmitting live reports. The next day the scene was repeated at 40,000 post offices from coast to coast, resulting in massive local publicity.

The first printing of 300 million stamps was followed by an unprecedented sold-out second printing of 200 million. The Elvis issue instantly became the bestselling U.S. postage stamp of all time. The Postal Service broke even on the printing costs for the ballot that cost voters nineteen cents to mail and turned a profit of $29 million on the sale of the stamps. Postal officials estimated that 15 percent of the stamps would never be used to pay for postal services. The Postal Service also did a big business in T-shirts, coffee mugs, and related Elvis merchandise.

Flush with success from its bestselling Elvis issue, the Postal Service embarked on a series of stamps honoring popular legends. On what would have been her sixty-ninth birthday, the Postal Service rolled out a new stamp honoring screen goddess Marilyn Monroe. Well-publicized parties were held in post offices and Planet Hollywood restaurants around the country, complete with Monroe impersonators and Marilyn merchandise. *Stamps, etc.,* the official Postal Service collectors publication, acknowledged the role of publicity in making the Marilyn issue, with 400 million sold, second only to Elvis: "Marilyn has attracted a tremendous amount of media, bringing stamps into the public eye in a big way."[3]

The "Legends of Hollywood" series continued in 1996 with the issuance of the James Dean stamp. By this time, the U.S. Postal Service recognized the value of staging special ceremonies in locations conducive to photo ops. The stamp was introduced on the lot of Warner Bros. Studios where Dean made all three of his feature films. Postmaster General Marvin Runyon was joined by Warner Bros. Chairmen and Co-CEOs Robert Daly and Terry Semel. Stamp collectors and fans of the late movie star gathered on the studio back lot and at the Warner Bros. tour office to purchase stamps with the official first-day postmark.

As part of the first-day activities, Warner Bros. Studio Stores across the country held special celebrations where stamps were sold and a special pictorial postmark applied. Overlooking no opportunity to attract attention and publicity, the Postal Service also held a special celebration at James Dean's hometown, Fairmount, Indiana. Collectors and fans who wanted more information on ordering the James Dean or Marilyn Monroe stamps could call the Postal Service toll-free 800 number or refer to USPS or Warner Bros. Web sites on the Internet.

The James Dean stamp was the most popular U.S. postage stamp of the year and the second only to the Centennial Olympics issue as the most-saved stamp with thirty-one million saved. The unchallenged record holder in the saved category was the 1993 Elvis. Marilyn topped the list in 1995 with 46.3 million stamps saved. The success of the "Legends of Hollywood" has been good news because revenue from stamps saved helps contribute to lowering the overall operating expenses of the Postal Service.

Lessons Learned

- Involve the customer with the product.
- You can sustain a story for months with good planning.
- Make each event special. Unveil. Reveal. Put on sale. All with flair.
- Choose an unexpected location for your announcement.
- Names make news and add to the glamour.
- Make it fun. Put up a tent. Send in the bands.
- Make customers want to be the first on their block to own one.
- If you are really hot, celebrate with midnight madness.
- Find ways to replicate the national doings locally.
- Don't forget the deejays.
- Tie in with a retailer with lots of locations.
- For best results, turn a product story into a human-interest story.

The One and Only Wonderbra

When Sara Lee Corporation introduced Wonderbra in the United States, it called on its public relations firm, Marina Maher Communications, to differentiate "The One and Only Wonderbra" from competitive push-up bras already on the market. Sara Lee's strategy was to shift media attention away from a competitive product to the "bra wars" that would begin when Sara Lee introduced the original cleavage-enhancing bra in the United States two months later.

The marketing counterstrike was launched at Macy's famous department store in New York. A "Cleavage Caravan" of armored cars, trucks loaded with the first shipment of Wonderbras, passed under a spectacular Wonderbra billboard in Times Square, followed by stretch limousines carrying a team of "Wonderbra Women" to Macy's where they were greeted by dozens of women carrying homemade signs and balloons and throwing confetti. Accompanied by marching musicians, the models paraded down the center aisle to the lingerie department for the formal unveiling and a fashion show where customers could see how the product looked on an identical set of clothed twin models. A Wonderbra was sold every fifteen seconds on the day of the launch at Macy's and two other participating New York department stores. The entire shipment was sold out by the end of the first day. The media fallout from the New York launch was so successful that top retailers nationwide committed to carry and promote the line.

Scenes from the New York caravan were transmitted nationwide by satellite resulting in more than 100 telecasts. Customized events were staged in ten other major markets later, attracting major coverage in local as well as additional national media. Cable-car caravans appeared in San Francisco, Wonderbra helicopters landed in Los Angeles, and pink Cadillac caravans drove through Miami.

The battle of the bras was a headline writer's dream. Among them: "Tempest in a D-Cup" (*Newsweek*); "Keeping Abreast of the Battle of the Bras" (*USA Today*); "For Some Women a Little Can Become a Lot" (*San Francisco Chronicle*); "Bra Wars: The Battle for the Ultimate Cleavage Machine" (*Dallas Morning News*); and "Dramatic Upheaval in Lingerie" (*Cleveland Plain Dealer.*) Wonderbra made headlines in the marketing media, too. *Advertising Age* headlined its story with "It's USA or Bust for Sara Lee's Wonderbra."

Wonderbra was the subject of good-natured kidding in a *New Yorker* cartoon, Dave Barry's syndicated humor column, a Jay Leno monologue on *The Tonight Show with Jay Leno,* and an appearance on the Top Ten List on CBS's *Late Night with David Letterman.* It got laughs on network sitcoms and was even mentioned on *Wall Street Week* on PBS.

During the ten-month launch period, Wonderbra was featured in publicity resulting in nearly 400 million impressions. Within months of national availability, with virtually no advertising and with public relations as the key marketing tool, Wonderbra became the number one push-up bra in the United States. Consumers were convinced that "Wonderbra was the one worth waiting for."

To sustain a high degree of media coverage, Marina Maher created a post-launch campaign directly linked to the target market of young women. "The Wonderbra Model Search," a nationwide search for a brand ambassador, was designed to keep the Wonderbra in the news in year two in a way that reinforced its sensual, fun image.

The contest, publicized as "the biggest talent hunt since the search for Scarlett O'Hara," set out to find a woman who "embodied Wonderbra's self-confident, slightly mischievous appeal in both personality and appearance." Open casting calls were held in New York and Los Angeles, supported by publicity and a tiny ad budget of $500 per market for commercials on local radio stations and *Variety*. Renowned casting director Linda Godlove was retained to help select three finalists from 1,200 contestants.

Marina Maher arranged for *Entertainment Tonight* to cover the ballot shoot exclusively. The finalists, clad in Wonderbra yellow-and-black jackets, arrived by white Mustang convertible at New York's Bloomingdale's for a news conference. Their introduction was followed by a fashion show featuring models wearing Wonderbras under various ensembles.

The public was asked to vote for one of three finalists pictured in ads in the *New York Times, People,* and *USA Today.* Wonderbra hangtag ballots were also made available in retail stores, assuring a large voter turnout of more than 52,000 consumers. The winner was announced at yet another New York press conference, this one at Macy's. Media were treated to a slice of an oversize, Wonderbra-shaped cake to celebrate Wonderbra's first birthday. A video of the event was instantly satellited to TV stations across the country. The winner made personal appearances at the brand's largest retailers and conducted a multimarket satellite media tour.

"The Wonderbra Model Search" contest generated nearly 100 million media impressions at a cost per thousand of only thirty-one cents. Despite competition from similar products, some at considerably lower prices, and no new product news, Wonderbra ended its second year on the U.S. market as the top-selling bra in its category.

Wonderbra continues to generate excitement in the marketplace. When Wonderbra introduced the Wonderbra Lift Bra, a bra for women who want a lift and comfort without dramatic cleavage, the excitement was captured by the product's dramatic arrival by air in Manhattan.

The media were invited to what was guaranteed to be an uplifting experience from the One and Only Wonderbra with a sky blue teaser that asked the question, "What Would Chicken Little Say if He Got Wind of This?"

When launch day arrived, an all-female skydiving team led by Cheryl Stearns, the world's most successful competitive diver, delivered the first Lift

The finalists of "The Wonderbra Model Search" are introduced at a New York news conference. (Courtesy of Sara Lee Corporation)

Bra to the women of New York via a skydive airlift over the Hudson River, landing on a tiny target steps away from a cheering crowd.

Women who traveled to Weehawken's Port Imperial to witness the landing were rewarded with coupons for free Lift Bras from Lord & Taylor, Bloomingdale's, and Macy's, where the bra went on sale prior to national distribution.

Following the skydive, a Wonderbra fashion show was held at the drop site featuring hot spring looks from a quartet of top designers. To cap off the event, the fashion models and skydivers boarded a ferry bound for Manhattan to deliver the Wonderbra Lift Bras to New Yorkers. It was another chapter in Wonderbra's now famous penchant for unusual deliveries and a publicity triumph for the brand and its public relations firm, Marina Maher Communications.

Lessons Learned

- Preempt the competition by telling the world the best is yet to come.
- The media love a good battle. If you are in ladies' underwear, so much the better.

- Dramatize the arrival by land, sea, and air.
- Enlist some friends to carry signs, toss confetti, and lead the cheers.
- Armed guards say something big is coming.
- Do something dramatic for the retailer.
- Merchandise your success to other markets.
- Build up excitement nationally before launching locally.
- Give a local twist to every major market intro.
- Become the talk of the town. Move from niche news to must news.
- You have arrived when Letterman, Leno, and *Saturday Night Live* know their audiences know your product.

Public relations alone continues to generate excitement in the marketplace that can lead to stunning sales success.

CHAPTER 6

Introducing New Products
Before the Advertising Breaks

MOST MARKETERS, INTEGRATED AND OTHERWISE, UNDERSTAND THE IMPORTANCE OF marketing public relations in generating awareness of and building up anticipation for new products. Most also understand that prelaunch publicity offers a unique window of opportunity to make headline news.

It's an opportunity that comes only once in the product life cycle and marketers should take full advantage.

The integrated marketing timetable must assure that the product news precedes the advertising break. Successful integration delivers a one-two punch, with publicity in media and online building excitement in the marketplace, receptivity to the advertising, and anticipation for the product.

In his 1996 book, *The New Positioning*, marketing guru Jack Trout states:

> The new general rule of marketing is PR first, advertising second. PR plants the seed. Advertising harvests the crop. The truth is that advertising can't start a fire. It can only fan a fire after its been started. To get something out of nothing, you need the validity that third-party endorsements bring. . . . When a company is using positioning as its basic advertising strategy, then it simply makes sense to use positioning strategy in its PR. Especially since the PR ought to precede the advertising.[1]

A Snapshot Heard Around the World

The nature of the product, in some ways, dictates the nature and tone of the public relations plan. But not always. Many experienced marketers have thrown away the book and are inventing new ways to maximize exposure before the advertising breaks.

Today many major international marketers are unleashing their megamarketing firepower with simultaneous introductions of major new products throughout the world.

Eastman Kodak Company introduced its complete line of Advanced Photo System (APS) products at news conferences on three continents. The significance of the announcement was underscored by Kodak Chairman George Fisher who said APS was "reinventing consumer photography." The system combines innovative film, camera, and photofinishing technologies that Fisher said would have far-reaching implications for the future of photography.

The introduction of Kodak cameras and films under the Advantix brand was backed by the largest marketing budget in the company's history.

The APS is based on a new film format smaller than 35mm, and is contained in a sealed cassette that delivers sharp, clear prints and frees consumers from ever handling film. The film has a magnetic coating on which cameras input information that ultimately improves print quality. The system affords the consumer the convenience of drop-in film loading and the option of three different print formats.

Eastman Kodak Company led a consortium of camera makers Canon, Minolta, and Nikon, and film competitor Fuji in developing APS and bringing compatible system products and services to market.

More than 200 reporters attended the U.S. media event to see the first Advantix cameras and films. Among them was Newsweek's Kendall Hamilton who reported that "Kodak didn't merely 'introduce' or 'launch' its Advanced Photo System last week; it hosted a worldwide 'premiere.' In Hollywood, no less. Searchlights swept the audience at the company's press conference. A stand-up comic prepped the crowd. Actress Jane Seymour showed off snapshots of her new twins. An oversize film cassette, perhaps five feet tall, arced across the room on cables. If you owned the word 'exciting,' you'd have been collecting some pretty fat royalty checks."[2]

Kodak traveled from its Rochester, New York, headquarters to California not just to bathe its product line in Hollywood stardust but because by prior agreement with the other APS consortium members, the news was embargoed until midnight. Midnight is not a very popular time for companies to hold press conferences, no matter how exciting the news. Besides, midnight in New York is 2 P.M. in Tokyo, which would give the Japanese members of the consortium a jump on the news break. By moving the announcement to California, Kodak was able to move up its media event to 9 P.M. Pacific Standard Time. Kodak

Actress Jane Seymour shoots a picture of George Fisher,
Kodak Chairman and CEO, at the worldwide launch of
Kodak Advantix cameras and film in Los Angeles.
(Courtesy of Eastman Kodak Company)

hosted more than 200 reporters to its bash at the Academy of Television Arts
& Sciences in Los Angeles while hosting a simultaneous event in Tokyo. Satellite feeds connected the two and also linked Rochester, where employees
attended a black-tie gala at the historic George Eastman House, and London,
where Kodak introduced the Advantix line a few hours later. The London event,
like those in Los Angeles and Tokyo, grabbed media attention. It displayed not
only the products but supermodel Carla Bruni clad in a ball gown made of pictures shot on Advantix film.

Media covering the story received a comprehensive news kit with tabbed
sections providing detailed information about the Advantix system, films, cameras, photofinishing, and marketing and, of course, replete with Advantix print
samples and product photography.

Accompanying the press kit was an elaborate suitcase-size "product kit." It contained a top-of-the-line Advantix camera, several Advantix film cassettes, and other goodies, including a Memory Keeper, a storage device to keep the film cassettes and proof sheets after getting them back from the photo processor.

Kodak used the kit for two purposes. First, it provided the media attending the Los Angeles, Tokyo, and London press events the opportunity to experience the new Advantix cameras and films firsthand. To give journalists interesting subjects to shoot, Kodak erected 12 × 12–foot photo-taking sets at each site featuring jungle scenes with live exotic birds, race cars, movie scenes, and more. The company also offered on-site film processing so journalists could soon see the fruits of their labor—and the spectacular results achievable—with the new photo system.

The kit helped stimulate photo buff magazine editors to "test-drive" the new cameras and films and to report on their own experiences. These firsthand reviews would entice readers to try and ultimately buy new cameras and film.

For months prior to the introduction, Kodak had taken steps to sell the value of the system and defuse some initial skepticism. Its preannouncement strategy included inviting the trade press to the company's laboratories in Dallas, Texas, and Paris, France, for an advanced look four months before the launch, bringing in customers for a test run and showcasing its photofinishing equipment at the Photo and Imaging Expo '95 in London. When Kodak introduced its cameras and film to the media, the sell-in of finishing equipment was well under way. By the time the product began to appear in stores, tens of thousands of locations were ready to process Advantix film.

Led by Kodak's communications and public affairs group in Rochester, a team of PR firms worldwide, including the launch's primary agency, Burson-Marsteller, worked seamlessly to produce spectacular results.

The worldwide introduction was covered by news media in twenty-three countries, producing an astounding 1.68 billion worldwide impressions. Kodak saturated media in the United States, its largest market, securing coverage in all news weeklies and major newspapers and on all TV networks. In international markets, the Kodak story was covered by virtually every major newspaper, magazine, wire service, radio/TV outlet, and trade publication. Kodak's media-embargo strategy enabled the company to dominate the headlines versus the competition. Ninety percent of the coverage identified Kodak as the innovator of the Advanced Photo System. Virtually 100 percent of the two primary target markets, casual picture takers and advanced amateurs, were reached by the media.

The New York Times reported that the company had accepted two million orders for Advantix cameras by the time they were ready to be shipped.

Despite the fact that production problems caused some delays in deliveries, a year after the introduction the Wall Street Journal reported that Advantix cameras were selling well and that "Kodak is counting on the new system to energize the U.S. photography market, the world's largest, and the whole industry is ardently hoping that the new system will catch on.[3]

Lessons Learned

- Global media coverage is greatly multiplied when product news is announced in world markets simultaneously.
- Timing is everything, especially when you are competing for headlines.
- End the speculation and eliminate the negatives by inviting media to a preview.
- Invite key customers for an advanced look and to answer their questions.
- Go to where the action is. Have your own preopening and become the talk of the show.
- Dramatize the news with events in key cities around the world.
- Assemble a client-agency team to maximize key world market coverage.
- There's no business like show business to launch a product. Comedy. Music. Action.
- Pick a great and unexpected location for your party.
- Trot out the CEO to pronounce the importance of the occasion.
- What's my line? Provide media with everything they want to know about your line but weren't afraid to ask.
- Give reporters the product to "test-drive" so they can report on their personal experience firsthand.

The Unleashing of Nintendo 64

Launched in the United States in the fall of 1996, Nintendo 64, the world's first true 64-bit home video-game system, quickly became one of the most successful product launches in the history of the consumer electronics industry. The entirely PR-driven prelaunch campaign created such high levels of consumer demand that many retailers were forced to break embargoes and sell Nintendo prior to the launch date of September 29. Before the product advertising campaign broke, 350,000 sets had been sold.

A well-orchestrated media relations campaign conducted by Nintendo's public relations firm, Golin/Harris Communications, had maintained consumer and media anticipation between the initial announcement in August of 1993 and the actual product launch in September of 1996. By implementing a strategic, ongoing public relations program that responded to new developments as they occurred, three years of successful coverage were secured for Nintendo 64 in all targeted media.

The firm's challenge was to position Nintendo 64 as "the Cabbage Patch phenomenon of the 1990s," promoting product sellouts and retail lineups.

The world debut of Nintendo 64 was held at the Shoshinkai trade show in Tokyo in November of 1995. Golin/Harris produced a video news release containing the first visuals of the system that was satellited to U.S. broadcast media. A transoceanic teleconference from Tokyo spread the news to key media and analysts around the world.

The U.S. unveiling was held six months later at the giant Electronic Entertainment Expo in Los Angeles in May of 1996. The news conference was paired with the first live product demonstration, bringing nearly 500 cheering journalists to their feet. Typical of the coverage was a color spread in *Time* titled "Super Mario's Dazzling Comeback." Correspondent David S. Jackson took Super Mario for a test run and reported that "Playing Mario 64 is like jumping inside the movie *Toy Story.*" His assessment: Nintendo 64 is "the fastest, smoothest action game yet attainable via joystick at the service of equally virtuoso motion."[4]

A few days before the launch day, Nintendo achieved advanced publicity by partnering with UPS and Boeing. Initial shipments of Nintendo 64 systems left Seattle aboard a brand-new Boeing 757 jet en route to retailers across the country piloted by a costumed Mario character.

Prelaunch and launch-day publicity generated 100 million initial impressions and drove consumer demand to unprecedented levels.

CBS's *This Morning* anchor Jane Robelot declared, "It's not even Halloween yet, but millions of kids already know what they want for Christmas. It's a new video game system from Nintendo called Nintendo 64." Consumer reporter Herb Weisbaum picked up the story saying, "The N-64 is truly breakthrough technology. Nintendo took the power of a $100,000 computer workstation and put it into an affordable home game machine. The result—some of the best video games ever made."

CNN called the system "dazzling," "a quantum leap," and "a whole new way of looking at games." Viewers were urged to "grab one quick because they're sure to be the hottest gift this Christmas."

Newsweek's "Cyberscope" said that Super Mario 64 "is unlike anything you've ever seen: incredible 3-D animation, so real it's dizzying."[5]

Business Week reported that "Children have been mobbing N-64 demonstrations since early September at the bustling "Toys 'Я' Us" in midtown Manhattan. Just one look, and kids get hooked." On its "Personal Business" page, the magazine advised its audience of businesspeople parents, "If you spring for N-64, there's little danger of it sitting unused in the closet."[6]

Newspapers from the *Times* of New York to the *Times* of Los Angeles weighed in with favorable reviews. The *Chicago Tribune* summed up the state of excitement generated by the prelaunch publicity with a story headlined simply "It's Here."

The result of all the excitement Nintendo 64 had generated in the marketplace was that widespread shortages occurred within hours of the launch. Within the first three days, Golin/Harris issued a news release with this headline, "Nintendo 64 Sold Out; Company Pushes for More Product; Frenzied Consumers Demand to Buy Before Product Officially Launches." It reported that 50 percent of the systems and software were sold even before they hit store shelves on the official launch day, September 29. And three days after the official launch, all of the 350,000 units initially sent to stores had been sold.

The Cabbage Patch analogy was furthered by Howard Lincoln, chairman of Nintendo of America, who said, "We're looking at a potential 'Cabbage Patch' doll situation for the holiday season. We want to do everything we can to ensure that there won't be kids disappointed that they didn't get what they asked their parents for."

After Los Angeles, Golin/Harris and Nintendo pulled out all the stops to give key media hands-on game-play experience. Team Nintendo Game Play Counselors personally visited long-lead video game and consumer media with prerelease versions of upcoming games. They traveled by "Holiday Van," equipped with Nintendo 64 systems and games to short- to mid-lead media offices in twenty-one top markets.

Nearly one billion gross media impressions were generated by the public relations effort between the May U.S. unveiling and the end of the year.

The power of public relations was summed up by industry analyst David Cole of DFC Intelligence, who told *Newsweek*, "It's incredible marketing. You have people fighting to get it from the stores."[7]

That was before the other pieces of Nintendo's $54 million integrated-marketing campaign kicked in. Another important strategy was to use database marketing to send a videotaped sales pitch to a half million potential customers. A sampling program with Blockbuster Video, the premier home-video entertainment provider, made the game available starting the day prior to the launch. Viewers could also pick up game pieces for a Spot the Dot Instant Win Game on Nickelodeon. The top TV kid's network offered prizes including Nintendo 64, Super Mario 64, and a walk-on role on the hit show *The Secret World of Alex Mack*.

Another tie-in was a "One in 64 Wins!" sweepstakes appearing on more than eighty million boxes of Kellogg's cereals. Four Grand Prize winners won their own exclusive neighborhood block party featuring a specially outfitted Nintendo 64 trailer complete with multiple game-play stations, driven right to their neighborhood, plus, of course, their own Nintendo 64 video game system and Super Mario 64 game.

At year-end the *Chicago Tribune* reported, "Some retailers are so ecstatic about Nintendo 64, they're calling it the Cabbage Patch of the 1990s. Not so. It's even bigger. Back in 1983, more than three million Cabbage Patch kids were sold within six months of their introduction, reaping $64 million in sales as well as some tussles in toy stores as parents struggled to find the funny-faced dolls amid a holiday-season shortage. But Nintendo's numbers are more impressive."[8]

The comparison was also apt because of the key role that marketing public relations played in each of these phenomena. The Cabbage Patch craze was fueled entirely by public relations. There was no advertising, or need for it, until sales plateaued after nearly every little girl in America had adopted her very own Cabbage Patch kid. Like the Cabbage Patch introduction, there was no advertising support for the launch of Nintendo 64.

At year-end *People Weekly* named Nintendo 64 "Best of Bytes" for 1996, describing Super Mario as "one small step for a plumber, one giant leap for Nintendo."[9]

The ultimate accolade for Nintendo 64 was its selection by *Time* as the machine of the year. A full-page color illustration of Mario and the Nintendo 64 machine appeared on the cover of the magazine's fourteen-page "Tech Buyer's Guide." Explaining its choice, the editors said, "The new Nintendo 64 has done to American video-gaming what the 707 did to air travel. Since arriving on these shores in late September, the 64 has set records for sales, hype, and, most important, slack jaws. The pure mix of art and technology implicit in the machine's design and the games that run on it help it transcend the category of mere amusement."

"No surprise then that the world—or at least the world's allowance-bearing teens—are beating a track to Nintendo. The 64-bit machines show every sign of being the over-the-top smash-hit consumer-electronics item of the year."[10]

Nintendo 64 not only became the star of the 1996 holiday season, it became the fastest-selling video-game system in history with 1.75 million unit sales in the United States in thirteen weeks.

Lessons Learned

- Have a long-range strategy to build media interest and consumer anticipation.
- Line up expert endorsements.
- Target key media for prelaunch test drives.
- Know the consumer. Don't overlook any media opportunity to reach those that play and those that buy.
- Originate prelaunch publicity at the biggest industry trade show.
- Create a great photo op with a prelaunch stunt.
- Use video to demonstrate the product and build marketplace excitement.
- Fan the frenzy with reports of consumer demand.

- Don't disappoint eager consumers. Announce that product shortages won't last.

- Publicize your product as top-of-gift-wish lists.

McDonald's Biggest Introduction

McDonald's new adult hamburger, the Arch Deluxe, was two years and 500 combinations in the making.

It was the biggest product launch in McDonald's history and the occasion for the company to stage its biggest PR event ever. McDonald's wanted a single, simultaneous event where the entire U.S. and Canadian McDonald's system, customers, and media could share in the unveiling of the new "brand" for grown-up customers.

The company also wanted to maximize the launch impact at the grass-roots level by providing a road map for local market activities to work in tandem with the national launch.

For a month prior to the "McMoment" of the product unveiling, McDonald's longtime public relations firm, Golin/Harris Communications, arranged for McDonald's famous clown, Ronald McDonald, to make "surprise publicity appearances" at high-profile "grown-up" events. The goal was to build anticipation and momentum for the launch by signaling that something new and different was happening at McDonald's. The Ronald sightings teaser campaign was designed to create a buzz about McDonald's without giving away the name or nature of the new product. The newly tuxedoed Ronald was "spotted" by media at such nationally televised adult events as the Academy Awards, Kentucky Derby, Masters Golf Tournament, and New York fashion shows. He was even seen comparing red-hair styles with Dennis Rodman at a Chicago Bulls game. Locally, hundreds of Ronald sightings at community events were captured on TV and in newspapers across the country.

An ad campaign based on the Ronald sightings PR concept hit the airways before the national launch. The teaser commercials found Ronald indulging in uncharacteristically adult pursuits such as disco dancing, playing golf, and shooting pool. Posters of Ronald in black-tie appeared in McDonald's restaurants to further the teaser program. These stunts complemented the advertising message "Looks like McDonald's is becoming a little more grown-up." Posters of Ronald in tuxedo garb appeared in McDonald's restaurants throughout the United States, furthering the integrated teaser campaign. Consumer research revealed a 34 percent unaided awareness that "something is going to happen at McDonald's" as a result of the Ronald sightings campaign. In addition, 59 percent of consumers claimed to have seen at least one Ronald teaser spot.

On launch day, the national media and the McDonald's employee family in every community witnessed the product unveiling simultaneously via live satellite. Two thousand-plus home office employees alone participated in a special lobby rally.

The *Chicago Tribune* not only covered the product story but ran a business feature titled "Making McSplash in News Media: Hamburger Hype-Fest Shows U.S. Firms' Burgeoning Appetite for Free Promotion." *Tribune* reporter Nancy Millman reported that the introduction of the Arch Deluxe hamburger in the United States and Canada was "an intricately staged media hype-fest designed to augment the front-page exposure the company garnered in *USA Today* with press and broadcast news coverage in every major city in the two nations."[11]

McDonald's staged events in about forty cities that linked simultaneous press conferences originating from New York's Radio City Music Hall; Los Angeles's Pacific Cinerama Dome Theater where a seven-story Arch Deluxe, dubbed "the biggest burger the world has ever seen," was unveiled by helicopter; and Toronto's Sky Dome, where thousands of McDonald's employees, franchisees, and suppliers formed a huge McDonald's Arch.

At the New York event, McDonald's Chairman and CEO Michael Quinlan revealed the company's new strategy of giving adult customers more reasons to come to McDonald's. Executive Chef Andrew Selvaggio introduced the new

Ronald McDonald with the Radio City Rockettes help kick off the launch of McDonald's Arch Deluxe at Radio City Music Hall in New York. (Courtesy of McDonald's Corporation)

sandwich consisting of a quarter pound of beef topped with American cheese, tomato, leaf lettuce, onion, catsup, and a special Dijon-style mayonnaise sauce on a potato roll, with hickory-smoked pepper bacon available as an option. The media got a sneak preview of new TV commercials that would blanket the airways that night. Also playing a prominent role was Ronald McDonald, appearing in black-tie and dancing in a kick-line with the Radio City's famed Rockettes in a tribute to the Arch Deluxe.

CEO Quinlan gave the official order for every one of the 12,500 McDonald's restaurants in the United States and Canada to "fire up the grills and begin serving the Arch Deluxe."

The national launch event was supplemented by a full complement of PR activities, including "Deluxe Deliveries" to remote media and a satellite media tour and live national media appearances by Chef Selvaggio.

The carefully orchestrated teaser campaign was geared to provide momentum to a massive marketing effort that was totally integrated from day one.

On the evening after the press introduction, the new campaign for "the burger with the grown-up taste" blanketed the airways.

Mark Goldstein, president of Fallon McElligott, the advertising agency for the launch, told Advertising Age that the PR drove the advertising and that "what people remember most is the teaser spots that grew from the PR strategy."

The introduction of the Arch Deluxe generated more publicity than McDonald's had ever received for a public relations program. Nearly 500 million impressions were recorded during the first week alone. In all, the public relations campaign yielded more than two billion print and broadcast impressions. The story received more than fifty hours of television coverage, including nine mentions of the product on CNN and a dozen more on the late-night talk shows. Content analysis revealed that the adult positioning was communicated very clearly with 90 percent of the stories describing the Arch Deluxe as "the burger with grown-up taste."

Telephone surveys showed that within five days of the national launch, five out of every eight Americans knew that McDonald's was offering a new burger called the Arch Deluxe. By the ninth day, awareness levels reached 81 percent.

McDonald's new adult hamburger got off to a good sales start. Launch sales exceeded projections by more than 30 percent. One month after the introduction, Ronald McDonald appeared on the floor of the New York Stock Exchange to serve the 100-millionth Arch Deluxe to the exchange's president.

The enterprising publicists at Golin/Harris were able to arrange for a Newsweek interview with Chef Selvaggio. The former executive chef at Chicago's elegant Pump Room told the newsweekly that "it was fantastic if he sold twelve of his favorite entrées a night at the Pump Room."

"Arch Deluxe, the first month, 100 million orders. I'm touching that many people's lives. To exceed the expectations of someone who's eaten burgers all his life—what a challenge for a chef!" he exclaimed.[12]

Media coverage for the Deluxe sandwich line was so extensive that in McDonald's 1996 Annual Report, Chief Financial Officer Mike Conley commented that "the press—possibly as a result of our exuberant product-launch publicity—seemed to think this line would single-handedly change the momentum of the U.S. business. Considering the size and breadth of McDonald's business, that was never our intent. What we did intend for this line is happening: these sandwiches are helping position McDonald's over the long term as a great place for adults as well as kids."[13]

Despite the initial success of the Arch Deluxe, its future is, at this writing, uncertain.

Lessons Learned

- Build anticipation for the big announcement by combining teaser advertising with publicity stunts and leaks.
- If you have an instantly recognizable spokescharacter, send him or her where the cameras are.
- If he's the world's best-known clown, have him clown it up.
- After the clown has his or her day among grown-ups, send your clown back home with the kids.
- There's no business like show business. Stage an extravaganza the media can't miss.
- Make the product the star. Bring in the brass as supporting players.
- Link big events from coast to coast and Canada, too.
- Use closed-circuit coverage and local stunts to grab coverage in key markets.
- Position your product directly to the target market. Make sure consumers know it's for them.
- Unite your employees behind the line by conducting a closed circuit telecast.
- Encourage local promotions.

CHAPTER 7

Introducing High-Tech and Health-Care Products

Two of the hottest growth areas for marketing public relations are health care and high technology. Together they now account for more than one-third of fee income of the top 50 public relations firms, according to *O'Dwyer's Directory of PR Firms*. There is every reason to believe that their rapid growth will continue to outpace all other practice areas. That is why the use of MPR to drive integrated campaigns that build excitement about new products in these categories is deserving of special attention in this chapter.

A new breed of public-relations specialists in high-tech and health care has emerged. The major public relations firms have either built their own specialty practices in these areas or have acquired independent specialist firms. The importance of the technology practice was underscored when the giant Interpublic Group, one of the last advertising-based communications conglomerates to enter the public relations field, acquired a leading technology public relations firm, the Weber Group, in 1996 with the intention of building a full-service public relations operation around it.

In the foreword to the 1996 edition of his number one *New York Times* bestseller, *The Road Ahead,* Bill Gates, Chairman, CEO, and cofounder of Microsoft Corporation, noted that:

> ❝ During the PC industry's infancy, the mass media paid little attention to what was going on in the brand-new business. Those of us who were enthralled by computers and their possibilities went unnoticed outside our own circles. We were hardly what you'd call trendy.
>
> But this next journey, on the so-called information highway, is the topic of an endless stream of newspaper and magazine articles, television and radio broadcasts, and rampant speculation. There has been an unbelievable amount of interest in the communications revolution during the past few years, both inside and outside the computer industry.[1] ❞

Regis McKenna believes that "in new and fast-growing industries, journalists can play the role of evangelists. They can preach the new technology. The large number of computer enthusiasts among the press corps certainly has helped expand the markets for personal computers. The press can help reinforce and broaden the credibility the product and company have already gained. It can educate, ease fears by making customers feel secure about new technologies."[2]

Interest in technology products has spread from the scores of technology publications to the mainstream media. The tech beat is covered with the intensity once reserved for the automotive and entertainment industries. Network news and morning shows review the hot new items introduced at the giant Comdex show and high-interest high-tech consumer products throughout the year. *Newsweek* runs a weekly "Cyberscope" page devoted to new computers, software, CD-ROMs, Internet, and online products. *Business Week* runs a weekly front-of-the-book "Technology & You" page for executives. Even *Playboy* runs a monthly column called "Wired" on new-technology products. The emergence of high-tech products as the most newsworthy of all product categories can be seen by the fact that *People,* the most mainstream of all weekly magazines, picks the "Best of Bytes" (and Worst) along with "Best of Tube," "Best of Screen," "Best of Song," and "Best of Pages" (i.e., books) in its annual year-end special double issue.

Reputation Management editor Paul Holmes says that "technology marketers are talking less and less to their fellow wireheads and more and more to business managers, housewives, and thirteen-year-old Doom addicts."[3]

John Brodeur, president of Brodeur Porter Novelli, a leading high-tech public relations firm, says, "what we are seeing is a convergence of the consumer market and the technology market."[4]

There is no better example than the headlines generated worldwide when an IBM computer named Deep Blue defeated Garry Kasparov, the greatest chess champion in history. The *New York Times* reported that "in the course of defeating Mr. Kasparov in a six game match, Deep Blue accomplished a feat that computer scientists have dreamed of for decades, capturing the imaginations of millions of people around the world."[5]

The media were quick to point out that the victory had, as *Time* magazine put it, "been a PR bonanza for its creator." The *Wall Street Journal* headline was "Checkmate! Deep Blue is IBM Publicity Coup." It reported, "International Business Machines Corp. portrays the contest as a triumph of technology. That may be, but it looks more like a triumph of public relations. The match has appeared on the cover of *Newsweek,* in a *Washington Post* editorial, a commentary on National Public Radio, on network newscasts, and in countless stories in hundreds of newspapers worldwide. Even Letterman and Leno weighed in. The tone of the breathless coverage makes it seem like some world-changing event. Only if your world is marketing. IBM spent an estimated $5 million on the match—including publicity, prizes, and building and programming the computer. But it says it has already reaped the equivalent of more than $100 million worth of favorable and free publicity. IBM's Internet site, which is covering the competition live, drew an astonishing one million viewers during Tuesday's match, the company says, perhaps the most highly trafficked event ever on the World Wide Web."[6] And that was days before the inscrutable computer crushed the world's champ, making the match the number-one news story around the globe.

The event reached a total worldwide audience of more than 2 billion and was spectacularly successful in communicating IBM's technology leadership and reinforcing its positioning as the company that finds "solutions for a small planet."

Bill Gates's Excellent Adventure

Then there was the introduction of Windows 95.

Paul Holmes says, "The software giant was able to take what was essentially an upgrade of an existing operating system, and use mainstream consumer marketing and public relations techniques to create a phenomenon unlike any new product introduction in living memory."[7]

Microsoft's master marketer Bill Gates indeed pulled out all the stops and out-hyped the marketing geniuses of the entertainment business when he introduced Windows 95 to the world.

His take-no-prisoners public relations plan was so brilliantly crafted and flawlessly executed that Windows 95 had achieved near-universal awareness weeks and months before the product hit the stores and the ads went on the air.

The public relations campaign was designed to position Windows 95 as a "milestone" in computing. Its promise was to make computing easier, faster, and more fun for everyone. The objective of the MPR campaign was to establish Windows 95 as a "must-upgrade" and position it as the standard in computing. To accomplish this, public relations had to communicate the technical superiority of Windows 95 and preempt negative news by focusing on the positive.

Microsoft used two public relations firms to maximize opportunities with the trade and the general interest media, respectively. Its technology agency, Waggener Edstrom, worked with the technology media while consumer marketing specialist, Patrice Tanaka & Co., expanded coverage with magazines, newspapers, radio, and TV.

The massive communications effort to consumers, corporate customers, and industry analysts was sustained for twenty months without the benefit of advertising support. To gain the critical support of industry, almost daily communications were maintained by Microsoft and Waggener Edstrom with the top fifty trade editors and analysts. They were asked for their opinions and suggestions. The result of their involvement was positive coverage that provided readers with reasons to upgrade to Windows 95. This endorsement of the trade media was invaluable in shaping positive coverage in the leading business and news media.

To reach consumers, Microsoft staged a Windows World Tour and gave 50,000 consumers in twenty-three cities an opportunity to experience Windows 95 and many of its new applications prior to the launch. The endorsements of some of these consumers were featured in the media.

With the help of Patrice Tanaka, the company staged an event at New York's Lincoln Center to bring Windows 95 to life for reporters from 200 key consumer media. A series of real-life vignettes involving families, small business owners, and executives demonstrated how Windows 95 could accomplish tasks in the home and on the road that would have been difficult to do in the past.

The events of August 24, 1995, were truly global in scope. Television coverage kicked off west of the international dateline when CNN satellited coverage of the sale of the first copy of Windows 95 from New Zealand. In neighboring Australia, a giant Windows 95 balloon was floated on a barge in Sydney Harbor. The company painted fields in southern France with the Windows 95 logo for the benefit of passing jets, threw a party for 7,000 at the Palais des Congrès in Paris, and handed out an entire day's run of 1.5 million copies of the London Times free to all passersby. Microsoft displayed a 600-foot Windows 95 banner from the world's tallest freestanding structure, Toronto's CN Tower, and bathed New York's Empire State Building in the red, yellow, blue, and green of the Windows logo.

More than 2,500 invited guests, including more than 500 journalists, attended the unveiling ceremonies at the company's corporate headquarters campus in Redmond, Washington. The opening-day closed-circuit television extravaganza hosted by Bill Gates and Tonight Show host Jay Leno was beamed to by-invitation-only gatherings of corporate customers in major U.S. business centers and press who didn't attend the celebration in person. Crowds of thousands of others tuned in to an exclusive telecast at Tandy Corporation's 6,600

Computer City, Radio Shack, and Incredible Universe stores. Others logged on to the festivities on the Internet.

Bill Gates was omnipresent on the TV news and talk-show circuit. Back-to-back interviews were scheduled for key media attending the Redmond event. When Gates gave viewers of ABC's *Good Morning America* a personal demonstration of Windows 95, host Charles Gibson repeatedly compared the launch of Windows 95 to the kind of hype reserved for big Hollywood films.

The *Wall Street Journal* estimated that 3,000 headlines, 6,582 stories, and more than a million words appeared in U.S. media in the two months preceding the launch day. The extent of the news coverage was itself a major story. Three weeks before the launch, *USA Today*, which had itself already run numerous stories about Windows 95, ran a cover story headlined, "Windows 95 Basks in Free Publicity," illustrating the point with a publicity shot of Orlando Magic star Shaquille O'Neal hoisting Bill Gates instead of a basketball. It quoted marketing authority Al Ries, who said, "The lesson in this is that good advance PR on a product could be just as effective as spending millions on ad campaigns."[8]

The combined efforts generated a grand total of twenty cover stories in major trade books and national news publications, 13,000 consumer news stories, 2,000 TV segments, and 100 syndicated radio spots.

As a result of the twenty-month coordinated public relations campaign, an amazing 99 percent of Americans were aware of the product at its launch.

Microsoft followed up arguably the most effective public relations campaign in technology history with a massive advertising and promotion campaign. It was estimated that the company spent an estimated $150 million in media advertising, winning more headlines by appropriating the Rolling Stones song "Start Me Up" for its commercials because it was the first time the Stones had ever commercially licensed one of their songs.

Sales began on August 24 at astounding levels, far exceeding $110 million in the first two months. A year later, Windows 95 was still the top-selling software program. The interest and excitement created by the Windows 95 PR-driven marketing campaign stimulated record sales for PCs, nearly all of them loaded with Windows 95.

Postscript: The song had long since ended, but the melody lingered on. On November 19, 1996, the *Chicago Tribune* reported that Microsoft stock had hit a record high $149 "after the company said it had sold 44 million copies of its Windows 95 operating system software since the product premiered with great fanfare in August of 1995."[9]

Lessons Learned

- Think Big. Big. Big.
- It's your choice. You can make it big news. Even if it's only an upgrade.

- Think global. Search out ways to make a splash in major world markets.
- Make the product and the CEO inseparable. Practice "gelt" by association.
- Make your product part of your vision for the future.
- Make the product's unveiling a party. Put your customers and the media in a festive mood.
- Invite several thousand of your best business friends to see you live or on closed-circuit TV.
- Bring in a big-name celebrity to emcee the event.
- Let public relations lead the way. Use it to dramatize the news and set the stage for advertising and sales.
- Nurture the technology press. Its endorsement opens the gates to techie heaven.
- Make a special effort to reach the rest of us where we live via what we see, hear, and read.
- While the story is hot, take the show on the road to major business centers.
- Make your chairman the star.
- It helps if he is one of the richest men in the world and everybody knows it.

Microsoft Sets Out to Conquer the Internet

Windows 95 was a stunning success, further solidifying Microsoft's position as the world's biggest and most powerful software company. Nevertheless, the company belatedly recognized that the future belonged to the Internet. Microsoft's single-minded dedication to become the dominant force in the Internet market was declared loud and clear by Bill Gates barely two months after Windows 95 was launched.

On December 7, 1995, Bill Gates hosted an all-day program for 300 analysts, journalists, and customers at the Seattle Convention Center to announce Microsoft's frontal attack on the Internet market and to declare war on Netscape, the dominant player in the browser market. A *Business Week* cover story, "Inside Microsoft: The untold story of how the Internet forced Bill Gates to reverse course," reported that at midnight before the big show, a public relations executive told Gates the presentations were overwhelming and that they needed a three-point summary for reporters. Gates blurted out, "I just want them to get that we're hard-core about the Internet."[10] Gates left no doubt that Microsoft had every intention of playing—and winning—in the new software game.

The date was not accidental. According to *Time,* "Gates hit a rare rhetorical high, offering up what amounted to his new digital gospel. To hammer home the message, he reached back into history, recalling the words of Admiral Isoroku Yamamoto on the day Japan attacked the United States: 'I fear we have awakened a sleeping giant.' It was December 7, 1995, and Bill Gates was taking Microsoft to war."[11]

Gates's declaration that every Microsoft division would be refocused to develop products for the Internet was widely quoted in the business and news media.

Over the next three months, Microsoft put actions into words by introducing a stream of Internet products. The company demanded attention and won headlines with software giveaways and events such as programmers' conferences staged simultaneously in forty movie theaters. *Time* stated that "The gang from Redmond, Washington, has pressed home one message: Microsoft is playing for keeps."

Enter Internet Explorer 3.0

In August, Gates proclaimed that the battle of the browsers would begin for real. At a lavish launch event in San Francisco, Gates unveiled Explorer 3.0, Microsoft's newest Web browser to compete with Netscape's Navigator, with a flurry of news. Gates told reporters, "This is a milestone. Today marks the starting line."

Microsoft issued a news release announcing "the immediate availability of technology to enable fast and safe download of Web application" and the offer of free content from top Web sites. Explorer 3.0 was officially made available for download at midnight and Gates urged customers to wait up and log on to get a copy. A media alert headlined "Surfing in Your Slippers. Who Needs Leno and Letterman? Microsoft Hosts 'Midnight Madness' Tonight to Launch Microsoft Internet Explorer 3.0." By dawn the next day, 32,000 people had downloaded the program. In its first week online, the number was more than a million.

Another media alert was required to announce that the record demand for Explorer 3.0 was overwhelming download servers and to apologize for download delays.

The launch was accompanied by massive media coverage. Bill Gates was inevitably interviewed by all major print and broadcast news media.

A dedicated Explorer 3.0 Web site was effectively utilized to reach specific audience segments. For the media, there was a comprehensive chronological collection of every press release and press kit issued by the company. The company also took the unusual step of printing summaries of Explorer 3.0 reviews. Microsoft welcomed the media to its "Internet Explorer Online Press Room," stating, "If you're a reporter, columnist, reviewer, or anyone else interested in Microsoft Internet Explorer press resources, you've come to the right place. Here, you'll find plenty of information to help you spread the word about Microsoft

Internet Explorer. You'll also find links to articles and reviews written by members of the press. And who knows? Perhaps we've included something you've written about the Internet Explorer."

The Web site included technical white papers, a complete file of press releases, and reproducible press graphics. The Web site capitalized on the value of third-party endorsement, saying that "Sure, we're bound to say good things about our own products. But why not see what everyone else is saying about Microsoft Internet Explorer? In almost every case, we couldn't have said it better ourselves." Included are capsule reviews and "defining quotes" from diverse media from the tech books (*C/Net, Hotwired, CRN, PC Week, PC Magazine Online, Infoworld, Tech Web, Computer World,* and *The Net*) to daily newspapers. Among those quoted: the *Wall Street Journal* ("Internet Explorer seems to have been designed with more attention to the needs of average, nontechnical users. On top of that, it's free."); *USA Today* ("Microsoft's technology is as simple as click-and-update. Netscape's system is, by comparison, clumsy."); *Boston Globe* ("Microsoft's browser is a Netscape killer."); and even the morning network talk show *Good Morning America* ("Explorer is free. A knockout blow to Netscape.").

Within a month, Bill Gates appeared (again) on a *Time* magazine cover with this banner headline: "He conquered the computer world. Now he wants the Internet. If Microsoft overwhelms Netscape, Bill Gates could rule the Information Age." The magazine declared that the transformation that set Microsoft on the road to a Net-based future had certified the emergence of Bill Gates into a world-class CEO. "Microsoft's warp-speed reinvention may set the standard for information-age corporate agility."[12]

By December of 1996, a year after Microsoft had announced its militant assault on the Internet market, *Newsweek* was ready to emblazon Bill Gates's remarkable achievement by declaring "The Microsoft Century." The newsweekly reported that "Far from hampering Microsoft's progress, the Internet has turbocharged it. Revitalized by its cyberspace initiative, the company is ready to gobble up the limitless opportunities that will come from the Net's restructuring of commerce itself."[13]

Gates pointed to the critical importance of media endorsement when he told *Newsweek*, "In December, no one inside or outside of Microsoft would've said that by August we'd be winning virtually all of the browser reviews."

Gates, who had so successfully barnstormed the business community for Windows, once again took the road to deliver speeches on Microsoft's Internet strategy to major business forums, trade associations, and educational institutions.

His year-old campaign culminated at the Comdex Conference in Las Vegas where he delivered a widely covered speech he called "Information at Your Fingertips: A Challenge for the PC Industry." The main hall was dominated by Microsoft's massive 40,000-square-foot display.

The business world's most-persistent cover boy was also out promoting the paperback edition of his 1995 bestseller, *The Road Ahead*. Gates told the *New*

York Times that a revision of the book was needed because when he peered down the road ahead a year earlier, the view looked far different. He acknowledged that he was late to grasp the significance of the Internet's explosive growth, so the book was rewritten to give it prominence.

The *Times* pointed out that in the year since the Pearl Harbor day speech, "Microsoft has gone head-to-head with Netscape Communications in a war over competing software to browse the World Wide Web; entered a partnership with NBC on a cable news channel and Web news site, MSNBC, and redesigned the Microsoft Network, with 1.6 million subscribers, to be primarily an Internet provider."[14]

As this is written, the question of whether Microsoft's operating system and its Internet browser are two distinct products or whether they should be considered one integral product has not been resolved. The Justice Department has charged Microsoft with requiring personal computer makers that license Windows 95 to install the Internet Explorer in all of their computers. Microsoft planned to release Windows 98, an upgrade of Windows 95 that integrates the Internet Explorer, in 1998. It has become clear that Microsoft is moving beyond personal-computer software and even the Internet to become a media company for the 21st century.

Who knows what wonders Microsoft will reveal and how many more Bill Gates cover stories will appear by the time you read this.

Lessons Learned

- Declare war on the enemy.
- Dedicate every waking moment to winning the war.
- Dramatize your message to convince customers, analysts, and the media.
- Maintain high expectations with new news.
- Pull out the stops in announcing major product news.
- Line up industry allies.
- Line up support from media before the announcement.
- Declare yourself the winner.
- Let media in on the inside story.
- Rewrite your vision, your mission, and your book.

Pharmaceutical Marketing Meets Public Relations

Like high-tech PR, health-care public relations is becoming more and more directed to the consumer. This is a comparatively new development in a fast-growing field that traditionally targeted doctors, nurses, pharmacists, and other health-care professionals.

Marketing consultant Tom Chetrick of NCI Consulting told *Advertising Age* that "we're going to see more and more brands use PR in the future—if you have a message that's newsworthy." The reason: "Media costs keep going up above the rate of inflation."[15]

Edelman Healthcare Worldwide, one of the pioneers in health-care public relations, now subscribes to a "convergence marketing" strategy that combines health-care knowledge, consumer lifestyle marketing expertise, and interactive technology capabilities "that satisfy the new, better informed, and more self-reliant consumer." Nancy Turett, managing director, told *O'Dwyer's PR Services Report* that "Health-care marketing today calls for increasingly melding the creativity and mass appeal of consumer marketing with the credibility and professional targeting associated with ethical pharmaceutical marketing. In addition to symposia and dissemination of materials to medical trade media, health-care marketers are applying approaches that have been most successful in the consumer PR area."[16]

Edelman blended health-care, consumer, and technology expertise to introduce AXID AR, a new over-the-counter heartburn medication from Whitehall-Robins. The public relations platform integrated a university-conducted epidemiological study, a computerized self-profiler, and publicity-producing consumer marketing strategy.

The study conducted by the New York Hospital–Cornell Medical Center demonstrated the link between heartburn and lifestyle and identified eight heartburn profiles. Reporters attending a launch event were invited to take the "AXID AR Heartburn Challenge" by taking a sample on arrival and, after the briefing, eating a heartburn-inducing lunch consisting of a hot dog, chips, soda, and chocolate brownie. The briefing was followed by a public lunch where more than 1,000 New Yorkers were given box lunches, branded T-shirts, hats, educational brochures, and product samples. Hand-held computers and touch-screen computer monitors were used to conduct the first-ever public heartburn screening. The integrated program also used advertising spokespersons to conduct media interviews via satellite media tour.

Today health-care news is widely reported on network and local news. The TV networks employ full-time "medical editors" and provide frequent guests who discuss health-care "news you can use." Research findings reported in prestigious medical journals such as the *New England Journal of Medicine* and the *Journal of the American Medical Association* (JAMA) are closely followed by the mainstream consumer media. So are the introductions of important new prescription pharmaceuticals and over-the-counter products. Products from "Aspirin the Wonder Drug" to Prozac to Redux have become cover-story subjects in the newsweeklies.

The success of Quigley Corporation's Cold-Eeze is attributable to a report on ABC's *20/20* news magazine about a study conducted by the Cleveland Clinic published in the *Annals of Internal Medicine* that claimed the zinc lozenges relieved symptoms of the common cold within three days. The *Tampa Tribune* reported that moments after the program ended, thousands of Walgreens pharmacies, primary carriers of the lozenges, received calls from congested consumers desperate for relief. "When other mainstream media picked up on the story, they reported that the study had generated a minor media frenzy."[17]

Tagamet HB and the Heartburn Wars

Public relations has, in recent years, played a key role in the introduction of over-the-counter pharmaceutical products in nonprescription doses. The importance of MPR is magnified in the case of billion-dollar categories such as painkillers and heartburn medications. The challenge is to find new ways to generate consumer excitement and interest about products that previously were marketed primarily to the medical profession.

The successful introduction of the heartburn medication, Tagamet HB, in over-the-counter form resulted in the largest first-day sale in SmithKline Beecham's history. The company attributed this achievement and the fast and widespread acceptance of the product entirely to the public relations program because the nationwide advertising campaign and other promotional efforts had not yet started.

SmithKline Beecham and its public relations firm, Porter-Novelli, had to overcome several critical obstacles to ensure product success. Pepcid AC was the first of the prescription heartburn medications, known as H_2 antagonists, to make the prescription to over-the-counter switch. Consumers were already wholeheartedly embracing the H_2 category, making Tagamet HB the underdog. Adding to the challenge, Pepcid AC launched a strategic campaign that emphasized a "prevention" claim that Tagamet HB would not have at the outset. Pepcid publicized "no side effects," while Tagamet had on-package side-effects labeling.

To maximize national media coverage, Porter-Novelli planned a two-tiered media relations campaign. The first phase was a massive publicity campaign around the approval announcement. Immediately on FDA approval, senior SmithKline Beecham officials conducted an interactive telephone briefing with major media from company headquarters in Pittsburgh. A video news release package was overnighted to 200 broadcast stations.

The company claimed that Tagamet provides relief in a way that no antacid could by blocking the production of stomach acid. The message strategy was based on the Nobel Prize–winning development of cimetidine (the chemical name for Tagamet), which differentiated Tagamet HB from Pepcid AC and antacids. The announcement capitalized on Tagamet's seventeen-year prescription use.

Some 237 million prescriptions had been written for twenty-three million people in the United States alone. The product was positioned as a new category of treatment, differentiating it from antacids and from Pepcid on the basis of pricing and dosage as well as on scientific heritage.

Local physicians in the top fifty U.S. markets were recruited for local media interviews. Press materials were localized in each market with information and graphics showing the estimated number of local heartburn sufferers.

Massive media coverage included stories on the Associated Press and Reuters wires that ran in hundreds of newspapers and radio and television stations, a front-page story in *USA Today,* and the first of three stories in *Time.* In its year-end review issue, the magazine named the science behind the product "the Best of 1995."

The media coverage of the approval generated a high degree of consumer and trade interest in and anticipation of Tagamet HB. To meet retailer demand, the company worked around the clock for two months before the product was ready to go to market.

The Product Launch

A second publicity campaign was unleashed when Tagamet was ready to hit the shelves. The new phase was designed to regenerate interest in and excitement about the product. Because most media had covered the story at least twice during the year, creating another big story was a challenge. Porter-Novelli met it by tailoring stories about heartburn prevalence and product usage for national and local media outlets. The data compiled by SmithKline Beecham was also used to identify and target a group of southeastern cities with a higher prevalence of heartburn than the national average, which was dubbed "Acid Alley."

Launch publicity efforts also capitalized on the battle between Tagamet HB and Pepcid AC for market share. The "Heartburn Wars" provided media with a new story angle. Another story line used effectively by Porter-Novelli was the tremendous effort to meet retailer demand for the product. The largest single-day product delivery in company history was given the name "Operation Heartburn."

"Heartburn Wars" and the availability of Tagamet HB in stores set off another wave of major stories in newspapers, newsmagazines, and television news, including features on *Good Morning America* and the *Today Show.*

The two-tiered public relations program drove product acceptance and record first-day sales. Massive advertising ("One of the Most Prescribed Medications in History: Now Available Without a Prescription for Heartburn Sufferers") kicked in after the initial success, building on the excitement generated by the publicity and resulting in one of the most successful integrated marketing campaigns in the pharmaceutical industry.

Lessons Learned

- Plan well ahead.
- Be ready to go on D-Day at H-Hour (for products requiring FDA approval).
- Lead off the marketing effort by maximizing news coverage.
- Focus on consumer benefits of both packaging and product.
- Cite research that reveals new information on the problem your product solves.
- Have another go at it when the product hits the market.
- Enhance the product message with a public-education component.
- Make it easy for consumers to get information materials with a toll-free number.
- Gain public endorsement of relevant health organizations.
- Select an established authority in the field as your national spokesperson.
- Announce all of the above at a news conference at an appropriate non-commercial location.
- Dramatize the news by setting up a satellite media tour.
- Recruit local physicians in key markets for media interviews.
- Localize the story with information about the incidence of the condition your product treats in major markets.
- Generate headlines by publicizing the battle for brand share.
- Tailor public information components to discreetly target health-professional audiences.
- Trumpet news of the marketing effort behind the product to business and trade media serving major retail categories of trade.

CHAPTER 8

Introducing New Products When There Is No Advertising

IT IS WIDELY ASSUMED THAT THE INTRODUCTION OF A NEW CONSUMER PRODUCT must be supported by a substantial advertising campaign.

But it ain't necessarily so.

CNS, Inc., a small company with a small advertising budget, achieved remarkable sales success using marketing public relations exclusively to introduce Breathe Right, a nasal strip designed to aid breathing and reduce snoring.

Like Gatorade, a product that achieved high visibility and extraordinary sales success through its involvement with sports and particularly with trainers of professional football teams, CNS's strategy was to showcase widespread use of the Breathe Right strip by sports heroes to motivate consumers.

The product, which was invented in 1987 by a Minnesota contracting engineer seeking relief from a lifetime breathing problem, was approved for use by the FDA in 1993, but it had achieved only moderate sales until CNS embarked on what *Reputation Management* magazine called "one of the most inventive small-budget marketing programs of recent years."[1]

The magazine reported that CNS Chief Executive Dan Cohen commissioned research that demonstrated that Breathe Right could reduce nasal airflow resistance by as much as 31 percent. He initially felt that the product would most benefit patients with allergies, colds, and sinusitis, and excessive snorers, and had marketed it to otolaryngologists and allergists. While its use by athletes was less known, it seemed logical that Breathe Right would benefit performing athletes.

CNS engaged the Minneapolis office of Shandwick USA to evaluate the interest of both athletes and the media. It sent free boxes of the product to the trainers of every National Football League team who were quick to recognize the health benefits it offered the players who wear mouth guards, forcing them to breathe through the nose.

When Herschel Walker of the Philadelphia Eagles caught a cold and wore a Breathe Right strip during a game, an enterprising reporter from the *Philadelphia Inquirer* wrote an article about it on the front page of the sports section, launching what would become widespread media coverage of this strange-looking product that had piqued fans' curiosity.

Shandwick conducted an audit of all NFL trainers to find out what players thought of the product and a survey of sports media to determine their awareness of the product. The agency also conducted focus groups to determine the product's strongest selling points.

Based on their findings, a concise message about the product's benefits to performing athletes was crafted and a widespread effort undertaken to spread the Breathe Right sports story to print and broadcast media. A Shandwick spokesperson told *Reputation Management* that "we needed to create a buzz about the product among consumers by educating the sports media about Breathe Right and encouraging coverage. Because of the product's quirky nature, we aimed to give it a lighthearted brand image, while retaining a proper emphasis on its serious medical attributes."

Shandwick's work reinforced a simple message: "If players can wear it on national television, you can wear it while you sleep."

Additional product was provided to trainers explaining the benefits experienced by trainers and players who used it. Superstar wide receiver Jerry Rice of the San Francisco 49ers attracted fan and media attention by wearing a Breathe Right strip in a game on ABC's *Monday Night Football*. In postgame interviews he explained the strip to curious reporters. He said that the device helped him take in more oxygen more easily while running flat out with a gumshield in his mouth.

Rice was such an effective and visible spokesperson that Breathe Right signed a consulting agreement with him in time for Super Bowl XXIX. An interview with Jerry was filmed and distributed to television stations via satellite for use as a Super Bowl sports feature.

To enhance media involvement with the product, samples were distributed to all reporters covering the Super Bowl. They also were given Breathe Right plastic-nose pencil sharpeners that were so popular with the media that the company rushed in 1,000 more sharpeners to fill requests.

During the Super Bowl telecast, there were 140 different Breathe Right exposures. The product was seen on air for about seven minutes. If these seven minutes were converted into its advertising equivalent at $1 million per 30-second Super Bowl commercial, the value of this free publicity alone would amount to $14 million. Breathe Right was where the action was. Eight touchdowns were scored by players wearing strips. Football analyst John Madden also discussed the product at length on Fox TV.

Publicity about Breathe Right nasal strips generated more than fifty-six million consumer impressions in three months, culminating with the Super Bowl. Media that covered the story included the popular morning shows *Good Morning America* and *Live with Regis and Kathy Lee* and articles in print media as far-ranging as the *Wall Street Journal* and *Better Homes and Gardens* as well as the sports media. Even Rush Limbaugh talked about Breathe Right strips on his syndicated radio and TV shows.

More than half of the broadcast and print stories focused on the product's health uses for nonathletes.

The proof of the success of this public relations–driven program is that Breathe Right sales for the first quarter of 1995 were twice its total sales for the entire previous year. Sales soared from $2.8 million in 1994 to $48.6 million in 1995. The program also opened a new distribution channel for the product—sports stores. The public relations effort had an equally impressive effect on marketing the company's stock. The value of CNS, Inc., stock more than doubled.[2]

Chicago Tribune reporter Nancy Millman wrote that "Although the company chief, who is a medical doctor, attributes the product's success to its efficacy, it was a stroke of marketing savvy that first got the strips on the tube for free."

Business resulting from public relations alone was so good that the company could afford to lay out more than $1 million to advertise for the first time on the next Super Bowl. The ads supplemented the publicity for what could now be called a fully integrated marketing communications program.

Lessons Learned

- Solid research is the first step to developing sound strategy.
- Keep the message simple.
- Think pictures. They can be more important than words in creating consumer curiosity.
- Influencing trusted influencers can create a bonanza of celebrity endorsements.
- If a popular celebrity likes your product so well that he talks it up with the media, sign him up.

- Provide samples to the media so they can test your product.
- Think media beyond where you would spend ad dollars.
- Even a serious product can be promoted in a lighthearted way.
- A medical story doesn't have to be a snore.

Crayola's High-Visibility MPR Strategy

The name Binney & Smith may not ring a bell, but everyone who has ever been a child knows the Crayola brand.

Each year Binney & Smith produces more than two billion Crayola crayons. Introduced in 1905, the first box of Crayolas sold for five cents. Today they are sold in more than sixty countries with boxes printed in eleven different languages.

One of the world's best-known brands has a tiny advertising budget for an international brand. In the United States, the company spends about $3 million on advertising.

Yet the brand has achieved high visibility by employing public relations as its principal marketing tool. Because MPR has proven its ability to leverage the brand's strength, Crayola has maintained a consistent level of commitment to its use both in introducing new products and keeping the brand top-of-mind among consumers and customers. Binney & Smith's small in-house public relations staff has been able to create news on a continuing basis for a seemingly unnewsy category. Its success is a function of the importance of the strategic role public relations as assigned in the marketing mix.

Brad Drexler, Manager of Corporate Communications at Binney & Smith, told *PR Reporter*, a public relations trade newsletter, that "We have been able to orchestrate several campaigns to introduce products or programs without the support of advertising and demonstrate that we can impact sales in a large way. That has helped strengthen the credibility of what public relations can accomplish. Our sales people can now recognize how we can help them do their job in a big way."[3]

Introducing Crayola's New Colors

In 1990, Crayola introduced eight new child-tested colors, the first new colors in eighteen years, and retired eight old ones. In line with the company's philosophy of listening to the consumer, focus groups were held with the primary market for crayons, children between the ages of four to ten. They were asked to review a variety of products and make recommendations on how they would improve or change them to make them more appealing.

Drexler told *Inside PR* editor Paul Holmes that suggestions ranged from packaging changes to product improvements, specifically adding bolder, brighter colors that would allow children to draw and color with hues that were prevalent in their lifestyles.[4]

Crayola made way for eight bright new child-tested colors by removing eight old colors kids found flat and dull—maize, raw umber, violet blue, blue gray, green blue, lemon yellow, orange red, and orange yellow.

The strategy was to use public relations to create awareness through a back-door program that focused initially on the discontinued colors. The old colors were referred to as "retired colors" and were enshrined in a Crayola Hall of Fame created at company headquarters in Easton, Pennsylvania. News of the new product introduction was held until the product was ready to be shipped to stores. When *USA Today* ran a front-page story, "New Crayons Let Kids Paint the Town Fuchsia," an avalanche of media coverage was unleashed.

The company also capitalized on a groundswell of protest from adults who objected to the banishment to crayon heaven of the colors they knew and loved. The company claimed that the protests were genuine and not staged to attract media attention, but admitted that they began to refer media to the protesters and invited them to the Hall of Fame ceremony. The good-natured sound bites from ad hoc groups such as the Committee to Reestablish All Your Old Norms (CRAYON), the National Campaign to Save Lemon Yellow, and Raw Umber and Maize Preservation Society (RUMPS) added a tongue-in-cheek feature that was irresistible to network TV.

The story touched a deep nostalgic vein among media types, who like the rest of us, grew up coloring with Crayolas. CBS's *This Morning* celebrated the new colors by rendering its logo for the day with the new colors. Over at NBC, the *Today Show* brought a company spokesperson to New York for an interview. Even the *Wall Street Journal* weighed in with "Roses Were Reds, Violets Blues, Till They Redid Crayola's Hues." Late-night viewers heard both Johnny Carson and David Letterman talk about the color change in their monologues.

The Crayola Hall of Fame is too far from New York and other media centers for live coverage of the enshrinement, so Crayola brought the story to network affiliates by satellite feed. A video news release included the enshrinement ceremony plus colorful live-action B-roll production footage of child color testing, Crayola crayons rolling off the production line, and even sound bites from protesters outside the event.

The low-cost public relations campaign generated 500 million gross impressions. Because there was no advertising support, the brand's record back-to-school sales results can be directly attributable to the public relations program. Binney & Smith credits public relations with a $6 million incremental sales increase.

Postscript: The company listened to its customers and reintroduced the "extinct eight" colors in a special collectors' edition a few months later. That generated a second wave of publicity recapping the company's decision to update its color selection that made some of its old customers angry. CBS correspondent John Blackstone replayed the story of the protests and hailed the return of raw umber "the only color for tree trunks."

When the company called in the media to announce that the eight retired colors were only semiretired, they demonstrated a sense of humor rare in corporate America. At the event, the beverage served was "New Coke," recalling Coca-Cola's marketing fiasco that didn't take into account the allegiance of core consumers to the "Old Coke."

Celebrating a Big Birthday

When the company celebrated its ninetieth birthday three years later, it introduced sixteen new colors and staged a contest to name them. Consumers were enticed by the chance to be enshrined in the Crayola Hall of Fame, win a free trip to Hollywood for the birthday party, and have their names printed on the crayon they named for a limited time.

Crayola recognized the value of extending media coverage by staging a year-long public relations campaign. Key media events began with contest announcements and culminated at the birthday party.

Each was supported by satellite-fed video news releases. Other publicity tools included an eleven-city satellite media tour and numerous press mailings. Because there were sixteen winners, hometown and regional publicity added a human-interest touch and proximity to the story. The total media reach topped 700 million.

Several major U.S. daily newspapers jumped at the opportunity to show off their new color-printing capabilities by running full-page reports that displayed the colors and explained the contest.

Binney & Smith received calls about the contest from more than 10,000 consumers on its 800-line telephone center. More than two million children and adults entered the contest, all attributable to the power of the company's publicity campaign.

The winners were announced on the brand's big birthday, which was the same day the ninety-six-color box went on sale. If that weren't enough, the company ran a poll to determine the top crayon colors of all-time. Top-tier celebrities from "Peanuts" creator Charles Schultz to TV's Mister Rogers to Whoopi Goldberg and Mike Myers were asked to reveal their favorite colors. Late-night television found both NBC's Jay Leno and CBS's David Letterman talking about Tickle Me Pink, Granny Smith Apple, Purple Mountain's Majesty, Robin's Egg Blue, and Macaroni and Cheese.

The company's sales force merchandised the high-visibility publicity campaign to customers and wrote a record number of orders for the new ninety-six-color box.

It became the company's most successful introduction ever, registering $23 million in sales. Total Crayola crayon sales rose 12 percent for the anniversary year.

High Technology Meets the Crayon

That was the headline on a 1995 Binney & Smith news release announcing the introduction of Crayola Magic Scent crayons, a new line that featured microencapsulated fragrances that release kid-loved aromas when they are used. The new crayons enable kids to make their own scratch-and-sniff artwork. Magic Scent crayons are named for their scents rather than their colors. They include bubble gum, banana, chocolate, strawberry, blueberry, cherry, orange, lemon, spearmint, lime, licorice, grape, rose, pine, coconut, and (would you believe) fresh air.

Crayola timed its introduction to coincide with the peak back-to-school crayon-selling season. It is also the season when media traditionally run back-to-school features and they found the story irresistible.

In announcing Magic Scent to the media, Brad Drexler pulled out a Yale University survey that found the aroma of regular Crayolas was among the top twenty most recognizable smells to U.S. adults. He said "We continually explore ways to add more pizzazz to the coloring experience, but this is the first time we've ever switched our renowned scent. Being able to draw pictures that smell like the real objects adds a whole new dimension to coloring."

Crayola also reassured the press and parents that testing had proved that children are no more likely to eat Magic Scent crayons than regular Crayolas and that they were nontoxic and harmless. More than 400 newspapers ran stories, many of them with an Associated Press color wire photo picturing a six-year-old taking a whiff of Magic Scent "fresh air." Lifestyle editors of newspapers throughout the country sampled the product with local kids who loved them. TV coverage included a clean sweep of network news, much of it including Crayola B-roll of kids scrawling and sniffing Magic Scents. The media had fun with the rejects as well, picking up on the smells the company rejected—unmagical scents such as blue cheese, leather, coffee, skunk, garlic, and hamburger.

Crayola Meets the Net

The ever-imaginative Crayola public relations people invited everyone with a color in his or her name to attend The Crayola Factory, a new multimillion dollar family visitor's center. Colorful individuals were invited to register by mail or on Crayola's World Wide Web site on the Internet. They were enticed by the opportunity to march in the ColorJam Parade of Color and participate in the world's largest finger painting. A crowd of 50,000 Browns, Greens, Whites,

Golds, Grays, and others showed up for the festival, doubling the entire population of Easton.

To celebrate the 100 billionth Crayola crayon, Crayola created a brand-new, "once in a lifetime color"—Blue Ribbon. The color was added to the Big Box for a limited time and kids were told to look for the special color wrapped in special gold foil. Ten kids, big and little, who found the gold-foil wrapped crayons were awarded a trip to Easton for the "ColorJam" parade and party. A random drawing determined the winner who could—and did—swap the 100 billionth crayola crayon for a $100,000 bond. The actual crayon was ensconced in the Crayola Hall of Fame. As a result of the 100 billionth celebration, Binney & Smith achieved a 30 percent increase above sell-through for the same period the previous year. Karen Barger, director of consumer promotion and merchandising said, "We've shown retailers that promotion with a lot of consumer involvement can really move packages."[5]

Crayola continues to find creative ways to reach kids and their parents online. Events featured on the Web site included the Crayola Storybook Maker contest, open to kids five to twelve, which offered the top winners the chance to have their very own book published and sold at book-signing events in their hometowns and put on the Internet.

Lessons Learned

- "First" and "new" are words that make a story. "First new" is even better.

- The media loves stories about kids.

- The proverbial good picture is worth a thousand words, especially if it's of kids and your product. If the picture moves, make that two thousand.

- Stage a fun event where the product is the star.

- With satellite transmission, it's not at all essential to have the media cover the event live.

- People love contests. Especially if there's a chance to become famous for fifteen minutes.

- You don't have to advertise the contest or give away the store to attract lots of entrants.

- Multiple winners multiply and personalize hometown media coverage.

- Stirring in a little good-natured controversy is a harmless and helpful device to attract media attention.

- Make company headquarters an attraction and tourist destination. Elevate the plant tour to a brand-building opportunity.
- Birthdays and other milestones are surefire ways to focus media attention on your company and its products.
- Both kids and their parents are becoming addicted to the Net.
- It helps to start with a product everyone knows and loves.

CHAPTER 9

Revitalizing Old Products

UP TO THIS POINT, WE HAVE DISCUSSED THE VITAL ROLE THAT MARKETING PUBLIC relations plays in introducing new products. Less well understood and less universally applied but equally important are the many ways in which MPR can be used to revitalize, reinvigorate, relaunch, and reposition existing products. This can be done at virtually any stage of the product life cycle.

In the chapters that follow, we will see how companies have effectively used public relations to keep mature products top-of-mind. When there is no real product news, the MPR effort may bring new attention to an old product by focusing on new advertising, packaging, or promotion. The MPR effort may involve identifying the product with a cause that people care about or a special interest of target consumers. It may be an interactive program that involves consumers with the brand or a newsworthy sponsorship. The news may be derived from finding new uses or benefits for the product. Or the product may be updated to meet changing consumer tastes and lifestyles. Nowhere is the job more difficult than in the world of fashion, but as we shall see, it can be accomplished with deft public relations.

Relaunching: "Hipping Up Hush Puppies"

That was the *Newsweek* headline for a 1995 story offering "definitive proof that *anything* can become hip: the Hush Puppies that used to look perfect for *Mister Rogers' Neighborhood* are now turning up in spring fashion shows." The report goes on to say:

> 66 Squishy-soled loafers and lace-up oxfords in rainbow colors are walking out of the stores, as twentysomethings too young to remember earlier uncool incarnations have pushed orders to 400,000 pairs nationwide. Hush Puppies fans can soon look forward to more hues, including wheat-field yellow, black coffee—and electric blue suede shoes a geriatric Elvis could wear around Graceland.[1] 99

The same week, the *New York Times* featured a report on what shoes the hottest celebrities were wearing. Headlined "Famous Feet Pick Old Favorites," the story reported that the biggest trend in Hollywood dressing was buying brands and that the most fashionable brands were Gucci, J. P. Tod, and Hush Puppies. You might ask which brand doesn't belong, but you would be wrong or at least uninformed.

The *Times* reported that the chic Pleasure Swell shop had opened a Hush Puppies boutique earlier in the year and had already sold 6,000 pairs. Customers included Hollywood stars such as Patricia Arquette, Ellen DeGeneres, Daryl Hannah, Lenny Kravitz, and Jean Tripplehorn. Rock star David Bowie and supermodel Iman were pictured by the *Times* "wearing four Hush Puppies (two each)."

"When celebrities go to be photographed for magazine covers, they are made over at the magazine's behest to look glamorous and Hollywood as the world outside sees Hollywood."[2] The paper says most celebrities these days show up in their own Hush Puppies and that when David Bowie was doing a promo from the new album and a press tour, you couldn't get them from the store because every stylist was pulling them.

These stories were the result of a marketing public relations campaign that supported the change in the Hush Puppies product mix from comfort dress to casual comfort.

Research conducted in 1993 had confirmed that Hush Puppies were perceived as conservative and appealing to an older audience. Consumers participating in focus groups described Hush Puppies as casual and comfortable, but they did not consider the shoes to be fashionable.

J. Walter Thompson Public Relations not only had to make the Hush Puppies brand name synonymous with comfort and casual, but had to change the negative perception that the shoes were old and staid.

The primary MPR objectives then were to attract a younger, more fashion-conscious consumer to the brand and to gain distribution in upper-tier department stores and specialty stores. The strategy was to capitalize on the retrofashion trend and reintroduce the company's classic suede footwear as hip and stylish and "must-have."

The original Hush Puppies shoe was reintroduced in December of 1994 in a holiday mailing to influential New York style makers, including key fashion editors, restaurateurs, retailers, stylists, and designers. The word of mouth that Hush Puppies were "in" again became word of media.

The new hip image was reinforced by a press conference the J. Walter Thompson people staged during Fashion Week in New York at the penthouse of the chic Royalton Hotel. The line was previewed by more than sixty newspaper and magazine editors covering the show. Their reactions were captured on video for use in a video news release for television.

A key to the public relations effort was the success of the public relations team in lining up designer endorsements. Agency President Joan Parker told *Inside PR* that "Recognizing an endorsement from the fashion world was a powerful tool of persuasion, Hush Puppies formed an association with leading menswear designer John Bartlett who showcased the classic suede shoes in bright colors in his February, 1994, runway presentation and prominently featured the shoe on the cover of his invitation." The *New York Times* feature traced the Hush Puppies revival to this show inspired by *Forrest Gump,* the immensely popular film in which Tom Hanks wore the shoes. A front-page story in the *Wall Street Journal* was headlined "Will Tom Hanks Wear Hush Puppies to the Oscars?"

Hush Puppies ensured equal exposure for the women's line when Anna Sui, one of the hippest women's fashion designers, featured them in her spring runway event. This resulted in a cover story in *Women's Wear Daily,* the influential publication that sets the news agenda for the newspaper and magazine fashion editors. Photos from both the Sui and Bartlett shows ran in the *New York Times* story.

Through publicity alone, the company completely revamped its brand identity, according to Joan Parker. A targeted MPR program made Hush Puppies a hip "must-have" shoe.

When Hush Puppies were named the Accessory of the Year 1995 by the Council of Fashion Designers of America, *Jack O'Dwyer's Newsletter* credited J. Walter Thompson "for turning an ordinary pigskin suede shoe, introduced in 1958, into a hot fashion trend."[3] He cited the brand's success in working with fashion designers and placing Hush Puppies on the popular TV sitcoms *Seinfeld* and *Friends.*

The brand generated more than 750 million consumer impressions in 1995 and achieved an advertising equivalency that represented an eighty-times return on investment. That media exposure in top markets was directly responsible for opening important new accounts in upscale department stores including Nordstrom, Barneys, Bloomingdale's, Saks Fifth Avenue, Lord & Taylor, and Macy's. Retail sales increased dramatically as did the stock of Wolverine Worldwide, the maker of Hush Puppies.

Lessons Learned

- You're never too old to make a comeback.
- Revamp the line. Ring in the new but don't ring out the old.
- Identify the trendsetters and get them to take a new look.
- Inspire them to spread the word.
- Form alliances with hot designers.
- Media outreach is the key.
- Showcase your product for the right media at the right places.
- Capture the enthusiasm on video for TV.
- Place your product in high-visibility movies and TV sitcoms.
- Win awards and make the most of them.

Repositioning:
Aspirin—the "New Wonder Drug"

My first test for public relations effectiveness is, Did the message reach me? My second is, Did it affect my own buying behavior? Every day when I take my adult low-strength enteric-coated aspirin tablet, I am reminded of the effectiveness of the Aspirin Foundation of America (AFA) public relations campaign repositioning aspirin as an exciting "new" wonder drug with many new uses.

When I asked my doctor about the efficacy of taking an 81-mg aspirin a day, he played back the message in the very words perpetuated by the public relations campaign. He called it a "wonder drug," citing studies that indicate it may reduce the risk of heart disease, stroke, and cancer.

That the good news about aspirin reached both my doctor and me testifies to the effectiveness of the program conducted for the AFA by Ketchum Public Relations. Its program focused on both informing the medical and health community about research concerning aspirin, and generating their support and endorsement in a broad-based communications campaign to reach the general public.

The campaign that caused Americans to take a new look at an old drug began in 1981 when several producers of aspirin met to discuss the formation of a trade association to reverse the decline in aspirin's image in the public mind and in the marketplace. The decline was caused both by health concerns that aspirin was unsafe and by the success of competitive products. During the 1970s, acetaminophen began to grow as a major competitor in the analgesic market. One element in that growth was the ability of Tylenol, the major acetaminophen producer, to create the impression among the medical and hospital community and consumers that their product was safe and aspirin was not. The newly formed AFA was dedicated to building credibility by nurturing and developing contacts in the medical, scientific, and health-care communities and establishing a strong and multifaceted scientific image of aspirin's benefits and safety profile.

Ketchum mounted a campaign to turn the situation around by repositioning aspirin as the "New Wonder Drug" while stressing its long history of safe use. The agency set out to challenge new competitive products by proving that new doesn't necessarily mean better.

The Aspirin Foundation Information Service (AFIS) was created to provide a focal point for collecting and distributing credible scientific information to both the medical and health community and the media. The Aspirin Foundation Scientific Advisory Board (AFSAB), made up of health professionals representing different areas of aspirin research, was formed to lend credibility to the message and to act as spokespersons.

The communications campaign was built around the information service, a consumer hotline, seminars and symposia, and aggressive media relations. The objectives of the public relations program were threefold. The first was to generate support of the medical and health communities and to gain their endorsement of aspirin as a safe, effective, and exciting drug. With this support, the media relations effort was designed to alert health, medical, and consumer editors to aspirin's overwhelming medical approval and to the fact that medical researchers were exploring a whole range of exciting new uses for old tried-and-true aspirin. The result was to remind consumers of aspirin's many traditional benefits and inform them of its newly discovered benefits in preventing serious diseases.

Seminars and symposia were held in conjunction with a number of credible scientific and public health groups focusing on both traditional and new uses of aspirin, such as its potential help in preventing heart attacks and strokes and in helping augment the immune system. Media tours were conducted in top markets featuring members of the AFSAB and other independent scientists speaking on aspirin's many benefits.

As a result of the media outreach program, positive stories on "The Miracle in the Medicine Chest" began to appear regularly in newspapers, on network and local television, and in major consumer magazines reaching health-conscious men and women.

In August of 1988, Business Week ran a cover story on aspirin titled "Miracle Drug" that proclaimed "Researchers are finding a cornucopia of exciting new uses for this old standby." It described what aspirin can do to: (1) lower the risk of heart attack and help treat those that happen; (2) bolster defenses against diseases from cancer to the common cold; (3) reduce the risk of cataracts and help treat other eye diseases; (4) curb dangerous high blood pressure that can end pregnancies; and (5) protect against second strokes and speed the recovery of stroke victims.[4]

In 1990, news media from network television to newspapers nationally, including the *Wall Street Journal* and the *New York Times,* reported on a study published in the *New England Journal of Medicine* proving that a daily dose of aspirin can dramatically reduce the risk of stroke from heartbeat irregularity that affects more than a million Americans. The next year another *New England Journal* story indicated that aspirin may reduce the risk of death from colon cancer, a disease that kills 50,000 Americans a year, and made headlines in the consumer media. *Time* magazine reported on the study that suggests "there may be yet another benefit from the world's most popular medication." It pointed out that less than a decade earlier, aspirin seemed to be losing its luster "but the wonder drug has made a wondrous comeback." *Newsweek* featured an aspirin tablet on its cover story, "What You Should Know About Heart Attacks: The Aspirin Breakthrough." Stories about the new benefits of aspirin continued to appear in major consumer media. *Reader's Digest,* one of the largest-circulation publications in the world, ran a feature in 1994 called "Aspirin: Not Just for Your Heart," which described how "a small, daily dose may also prevent stroke and other serious health threats." A "Column One" story in the *Los Angeles Times* the same year called "The Little White Pill That Could" said that "newer, more-expensive pain relievers pushed aspirin out of the spotlight, but it is making a comeback after researchers linked it to the fight against heart disease, cancer, and AIDS."[5] The story updated the latest of dozens of studies on the wide range of surprising benefits of aspirin by adding the notorious health hazard AIDS to the list. This AIDS study, conducted by scientists at Yale University, indicated that "aspirin may delay the onset of the disease by preventing the human immune deficiency virus from replicating." New research reported in 1997 prompted the American Heart Association to state that taking aspirin at the first sign of a heart attack could save lives.

Together, the continuous stream of new research on newly discovered benefits reported in medical journals renewed interest in aspirin in the medical and health-care communities, and the steady drumbeat of stories in the mainstream media updating the accumulated evidence of the benefits of aspirin effectively repositioned a century-old standby as a miracle drug. Today Americans consume an estimated eighty billion aspirin tablets a year.

Lessons Learned

- Support research that studies new product benefits.
- Report results in journals reaching professionals.
- Set the news agenda for mainstream media.

- Organize an information arm to collect and distribute credible scientific information.
- Create a scientific advisory board to lend credibility to the message.
- Designate board members as spokespersons.
- Send them on media tours to major markets.
- Target the medical and health communities first.
- Use their endorsement to gain credibility with consumers.
- Hold seminars and symposia with prestigious scientific groups.
- Conduct ongoing media relations support of new research.
- Adding new evidence enables you to retell your story.
- Research is the key to repositioning a product that has lost its luster.

CHAPTER 10

Maintaining Market Leadership

MARKETING PUBLIC RELATIONS HAS THE POWER TO HELP SUCCESSFUL BRANDS maintain market leadership.

When Chrysler introduced the world's first new minivan, no one could have imagined the role it would play for the company or the automotive industry. There was no known segment for the minivan. There was no customer base. There was no blueprint to follow.

The Chrysler minivan would become not only the benchmark for the industry but the primary building block from which the company would base its future. Chrysler ignited the minivan revolution with the U.S. introduction of the first minivan in 1984. The vehicle was an immediate success, accounting for 100,000 units in its initial model year. While competitors soon unleashed competitive minivans, Chrysler captured and maintained a whopping 50 percent of the minivan market share during the next decade by listening to the needs of customers and responding by continually improving the product and its value.

By the model year 1995, the minivan niche that Chrysler created had grown to become a major automotive market segment, accounting for one million in U.S. sales annually. More than five million Chrysler Corporation minivans had been sold in North America in the first twelve years. However, an onslaught of new minivans challenged Chrysler's market leadership. While Chrysler maintained its lead in the market with a commanding 40 percent, the company faced increasing competition from eighteen different nameplates. Ford was advertising its Windstar using a point-by-point comparison with Chrysler. Imports from Mazda, Toyota, and Nissan began to battle aggressively for the U.S. minivan market.

While Chrysler was introducing its all-new version of its minivans, top analysts and automotive journalists were claiming that the segment had reached a saturation point. The challenge was to position Chrysler as the past, present, and future minivan leader in a segment that was continuing to grow.

Chrysler was well aware of the growing competition in the niche it created when it decided to plan a direct assault with its 1996 model-year introduction of new minivans that would break the mold, address new features desired by minivan buyers, and provide them with other new features they hadn't thought of.

The new Chrysler minivans were developed over a thirty-two-month period at a cost of $2.6 billion.

Their two most desired safety and user-friendly features, the driver-side sliding door and the "Easy-Out" Roller Seats, became the focus of the public relations campaign.

Bob Eaton Led the Big Parade

Chrysler's marketing objectives were to drive showroom traffic and increase consumer awareness of the all-new minivan lineup while continuing to position the company as the dominant leader in the minivan market. Chrysler's milestone of selling more than five million minivans in twelve years was remarkable, especially considering the fact that it took Volkswagen thirty years to sell 4.9 million of its very popular Beetles. Public relations used the sale of the five-millionth minivan as the vehicle to generate extensive media coverage of Chrysler's continuing leadership of the minivan market it created.

To do this, Chrysler and Golin/Harris created a broadcast-friendly and exciting delivery event focused on the consumers who actually purchased the five-millionth Chrysler minivan.

The morning of October 9, 1995, dawned in Clintonville, Ohio, just like any other for Richard and Susan Lombard and their ten-month-old daughter. They knew that they had purchased the five-millionth minivan and expected the van would be dropped off by the owner of Bob Caldwell Chrysler-Plymouth.

At 7 A.M., a procession of more than 200 Chrysler dealership and corporate employees led by Chrysler CEO Bob Eaton began a half-mile parade to the Lombard home. The Lombards' 1996 Plymouth Voyager was perched on a rolling soundstage float accompanied by the local high school marching band, neighbors who had been clued in on the secret, a crew from the local McDonald's who provided breakfast, and the Goodyear blimp flying overhead.

Eaton appeared at the front door and presented the completely surprised Lombards with the keys to the car and told them it was theirs, free of charge. They were also presented with a minivan-shaped bank containing a $5,000 U.S. savings bond for their daughter's college education. Another surprise guest, Ohio Lieutenant Governor Nancy Hollister, presented the Lombards with a new vanity plate for the minivan (5MILNTH). An "Over Five Million Sold" logo was used on banners, promotional materials, news releases, and customized delivery team jackets and caps.

The broadcast strategy paid off. The story was covered by such national media as ABC's *World News This Morning*, CNN's *Moneyline*, CNN's *Headline News*, *Wake Up America*, and *Bloomberg Business News* and fed to affiliate stations by ABC and CBS. The radio actuality newsfeed alone reached 860,000 listeners in thirty-two markets. A story on the event in *U.S. News and World Report* positioned Chrysler as a strong and vibrant company focused on the marketplace.

Chrysler minivan sales continued to climb in record numbers. Sales for the fourth quarter, during which the five-millionth was delivered, established an all-time record with 123,764 units sold. Chrysler's minivan was named by *Motor Trend* as "Car of the Year," a first for the minivan. It was also named "Car of the Year" by an independent jury at the 1996 North American International Auto Show.

Lessons Learned

- You don't need a brand-new product to keep your product top-of-mind.
- Find ways to make news by dramatizing new models and features.
- Unveil your product at the big show of the year.
- Beat the competition by staging a "must" event for the media.
- Build excitement by keeping the set under wraps.
- Create a memorable theme that the media can play back.
- Plan a visual stunt that tells the tale.
- Enlist your top brass to set the stage.
- Bring on a surprise guest.
- Don't stop after the product is shipped.
- Plan an on-location special event that maintains the momentum.
- Make the special delivery a surprise and let the media in on it.
- Bring out the boss and a large supporting cast from the company.
- Add floats and a brass band and make it a parade.
- Use the event to reinforce category leadership.

Purina Dog Chow Search for the Great American Dog

Purina Dog Chow, the longtime leader in dry dog food, had no news to report and no meaningful product enhancements when it mounted a public relations program that generated unprecedented visibility for the brand and reinforced its market leadership position.

Proprietary Purina research revealed many dog owners frequently change dog foods. These brand switchers believe they are showing love for their dogs by putting variety in their diet. They do not know that such behavior can have a negative effect on the health of their dogs. Experts say that changing a dog's food or dressing it up with table scraps may cause stomach upset, vomiting, and diarrhea and that feeding the same nutritious food every day is the best way to ensure that your dog receives all the protein, vitamins, and minerals it needs. Purina's message: when it comes to diet, nothing is better for a dog's health and happiness than consistency. The same could be said of the company: brand switching could, of course, have a significant impact on Dog Chow sales.

Purina and its public relations firm, Cohn & Wolfe, set out to develop a program to educate dog owners of the peril of changing diets. The objective was to inform owners that the best way to show love for their canine companions is to feed them a 100 percent nutritionally complete and balanced food, such as Purina Dog Chow, every day. In the process, Purina would reinforce its position as a caring authority on pet care.

A segmentation study conducted by Purina revealed that the primary target for this effort was owners who share intense emotional bonds with their dogs. These folks view the relationship with their dogs as one of mutual reward and treat the dog as a family member. They share activities with their dogs and spend as much as six hours a day together. Finally, they have a strong desire to do what is right for their dogs and actively seek, respect, and follow the advice of established authorities on pet care.

This emotional involvement with their dogs and their respect for the advice of established authorities created the opportunity to deliver the Dog Chow message every day and motivate consistent feeding behavior. Cohn & Wolfe media research revealed a strong interest in the human-animal bond.

Determining that a creative approach would be well received, the firm came up with a national photo/essay contest to find that one special dog. It called the contest "The Purina Dog Chow Search for the Great American Dog." The press kit describes the Great American Dog as "the one dog whose special qualities truly distinguish him as an outstanding example of the dependable, devoted, and faithful friend we all know and love." Unlike other dog contests, the Purina contest did not focus on beauty, brains, or breed, but on best friends.

This platform enabled people to tell stories about how their best friends give them unconditional love every day. At the same time, it gave the brand the opportunity to tell dog owners about the best ways to return that love, by feeding Purina Dog Chow every day.

The search was launched with an intensive media blitz featuring noted dog trainer, behaviorist, and author Brian Kilcommons as spokesperson. He drew upon Purina research that profiled the ways dogs and their owners show love for each other every day. Their responses ranged from the tried and true—walking or running with their dog, taking pictures of their dog, and teaching their dog tricks—to such unexpected answers as sleeping with the dog in the dog's bed. Ninety-seven percent of dog owners reported they show their love by feeding their dog nutritionally balanced dog food. During his major market media tour, Kilcommons delivered the "Dog Chow Every Day" message while reporting on the survey results. In his interviews, he invited dog owners to enter their pet in the contest for a chance to win a grand prize of $10,000 and a lifetime supply of Dog Chow. Contest publicity in other markets included a toll-free 800 telephone number.

Purina received more than 4,000 entries with photos and essays completing the sentence "My dog is my best friend every day because . . ."

Fifty finalists each received a $500 savings bonds and a year's supply of Purina Dog Chow. Stories about them in local and regional media further delivered the "Dog Chow Every Day" message. A second round of judging by Kilcommons and the editor of *Dog Fancy* magazine yielded ten finalists. They were awarded all-expense-paid trips for two to Washington, D.C., for an Independence Day weekend, yielding another round of local media coverage. The winner, Peter Campione of Sarasota, Florida, and his dog Jake were taken by private jet to the nation's capital, where the media covered their arrival and limousine tour of national landmarks. On July 3, before a score of TV crews and reporters at the National Press Club, Hall of Fame pitcher and dog lover Nolan Ryan invited each finalist to read his or her entry as slides of their dog companions were projected onto a giant screen. Ryan read the winner's name and placed a gold medal around Jake's neck and introduced him as the Purina Great American Dog.

Cohn & Wolfe distributed a B-roll video package via satellite. Jake and his owner were taken to CNN's Washington studios for a live interview that ran on the network throughout the day. They were then flown by private jet to New York for a live prearranged Fourth of July interview on ABC's *Good Morning America*.

The first Purina Dog Chow Search for the Great American Dog generated 43 million media impressions; more important, the brand's key messages were successfully delivered. Media analysis revealed that 96 percent of the coverage supported Purina's caring authority position and 68 percent supported the Dog-Chow-every-day message.

Lessons Learned

- Find out all you can about why consumers switch brands.

- Use research to discover good reasons for them to stay with your brand.

- Build a program around the best reason.

- Make sure that everything you do communicates the reason why they should remain loyal to your brand.

- Use consumer research to generate news that support your positioning.

- Appeal to both reason and emotional attachments.

- Create a contest that anyone can win and offer a prize anyone would want to win.

- Give it a memorable name that incorporates your brand.

- Make multiple winners. Fifty winners open opportunities to deliver the message in fifty markets.

- Send an expert spokesperson to top markets. It helps if he can train a dog live on local TV.

- Bring finalists to a star-spangled event in Washington on July 4.

- Videotape their doings around town and the award ceremony.

- Send it on the satellite on a slow news day.

- Optimize publicity potential by engaging an appropriate celebrity presenter.

- Prearrange a big next-day TV hit by promising an exclusive interview.

Pampers Celebrates a Big Birthday

In 1956, while Procter & Gamble researcher Vic Mills was baby-sitting for his newborn granddaughter, he developed an understandable disdain for the labor-intensive process of changing and washing diapers. An idea was born! Back in the Procter & Gamble laboratories, he assigned a group to research the possibility and practicality of a diaper that was absorbent, prevented leaks, and kept babies dry, and that could be discarded after use. After extensive research, formulations, and trials, Pampers was created and a new product category, disposable diapers, was born.

Pampers filled a significant consumer need for having an "easy change" from the endless hours parents spent soaking, washing, drying, and folding cloth diapers. The new diapers also provided improved skin health compared to conventional diapers of the day. Pampers' unique three-piece construction was cited as a major reason for the product's early success. Through the years, Pampers researcher continued the tradition of innovation by introducing major improvements and upgrades.

In 1996, the Procter & Gamble and Pampers public relations firm, Manning, Selvage & Lee, created a thirty-fifth birthday program to underscore the brand's history of innovation and its continuing category leadership.

The message—the brand that "changed America" thirty-five years ago is still the leader today.

The company announced that Pampers would celebrate its major birthday by introducing a new generation of diapers. Two innovations were Pampers Baby-Dry and Breathable Pampers Premium, which employs a breakthrough technology that allows air to flow to babies' skin where they need it most. The new products were designed to simplify the diaper shopping experience and provide greater value and convenience.

The integrated program was the brand's biggest overall initiative in a decade. It included consumer and trade advertising, promotion and public relations, Hispanic advertising and public relations, a Web site, and employee communications. All the elements of the program were unified throughout the birthday year by using a special Pampers thirty-fifth anniversary logo developed by Manning, Selvage & Lee.

The marketing public relations program was designed to establish the brand as a leading source of practical child-care information and was directed to the Pampers key target audience of mothers of diaper-age babies.

There were four distinct elements of the MPR program. The first was "We've Changed America: Thirty-five Years of Dry and Happy Babies." It was directed to customers, employees, and target moms via the media. To reach the retail trade directly, Pampers delivered a special delivery package of Pampers historical photographs and samples of Pampers Baby-Dry and Breathable Pampers Premium. Pampers also became a sponsor of the Food Marketing Institute (FMI) convention, the biggest show of the grocery industry. The brand's booth featured the anniversary logo, the heritage, and the new products. All were featured in a special video produced for the trade.

A thirty-fifth birthday press kit featuring historical and new product information was widely distributed to consumer media in Pampers thirty-fifth birthday diaper bags. Other successfully employed media relations tactics included desk-side briefings with key consumer and trade media and a video news release package for television. The result was several hundred stories in long-lead women's and parenting publications, daily newspapers, and television and radio stations. Popular daytime TV talk-show host Rosie O'Donnell mentioned Pampers on seven different shows.

A special tie-in with MCI was a thirty-fifth birthday telephone card distributed to media and employees providing thirty minutes of free long-distance time to "call home on Pampers."

The second element of the birthday program was the "Pamper Your Baby Contest." Mothers were invited to submit a photograph of themselves and their babies. The contest was announced through print advertising in parenting magazines and publicity in major media including *USA Today*, *Family Circle*, *Parenting*, *Parents*, and *Essence*. The grand prize was a $35,000 college scholarship, an appearance in a future Pampers advertisement, and a personal house call from famed pediatrician Dr. T. Berry Brazelton, author and host of an Emmy award–winning show on Lifetime television. Four additional prize winners received $5,000 for college tuition, a professional photo session, and other prizes. A special telephone number—1-800-PAMPERS—that was set up for contest information handled more than 70,000 calls during the two-month contest period. Almost 23,000 mothers entered the "Pamper Your Baby Contest."

Dr. Brazelton was recruited to head the expert panel of the Pampers Parenting Institute (PPI), a first-of-its-kind information resource created by the brand in celebration of its thirty-fifth. The institute brings together some of the world's most-respected child-care experts to answer child-care questions and provide information for parents and professionals. Other panelists represent such leading organizations as the American Academy of Pediatrics (AAP) and the National Association of Pediatric Nurse Practitioners (NAPNP).

The formation of the institute was announced at a New York media event presented in a talk-show format with Dr. Brazelton and other members of the expert panel answering moms' questions live. A new PPI Web site, "Total Baby Care," was introduced at the event. It gave parents access to America's leading pediatric and child-care experts. The site was designed to make it easy for parents to access information on a specific issue or general information. Insights on feeding, communications, cognitive development, and motor skills were discussed on the site with the information arranged by a child's age, from newborn to toddler. The site offered parents the chance to have a personal house call with Dr. Brazelton.

To involve its employees, Procter & Gamble invited Dr. Brazelton to its headquarters in Cincinnati, where more than 500 employees heard him speak and were able to ask questions about parenting.

A special Pampers program was targeted to Hispanic mothers. All media materials for the birthday, new products, photo contest, and institute were translated into Spanish and provided to the Hispanic media. A special couponing effort promoted the contest to Hispanic consumers. In addition, a special photo contest, "A Smile for Mommy," was cosponsored with *Ser Padres* magazine. A Hispanic pediatric nurse was chosen to be a spokesperson to conduct interviews with Hispanic media.

Beyond the thirty-fifth birthday celebration, the PPI continued to maintain Pampers leadership position as a brand that really cares about parents and their babies—a position that distinguishes Pampers from the competition in the highly competitive disposable diaper market. Its stated mission: "In the long-standing tradition of Pampers' commitment to families, the Pampers Parenting Institute provides a forum for the world's leading pediatric and child-care experts to give parents information, guidance, and encouragement and to exchange ideas to meet the diverse needs of families today." The PPI, designed to meet the needs of babies from prenatal to toddler, reaches 90 percent of the target market of parents of diaper-age children. In the process, it enables Pampers to maintain its category leadership position.

Lessons Learned

- Use a big birthday to focus attention on the brand.
- Celebrate what your product has done to make life easier and better.
- Use the birthday as a platform to introduce new and improved products.
- Build birthday brand excitement with the trade.
- Cover all the media bases reaching key customers and consumers.
- Involve families in a contest.
- Select intriguing instead of expensive prizes.
- Nothing beats an opportunity to be in pictures—or ads.
- Promote the contest with a special toll-free telephone line.
- Pull your PR, advertising, and promotion together with a special logo.
- Create special materials and programs for special target consumer markets.
- Create a resource that fosters relationships with consumers for years to come.

CHAPTER 11

Making Advertising News
When There Is No
Product News

TODAY CONSUMERS ARE CONSTANTLY BARRAGED BY AN UNPRECEDENTED NUMBER OF advertising messages. Commercials must fight for attention. There are two ways to gain attention. The first, of course, is to create great advertising and spend big bucks to make sure that your ad reaches target consumers often. The second is to use public relations to build anticipation for and maintain interest in your advertising.

People are interested in advertising. They talk about new campaigns. As James W. Seymour, managing editor of *Entertainment Weekly* told the *New York Times*, advertising is increasingly becoming part of the popular culture. Commercials are the reason that television in America exists. They're a good part of what America watches, what shapes American opinion, and what tickles America's fancy.[1]

Some of the biggest advertising budgets are for longtime leading brands. When there is no product news to report, the next best thing is to make the advertising the news.

Phil Dusenberry, chairman of advertising giant BBD&O says that "When you get this type of publicity, it's like somebody coming along and handing you a whole pile of money you didn't have. The advertising takes on more value because it's being mentioned in a nonadvertising context."

He advises his clients that "any time you release a new campaign, you would be wise to bring in your PR people and ask 'Is there anything in this that can stretch it beyond our media expenditure?'"[2]

Legendary adman Jerry Della Famina takes it a step further. He told *USA Today* that his work doesn't stop with the ad and that "in many ways, the public relations overshadows the ads." He says that ads "should be more than just ads and that there should be public relations opportunities every time an ad is produced"—even if the ad never runs.

When President Ronald Reagan mentioned Joe Isuzu, a character in Isuzu automobile commercials in a speech, Della Famina convinced his Isuzu client to spend $3,000 to make a commercial about it. He told them that CBS would refuse to run the spot, which they did. He contends that the story that ran in the *Wall Street Journal* about CBS turning down the commercial was far more valuable for Isuzu than running the commercial would have been.[3]

The value added to newsworthy advertising by publicity is measurable. When three-year-old Andrew Thompson was selected from 65,000 kids to sing the Oscar Mayer jingle in a new commercial, he starred on *Good Morning America* and beyond. The company's marketing director, Mark Zander, told *USA Today* that "it really was a great success on two things that matter most to us. It significantly increased our brand awareness and we saw a double-digit increase in sales." That is especially remarkable when you consider that the hoopla was about a thirty-three-year old jingle. Whatever happened to what ad people used to call "wearout"?[4]

The Super Bowl of Advertising

Since Apple Computer's startling commercial introducing the original Macintosh during the 1984 Super Bowl, the Super Bowl has become the venue of choice for new product introductions and new campaign launches for old favorite products.

That's because it attracts the largest TV audience of the year. Year after year, half of the homes of America with TV sets have the game turned on. In a story titled "The Ad Game," *Newsweek* pointed out that "it's the spots that count on Super Sunday, the great American holiday and the only event that still pulls 140 million viewers into the same tent."

Advertisers who are spending more than $1 million per thirty seconds of airtime on the Super Bowl want to ensure the impact of their spots by mounting a supporting teaser publicity blitz. They have learned how to build anticipation by providing the same kind of sneak previews for the media for a thirty-second spot that Hollywood produces for its feature films.

Advertisers now distribute video news release packages that typically include a teaser of the commercial plus B-roll interviews with celebrities or actors appearing in the spot, producers and company spokespersons, as well as often hilarious outtakes of the making of the commercial. The variety of material enables newscasters and sportscasters to put together their own segments and voice-overs. This format has been used successfully by many Super Bowl advertisers.

They are particularly effective with commercials that feature well-known personalities. When McDonald's produced a series of "Nothing but Net" Super Bowl commercials featuring fantasy shooting contests between NBA greats Michael Jordan, Larry Bird, and Charles Barkley, outtakes and interviews from these commercials ran not only on sportscasts but during halftime breaks on NBA game telecasts.

Some advertisers have invited reporters from the print media to cover the making of a newsworthy TV commercial. McDonald's invited *USA Today* to the making of the "Nothing but Net" shoot exclusively and won a cover story.

USA Today is, in fact, so entranced with the ad game that it previews a commercial a day in the weeks leading up to the Super Bowl. On game day, the newspaper polls viewers moment-by-moment for their reactions. The next day it announces the winners and losers of the "Ad Meter" survey.

The Olympic Games have likewise become a prime vehicle for launching new ad campaigns. Nissan Motors Corporation chose the closing ceremonies of the 1996 Olympic Games to introduce a new $200 million brand-building nontraditional advertising campaign built around the theme "Life is a Journey. Enjoy the Ride." The spots featured an elderly fun-loving Japanese character based on former Nissan President Yutaka Katayama, known in the company as Mr. K. The new campaign was supported by a substantial public relations push. Don Spetner, Vice President of Corporate Communications, told Paul Holmes, editor of *Reputation Management*, "Six weeks before the launch, we took some of the themes from the advertising campaign like 'Drive Happy' and used them to create curiosity and build word of mouth. The idea was to create a buzz."

Holmes reported that "the company's determination to integrate public relations into the ad campaign is evident in its decision not to explicitly identify the Mr. K character in the ads." President Bob Thomas echoed one of the basis tenets of integrated marketing communications when he said, "We felt that it was more exciting if people found out for themselves. Rather than telling them, we provided a number of ways for them to learn his identity for themselves. People are more likely to retain something they learned, and once they learn it, they can't wait to share it with other people, and so we get this great word of mouth and it all comes from consumers talking to each other, not from us talking at consumers." The buzz was also helped by an Internet site called "Mr. K's Neighborhood," developed by Nissan's public relations firm, Porter-Novelli. The enormously popular campaign unleashed the latest adventures of Mr. K on Super Bowl XXXI.

The Nissan campaign was named the best of 1996 by *Time* magazine and *Rolling Stone*. The *Wall Street Journal* commented, "More than ever, agencies are scrambling to make ads that create a buzz but have little to do with the products they sell."[5] But Nissan believes that the entertaining campaign put its cars on everybody's shopping list and that tactics such as direct mail, print ads, the Nissan Web site, videotapes, and public relations deliver more specific product information.

You Don't Have to Be Real to Make News

Like Mr. K, some commercials have created their own stars. McDonald's Super Bowl buddies made it to the Super Bowl in Miami in time to make a morning full of lead-in appearances on *Good Morning America*'s pre–Super Bowl Show. These actors and others like the "I Love You, Man" guy from Budweiser commercials and the shirtless, diet Coke–guzzling construction worker ogled by office girls have become national celebrities.

Lucky Vanous of the diet Coke spots was so popular that the company sent him on a major market tour where he did media interviews, signed autographs, and had lunch with lucky local winners of diet Coke break fantasy contests. The previously unknown actor was even picked by *People* as one of "The Fifty Most Beautiful People in the World."

The Continuing Saga of the Taster's Choice Couple

The long-running Taster's Choice instant coffee campaign featuring a soap-opera couple named Sharon (Maughan) and Tony (Anthony Head) has made them stars like their counterparts on daytime TV. Their love affair has been chronicled in a series of commercials that began running in 1990.

The airing of each new episode signaled a publicity campaign, often tied to a contest or other promotion. Over the years, the Taster's Choice couple has been a major public relations coup for the brand. *Food Processing*, a grocery trade publication, reported that "The company realized they had a hit on their hands after the second spot in the series started airing in 1991 and calls and letters began pouring in. Recognizing a ready-made marketing opportunity, Nestlé hired a public relations firm to create tie-in programs."[6]

In 1994, when the brand asked consumers what they thought the names, professions, and hobbies of the coffee-drinking neighbors were, more than 100,000 people called in to reply. Another public relations event was a contest that invited viewers to write about what they would like to see happen next. The winner received a free trip for two, of course, to Paris.

In England where the campaign began and where the product is called Gold Blend, the drama is so popular that it is played out in the tabloids. Nestlé capitalized on the public's infatuation with the couple by commissioning a romance novelist to write a book about them called *Love Over Gold*.

The couple remained so popular in the United States that six years after the series began, *Good Morning America* booked them to preview their newest spot, breaking that night. The company had no trouble booking them on a satellite media tour where they got the celebrity treatment from the hosts of scores of local news and talk shows in major markets.

Print media were equally intrigued by the promise of the new spot as described in the press material from Taster's Choice public relations firm Manning, Selvage & Lee, which said, "Episode twelve will prove to be intriguing with an unexpected twist. How will an unforeseen situation draw the couple closer together or tear them apart? Will the mystery woman be able to say no to Taster's Choice instant coffee?"

Tony Adamich, Vice President of Marketing and Communication for the Nestlé's Beverage Company, says that the coffee is the real star of the series. "Because it is a spontaneous and convenient coffee, the couple and their guests are always able to share a cup of Taster's Choice. With Taster's Choice there is always a reason to stay, so one should have it on hand in case an unexpected guest should arrive."

Milk, Where's Your Mustache?
Print Makes Broadcast News

One of the best-integrated marketing campaigns of recent years is the one created for America's milk processors by the Bozell organization. Its advertising, public relations, and promotion agencies combined to cause a dramatic documented shift in attitudes toward milk, and stem a thirty-year decline in milk consumption. The campaign consisted exclusively of print advertising, specifically magazine ads, featuring well-known celebrities of stage, television, film, and sports wearing that badge-of-milk enjoyment, the milk mustache. The celebs were selected to appeal to key market segments. Supermodels Kate Moss, Iman, and Christie Brinkley were chosen to make milk seem hip to the young. Lauren Bacall and Joan Rivers were used to reach older women, and jocks such as Steve Young and Pete Sampras to reach male consumers. The *Wall Street Journal* reported that "In just a year, the campaign has done a job of worming its way into popular culture. Talk-show host David Letterman, quipping about moves Saddam Hussein could make to restore his image, suggested an appearance in the milk-mustache campaign. Comedian Sandra Bernhard made a stir posing in a parody poster and the campaign even turned up on the quiz show *Jeopardy*, where contestants had to name an ad that featured Vanna White, Nastassja Kinski, and Naomi Campbell."

The milk-mustache campaign was launched with an event at the American Museum of Natural History in New York that generated a burst of media coverage. Each new print ad provided an opportunity for additional public relations support. The photo shoot of *Good Morning America* cohost Joan Lunden was covered by her show, the mustached girls from *Friends* were featured in *TV Guide*, and Gabriela Sabatini was covered in the sports section of *USA Today*. A series of nationally televised "making of" milk-mustache ads featured exclusive footage of famous photographer Annie Leibovitz in action and on-camera celebrity endorsements of milk. In the first year, the campaign generated more than 1.3 billion media impressions, including heavy TV coverage, although the ad campaign was limited to print. The campaign also included a hot line for consumers, 1-800-Why Milk, with a series of recorded messages on a variety of milk-related topics, and staffed by registered dietitians and nurses to answer specific caller questions live.

Evaluative research conducted by Roper Starch shows the campaign caused a significant improvement in women's attitudes about the health benefits of milk and the fun of drinking milk.

Building on its success, the National Fluid Milk Processors Board held a press conference midway in year two to launch an expanded second phase of the campaign at double the ad budget. Features on network television news and in newspapers such as the *New York Times* and *USA Today* reported the new ads would feature an expanded list of twenty new celebrities.

The media reported that the new ads were directed to new target audiences, including girls twelve to nineteen, college students, and men eighteen to thirty-four, the ages when milk consumption drops off. New celebrities chosen for their appeal to these audiences included sportscasters Bob Costas, Frank Gifford, and Al Michaels who praise milk as a drink that replenishes nutrients. Film director and noted sports nut Spike Lee wearing a milk mustache over his real one tells readers that milk isn't just kid's stuff and that "the plot thickens as you discover your bones are still growing when you're thirty-five." Lee, Costas, and other top celebrities, from basketball star Patrick Ewing and baseball immortal Cal Ripken to legendary singer Tony Bennett and socialite Ivana Trump, appeared in a 1997 milk-mustache calendar.

Another new wrinkle in the next ads announced at the press conference was the creation of the milk board's newly established World Wide Web site.

The milk mustache had become so well known that the tag line in phase two was changed from "Milk, What a Surprise!" to "Milk, Where's Your Mustache?" Bozell Senior Partner Ken McCarren told reporters that the new theme was a fun way to ask consumers, "Why aren't you drinking your milk?"

Among the public relations vehicles used to support the integrated campaign was a *Seventeen* magazine photo contest that offered girls a chance to become the next milk mustache model, which elevated the image of milk as a hip drink for high schoolers. A traveling milk mustache photo studio toured 120 college campuses, attracting attention and offering students an opportunity to appear in a milk mustache ad in their college newspaper.

On the eve of the 1996 U.S. presidential election, the milk processors ran a full-page ad in *USA Today, Time,* and *Newsweek* asking consumers to "Vote: Strengthen America's Backbone." The ad featured stock photos of candidates Bill Clinton and Bob Dole wearing computer-generated milk mustaches. As a result of this integrated marketing effort, milk sales were up for the first time in thirty years.

Controversy Rings the Publicity Bell

An out-of-the-box newspaper advertisement was used to generate word of media and word of mouth for Taco Bell. On April 1, 1996, Taco Bell ran full-page ads in big-city newspapers announcing, "In an effort to help the national debt, Taco Bell is pleased to announce that we have agreed to purchase the Liberty Bell, one of our country's most historic treasures. It will now be called the Taco Liberty Bell and will still be accessible to the American people for viewing. While some may find this controversial, we hope our move will prompt other corporations to take similar action to do their part to reduce the country's debt."

Taco Bell's public relations firm, Paine & Associates, simultaneously issued a news release that said the Liberty Bell would rotate between its historic home in Philadelphia and Taco Bell's headquarters in Irvine, California. The company's CEO was quoted as saying, "People have been adopting highways for years. Now we're going one step further. For the first time in the country's history, a national monument has been purchased for commercial purposes. Taco Bell's heritage and imagery have revolved around the symbolism of the bell. Now we've got the crown jewel of bells."

Some consumers didn't get the joke or notice that the ad ran on April Fools' Day. However, a company spokesperson said that "The prank was a phenomenal success" and "We put a smile on everyone's face." In today's world where almost everything is corporate-sponsored, that announcement that a company had bought a national historic monument could be considered believable. In fact, Taco Bell received so many telephone calls that it had to install a Liberty Bell Hot Line. The Philadelphia Chamber of Commerce and Independence National Historic Park where the Liberty Bell is housed were flooded with calls from concerned citizens. To make amends to the patrons in Philadelphia it might have offended, the company donated $50,000 to the park service to maintain the Liberty Bell. But what Taco Bell calls its "publitisement" succeeded in attracting a huge amount of national news worth $500,000 in equivalent paid media and gaining attention for Taco Bell's new $200 million ad campaign appropriately themed "Nothing Ordinary About It." The company claimed that it had met its public relations objectives of breaking through advertising clutter to achieve massive awareness of its new campaign and enhancing the image of Taco Bell as a fun, hip company to its target youth audience. Instant sales increases were attributable to the ad and publicity topspin, which reached seventy million customers in two days.

Outdoor Ads That Are Both Seen and Heard

Infiniti used outdoor advertising to generate media coverage of its introductory campaign for the I30. When the luxury sedan with the affordable price tag of $30,000 was introduced, Infiniti invited the press to "come see what $30,000 can do," specifically to attend the unveiling of a heavily guarded outdoor board on Hollywood's Sunset Strip. The board was papered with 30,000 real dollar bills, the price of the car. Publicity was enhanced when the sign was disassembled and the dollars donated to Los Angeles charities. The board stopped traffic, generated headlines, and started people talking about the I30.

Infiniti papered an outdoor board with 30,000 real dollar bills to publicize the affordable price tag of its luxury I30 sedan. (Courtesy of Infiniti, Nissan North America)

Lessons Learned

- The media are ad-minded. They like ad stories and love ad revenue.
- Commercials with celebrities offer special behind-the-scenes interview opportunities.
- If you can't afford a celebrity, create your own and use PR to make him or her a star.
- People love outtakes, especially where somebody blows a line or a cue or breaks up the crew.
- Let the print media in on the making of a newsworthy spot.
- News value is enhanced if your spot will break on a big audience sports or entertainment event.
- The media likes to cover wars, even beer wars, burger wars, telewars.
- Local media like a local angle—go for it if the spot was shot locally, stars a local hero, or is about a hot new product coming to town.
- Bring your commercials to life at the point of sale.
- Help the print media with stills and scripts.
- Print ads can make news, too. Especially those that are interactive or outrageous.

CHAPTER 12

Making Promotion News When There Is No Product News

WITH A LARGER PIECE OF THE MARKETING PIE MOVING FROM ADVERTISING TO promotion, it follows that public relations should be used to gain higher visibility for major promotions in the same way that it is used to support advertising campaigns.

Gillette's Million-Dollar Bet

The Gillette Company has long been identified as a major sponsor of sports. Gillette's enduring "Look Sharp, Feel Sharp, Be Sharp" advertising campaign is indelibly etched in the memories of World Series past.

With the 1990s, Gillette began to move into major promotions tied to big sports events. Major league baseball was a natural. When the company staged its first Gillette Strike Zone Challenge in 1995, the company had been a sponsor of big-league baseball for fifty-six years.

The company sponsored a sweepstakes through freestanding inserts in newspapers and in-store retail displays. More than three million consumers entered, hoping to be picked to toss a million-dollar pitch at the World Series before a huge national television audience.

A major publicity effort supporting the event went into high gear in the days preceding the third game of the Cleveland–Atlanta series. It was the Indians' first World Series appearance in forty years, which made it that much more appropriate—and newsworthy—that an Ohioan, seventy-three-year-old Sam Danze was the winner. The media knew a good human-interest story and the events leading up to Danze's big day were covered not only on sports pages but on network television news. Gillette brought in Hall of Fame pitcher Rollie Fingers to be Sam's private pitching coach. All eyes were on Danze when he wound up and pitched a baseball sixty feet from the mound into a 30 × 18-inch target at home plate. He missed, but carried away a nice $50,000 consolation prize and the thrill of a lifetime.

Gillette carried away media coverage of the event not only on the World Series telecast but to a far larger audience than the game itself.

Jim Lamie, director of sports and event marketing, proclaimed that the Gillette Strike Zone Challenge was an exciting extension of a longtime association with the World Series that provided consumers with a personal sports megamoment.

A full-scale public relations program generated strong advanced media coverage during the weeks preceding the second Gillette Strike Zone Challenge in 1996, building awareness of and audience for the event. An Alabama student randomly selected from more than three million entrants missed the target in

NBA Hall of Famer Rick Barry coaches contestant Tom Gates at the 1996 Gillette Million Dollar Three-Point Challenge. (Courtesy of the Gillette Company)

Game Four of the World Series, but Gillette hit the mark. Total impressions generated by television were double those of the first year, and total impressions in all media increased 50 percent.

The Gillette Strike Zone Challenge was the latest in a series of Gillette Million Dollar Sports Challenges. Another well-publicized promotion supports the company's sponsorships of World Cup soccer where one lucky winner is given a free kick attempt worth $1 million.

At the National Collegiate Athletic Association (NCAA) Final Four, the premier college sports event of the year, Gillette sponsors a Three-Point Challenge. One randomly selected winner from up to three million entrants steps up to the three-point line to take a shot worth a million bucks. In 1996, the winner, Tom Gates, a fifty-two-year-old helicopter pilot, coached by Hall of Famer Rick Barry, missed the toss before a live audience at New York University and a huge national television audience between the Saturday night semifinal games on CBS-TV. He took home a $50,000 consolation prize and on Monday told host Charles Gibson on *Good Morning America* that the media coverage had reached the family of a fellow Vietnam chopper pilot who was killed in action. Gates was able to tell them the unknown story of the pilot's heroism under fire.

Gillette extends the media coverage of its NCAA sponsorship to the grass-roots level by offering $25,000 to fifty-five regional sweepstakes winners at five separate events. The regional contests are covered by the major TV networks newsfeeds.

The company moved into golf in 1996 by offering a consumer picked at random in a similar manner a chance to share the national spotlight with four of the world's best golfers, Tom Watson, Corey Pavin, Fred Couples, and Peter Jacobsen at the Skins game.

The pressure was on winner John Brinson and ABC sports television cameras trained on him as he attempted a one-time ten-foot putt after the foursome completed the first-day nine-hole round. He missed, but Gillette couldn't miss with every Sunday golfer identifying with the winner and knowing that he or she could have sunk it.

The public relations plans developed by Gillette and its public relations firm, Alan Taylor Communications, for all of the million-dollar events are designed to:

- Create awareness of the event.
- Increase traffic for participating retailers by motivating consumers to see Gillette's in-store displays promoting the event.
- Build anticipation of the event in the media.
- Generate maximum publicity about the event when it happens.

To achieve these objectives, Gillette typically employs tactics such as:

- Staging a media event to introduce the contest winner and the special big-name coach Gillette picks to coach the winner. Pitching great Rollie Fingers, former University of Notre Dame basketball coach Digger Phelps, and former ladies' professional golf star Jane Blalock have been enlisted to accelerate the publicity.

- Providing a complete press package to targeted national, regional, and local media as well as those covering the media event.

- Producing video news releases for use in pre-event television features. The video news releases introduce the winner and show him or her being trained by a personal coach for the big event.

- Producing a second video news release at the event for immediate transmission via satellite to stations across the country not covering the event and providing copies of the video news release to those covering the event live.

- Arranging preevent and postevent interviews for the contestant with major media.

Gillette typically reaches more than 300 million consumers per million-dollar event through stories on television, radio, newspapers, and magazines.

In 1996, Gillette's Million Dollar Sports Challenges captured an astounding one billion media impressions.

But it was another sponsor, Hershey Chocolate, that dished out the cash. At halftime of the 1997 Pro Bowl in Honolulu, a twenty-six-year-old New York investment counselor named Lance Alstodt kicked a thirty-five-yard field goal to win the $1 million prize and fifteen minutes of fame. He was mobbed by NFL players and news cameras. He was the media hero of an otherwise slow news day. Rival networks joined ABC, which covered the event in replaying the kick and interviewing the kicker. An AP photo of the winner of the "Hershey's $1 million Pro Kick" in action ran across the country. In the *Los Angeles Times,* it was captioned simply "1,000 words' worth." That newspaper commented that the million-dollar prize was "enough to buy plenty of candy bars."

Miller Gives Super Bowl Promotion "Legs"

Miller Brewing Company leverages its promotion investments by creating "news legs" that generate attention and sales. The National Football League is a major Miller Lite property and generating awareness of the brand's association with the NFL is a critical priority. Miller Lite ran a promotion around Super Bowl XXX that offered consumers the chance to purchase inflatable armchairs so that they could watch the big game wherever they were. This was a great promotional opportunity for retail outlets such as grocery and convenience stores.

Miller asked its public relations people and the Ketchum agency to create an additional hook that would break through all that Super Bowl clutter, build on Lite's association with the league and the game, and generate sales in bars.

They responded by creating the Miller Lite Armchair Quarterback Challenge, a nationwide interactive trivia contest. A series of competitions were run in bars across the country during the NFL playoffs that attracted more than 50,000 beer drinkers. They competed in more than 3,000 participating bars and restaurants to test their Super Bowl knowledge.

After each of two playoff rounds, the two highest-scoring contestants won a trip to the Super Bowl and a chance to go head-to-head in the finals. The Challenge was held at the NFL Experience, pro football's interactive theme park. The finalists were, of course, seated in Miller Lite's promotional inflatable armchairs. Celebrity coaches Pro Bowl Quarterback Jim Harbaugh and NFL Hall of Famer Ray Nitschke coached the contestants, doused the winner, and presented him with the Miller Lite Armchair Quarterback of the Year Trophy. The finals generated nearly twenty million targeted consumer impressions. The interactive contest raised incremental volume for Miller Lite in a majority of retail accounts.

Lessons Learned

- You can create excitement about a promotion by making it news.
- Tie in with an event that has built-in media coverage.
- A well-planned publicity support program can be phased over a period of weeks or months rather than be limited to one-day coverage.
- Never overlook the human-interest value. People are more interested in people than products—especially people just like themselves.
- Pick a well-known celebrity to take part in the event to enhance the news. OK, so you can't afford Michael or Shaq. There are plenty of affordable former stars around who welcome the chance to be back in the spotlight.
- If you have a company spokescharacter, use him or her or it.
- Make sure that signage is strategically placed so that TV cameras can't miss it.
- Provide participants with branded caps, T-shirts, or other apparel that will show up on TV and in newspaper pictures.
- Don't count on TV cameras. Shoot the event and send it up on satellite.
- Stick with the promotion. Make it an annual event the media anticipates.

- Keep it interesting by adding some new wrinkles every time you do it.
- Select an appropriate but offbeat location to stage a stunt.
- Make a special effort to obtain hometown and regional media coverage. The closer to home, the greater the news value.
- Remember that television is a moving medium that hates talking heads.
- Look for opportunities to bring promotion to life at the point of sale.
- Make it fun.

CHAPTER 13

Making Packaging News When There Is No Product News

REPACKAGING OF AN OLD FAMILIAR PRODUCT MAY BE A SIGNIFICANT MARKETING strategy involving a considerable investment. That doesn't mean that it will be readily apparent or stir a great deal of interest among consumers. Packaging changes per se are likewise of very little interest to media beyond the trade books. Still, with adroit public relations support, a packaging change can generate media attention, focus attention on the product, and materially affect sales.

H. J. Heinz made news in 1997 when it distributed 10 million bottles of its famous Heinz Ketchup with three different labels created by kids who entered a drawing contest sponsored by the brand. One featured red stripes of the American flag painted with ketchup, another a Heinz Ketchup-drenched hot dog that looked like a smile with two tomatoes as eyes, and the third pictured a huge tomato. George Lazarus, marketing columnist of the *Chicago Tribune*, commented that "the bottom line for Heinz is increased business and awareness of the brand."[1]

Governors Chip in to Introduce New Package

The most-used single video news release of 1995 was about a commercial for Doritos that would run on the Super Bowl. The commercial featured the nationally known and recently defeated governors of New York and Texas, Mario Cuomo and Anne Richards, discussing change. The twist was that the change was not political but the new package for Doritos. The governors' spot generated an avalanche of pre–Super Bowl media coverage in print as well as broadcast media that made it a "must-see."

Doritos also received some unexpected post–Super Bowl visibility for its new package when the spot was reprised in some unlikely places. The governors were seen reaching into the new package and munching Doritos during a Mike Wallace interview on CBS's *60 Minutes*, one of the top-rated programs on television.

When moderator John McLaughlin raised the propriety of the governors appearing in the Doritos commercial on the highly political *McLaughlin Group* on PBS, the panelists finally agreed on something—that if the Cuomo and Richards campaign commercials had been as good as the Doritos spot, they might have been reelected.

The Sucrets Early-Retirement Package

After sixty-two years, SmithKline Beecham decided it was time to replace the Sucrets tin package that had been a product trademark. Even though the new plastic container would keep the product fresher, the brand risked losing a key identifying mark and with it the business of loyal Sucrets users. In consumer tests, the tin was proven to be a main differentiating factor and competitive advantage for Sucrets.

The company wanted to make sure that it wouldn't have to buy back cases of the old tin containers from retailers when the new container went on sale. The public relations challenge was twofold—to help deplete inventories and to generate awareness of the new packaging.

From previous research, the company knew that more than one-third of consumers who purchased Sucrets kept the tin for later use. Sucrets PR firm, Ketchum Public Relations, conducted research to find out what consumers would do with Sucrets tins after the lozenges are gone. The new research confirmed that consumers valued the tin as a storage container and appreciated the product's heritage. The personal responses of more than 5,000 consumers served as a valuable database and guided strategy for the development of the Sucrets Early-Retirement program.

A historic search of Sucrets advertising revealed that Charles Kimbrough, news anchor Jim Dial on the popular CBS sitcom *Murphy Brown*, had appeared in a Sucrets commercial in 1977. Ketchum recommended that Kimbrough be the spokesman for the package change story because of his previous association with the brand and because Jim Dial's image was a good fit with the Sucrets brand character: steadfast, trustworthy, conservative, and likable.

Because a packaging change is not hard-core news, a highly visible event was needed to attract media attention. Since the tin was sixty-two, the big idea was to take advantage of its early-retirement age and build a program around retirement. This theme flowed naturally into a retirement celebration and a historical review of the tin's life. The challenge was to create a newsworthy program that would retire the tin but not the brand and introduce the new packaging in style.

To capture national media attention, Ketchum staged a retirement party/news conference at the Rainbow Room of New York's Rockefeller Center. The invitation consisted of a tin of Sucrets reclining in a miniature wooden rocking chair. When the box was opened, a voice chip was triggered to deliver a personalized message. The event featured Charles Kimbrough and Dr. Ramunas Kontratas, a curator of the Smithsonian, who accepted the tin into the National Museum of American History. Attention was focused on the new Sucrets package, which made its first public appearance at the retirement party of its predecessor.

Sucrets also announced a consumer sweepstakes with a chance to win retirement-related prizes, including a grand prize of $20,000 "to help retire the mortgage."

Media received a Sucrets Early-Retirement Package that contained a "Through the Years" retirement picture album, a jumbo tin of assorted Sucrets fruit lozenges, and B-roll production footage of the old and new packages.

USA Today listed the top items kept in the tins derived from the top-ten list in the press kit: sewing notions including buttons, snaps, bobbins, pins, and needles; desk supplies such as paper clips, rubber bands, staples, and postage stamps; and hair accessories such as bobby pins, clips, and barrettes. Readers were consoled not to "feel too bad about the retirement" of the Sucrets tin because "it's found a terrific new home: The Smithsonian's National Museum of American History national pharmacy collection."[2] The *New York Times* picked up an item from the press kit and reported that the English jeweler who reset the crown of Queen Elizabeth II in 1954 wrote the company to say that Her Majesty's jewels were stored for a time in a Sucrets tin.[3] Even the *Wall Street Journal* got into the retirement act with a story headlined "If You Like to Secrete Treasures in Sucrets Tins, Better Stock Up." It reported that Sucrets research revealed such creative uses of the tin as "the final resting place for goldfish and turtles, a velvet-lined case for a prize shooter marble, and a tooth-fairy repository."[4]

Sucrets brand management was elated and reported that sales went through the roof immediately following the retirement announcement media event. As a result of the promotion and the 100 million media impressions generated by the retirement story and in the absence of any advertising, sales jumped 40 percent in the first week of the campaign and remained 20 percent above average for two months after the program. All this happened during the summer, the historic lowest sales period for sore-throat lozenges.

Swanson Celebrates the TV Dinner

In 1994, Swanson frozen foods, a division of Campbell Soup Company, introduced new contemporary packaging for its entire line. The redesign made use of extensive company research that showed that consumers retain a strong association with the historic teal packaging of the Swanson line.

Campbell's corporate communications department seized on the fact that 1994 was also the fortieth anniversary of Swanson frozen dinners and told the story of how the new packaging evolved from the original package, the famous TV dinner package designed to look like a television screen.

The company selected Betty Cronin, a retired Campbell executive, who, as an employee of the original C. A. Swanson & Sons, had helped develop the original TV dinner. To add media appeal, she was dubbed "The Mother of the TV Dinner." Her recollections about the early history of the brand and factoids derived from an exhaustive search of the company's archives were woven into an updated history of the brand's leadership in the frozen-food category and to explain the reasons for the new packaging.

Publicists from Golin/Harris Communications developed story angles to appeal not only to food editors but to lifestyle, feature, business, and trade media and launched an aggressive national media relations campaign.

A birthday event was held in Omaha, Nebraska, "the birthplace of the TV dinner." Betty Cronin recalled the early days of the brand and Kathleen Mac-Donnell, President of Campbell's Frozen Food Group, discussed recent developments and introduced the new package. To maintain the brand's contemporary appeal, a five-foot-tall replica of the new turkey dinner package was positioned as the focus of the event. Retired Swanson employees who worked on the production lines of the earliest dinners joined in a rousing rendition of "Happy Birthday," while the candles on an oversize TV dinner–shaped birthday cake were lit. Immediately following the party, a B-roll video package was transmitted to television stations across the United States. Interviews were conducted in front of the giant new package to ensure brand-name retention, help to maintain a contemporary image, and to gain visibility for the new package.

Massive media exposure included a guest appearance of Betty Cronin on the *Today Show,* where she was interviewed by host Bryant Gumbel. She cited three factors that led to the creation of the TV dinner: (1) many women who had joined the workforce during World War II continued to work after the war;

(2) it was the heart of the baby boom and there were lots of five- and six-year-olds to feed; and (3) TV had come into its own and everybody was watching it at dinnertime. Bryant, cohost Katie Couric, and weatherman Al Roker all sampled a new Swanson turkey dinner and pronounced it "mmmmm good." Other television coverage ranged from *Good Morning America* and *Sunday Morning on CBS* to good-natured spoofs on *Saturday Night Live*, *Tonight*, and *MTV News*. Even President Bill Clinton made note of the occasion in a dinner address covered by ABC and C-Span. Radio and print publicity was equally impressive, adding to a total audience reach of well over 120 million.

Campbell marketing executives said the Swanson's TV dinner's fortieth anniversary was the company's most successful public relations program. The program was so effective that a planned $7 million advertising campaign supporting the new packaging was canceled. The public relations program had an impressive measurable impact on Swanson sales. In the absence of any additional national advertising or promotional support of the anniversary, sales of four-compartment dinners increased 44 percent over the previous year and brand share increased nearly two points. Swanson dinners experienced their strongest single-sales gain the week of the anniversary event.

Lessons Learned

- Bring attention to the new package by treating the old package as an icon.
- Dig up lots of fun facts about the package. The media loves trivia.
- Hold a retirement party and invite the press.
- Enshrine the old package in a museum.
- Tie it in with an anniversary or other company milestone.
- Designate someone with a historic association with the brand as spokesperson.
- Hold a party in the original plant and invite retired employees.
- Capitalize on celebrity spokesperson appearances live and on tape.
- If celebs appear in a commercial about the new package, tape and transmit interviews and outtakes.

CHAPTER 14

Using Databases to Communicate with Target Customers

PUBLIC RELATIONS HAS TRADITIONALLY REACHED MASS AUDIENCES THROUGH THE mass media and segmented audiences through special interest media. In recent years, public relations has also begun to borrow the techniques and technology of direct marketing to reach target individuals one-on-one. These individuals may be consumers, segmented by demographics, lifestyle, region, neighborhood, and ethnicity—and by their previous buying behavior. They may also be individual opinion leaders who exert an important influence on consumer attitudes and behavior.

In addition to supporting marketing goals, public relations is increasingly using databases in such vital areas as community relations, government relations, investor relations, and media relations. In the area of community relations, for example, direct techniques are used to build grass-roots coalitions in support of or in opposition to governmental policy that may have an effect on marketing. In the area of investor relations, databases are used to reach specialized financial markets and individual investors. In media relations, the use of up-to-the-minute databases is critical in reaching the right reporters, editors, and news program directors. Databases have evolved from simple media lists to include information that provides the sender with intelligence about the types

117

of stories favored by particular reporters and even their perceived editorial biases.

A clear distinction should be drawn between the uses of databases for marketing public relations purposes and their use in direct marketing. In its marketing support function, public relations uses databases to build brand equity, to inform and educate, to gain understanding, to build trust, to create a climate of consumer acceptance, and to give people reasons (and in some cases, permission) to buy. Public relations is in the relationship business and uses databases to build company-to-customer bonds. The purpose of direct marketing, on the other hand, is to cause an immediate response and to make a sale.

Paul Wang, professor of direct marketing at Northwestern University and a leading database marketing authority, says that the advent of database technology and relationship marketing is good news for public relations. It increases marketers' thinking about and measuring long-term rather than short-term success. He predicts that long-term goal assessment will lead to a greater appreciation of the ability of public relations to build positive attitudes about products and the companies behind them that eventually lead to sales.

He says that "database marketing should not be used as a replacement for media coverage, which typically generates a high amount of trust as well as a wide reach that database marketing cannot provide. However, particularly for marketers who target niche markets with a specific interest in a certain type of product, database marketing may provide a viable way to distribute information that might otherwise never reach these customers as mass media."[1]

The Pillsbury Bake-Off is discussed elsewhere in this book as the classic example of building person-to-person relationships with customers. Database technology has come to play a prominent role in the relationship-building process. It is used to attract entrants to the competition and to evaluate their recipes. The call for entries is announced through extensive publicity in print and broadcast media, an FSI listing, an 800 number, and an entry-form mail drop to all past entrants. Pillsbury has compiled a database of hundreds of thousands of prospects. After an elaborate screening, testing, and tasting process, Pillsbury conducts a critical originality check by searching another database of 10,000 recipes, its own and those entered in past Bake-Offs, before selecting 100 regional winners to be invited to the contest site.

Here are some other examples of how public relations uses database marketing to reach target individuals one-on-one.

Chrysler Targets VIPs

To get its LH sedans, the Chrysler Concorde, Dodge Intrepid, and Eagle Vision, off to a quick start before advertising began, Chrysler marketing and public relations joined forces on a program targeted to a high-profile, high-exposure potential audience across the country. Chrysler and its public relations firm, Golin/Harris Communications, identified VIPs in key markets and personally offered them the opportunity to test-drive a car for two or three days. The cars were delivered to them and picked up when they were finished. As part of its national press previews in New York and Los Angeles, Chrysler again created a database to invite a select list of VIPs to receptions where they were invited to sign up for test drives. The program stimulated extensive word-of-mouth anticipation before Lee Iacocca showed off the LH cars to the car-buying public in his last commercial as the company's CEO.

Delta Taste-Tests Its "Air Fare"

When Delta Airlines introduced gourmet cuisine to its first-class and business-class fliers, it identified specific Delta customers to participate in the menu-selection process. They included Delta frequent fliers who had flown domestic first class on a long haul in the previous twelve months, and business travelers from Delta destination cities with a high concentration of resident frequent fliers. Delta's public relations firm, Ketchum Public Relations, conducted a coordinated target media relations campaign designed to strengthen the airline's relationship with frequent fliers. The unlikely juxtaposition of gourmet food and airline fare piqued media amusement and interest. Reporters were invited to participate in the food selection to finalize the menus. They were able to both observe consumers' reactions and taste-test for themselves. After the menus were finalized, the media were invited back to sample the new "air fare." This media involvement led to positive coverage in key print and broadcast media nationally as well as in key destinations. Ninety percent of the frequent fliers that attended the taste tests perceived the experiences as positive reinforcers of their relationship with the airline. This was expressed by one business traveler who said, "This kind of research involvement exponentially increases my loyalty to Delta." Typical of the destination-city media commentary was this from Salt Lake City: "Besides catering some great food, customers walked away having associated with a few of the faces that work behind the big red doors at Salt Lake International."

Food Fan Clubs

Some food marketers have created clubs that build relationships with their best customers. Recipe clubs for its clients created by Toronto public relations firm Langdon Starr provide useful information to core consumers. For McCormick Canada, Langdon Starr created the McCormick Dinner Club to promote the use of the company's entire line of spices. More than 70,000 Canadian homemakers responded to initial publicity about the club by calling an 800 number or writing the company. The growing list of members received a number of mailings a year, including newsletters, recipe cards, coupons, and trial-size samples.

For Pepperidge Farm, Langdon Starr created the Pepperidge Farm No Fuss Pastry Club. The club communicated directly to known users, showing them how to make dozens of easy-to-prepare meals with frozen puff pastry. The club generated members through a magazine mail-in offer, an offer on the package, point of sale, and publicity. Newsletters and recipe cards were mailed to members throughout the year. Member surveys were used to gain marketing information, build interactive relationships, and refine the database.

Pharmaceutical Companies Target
Their Customers

Pharmaceutical companies routinely use database marketing to explain the benefits of their products to medical specialists. The Upjohn Company took a different approach. To promote Vantin, its antibiotic for treating ear infections, Upjohn created an innovative newsletter to help pediatricians understand more about their patients.

Vantin's PR firm, Manning, Selvage & Lee, created *What's Hot Doc?*, a triannual newsletter to pediatricians to learn what's in and what's out with their patient population. Each newsletter contains approximately twenty articles and a children's activity pullout. Content is based on information gathered by the agency through interviews with fashion editors, by attending toy trade shows, and reading hot kids publications and youth trend reports. The newsletter is mailed to a database of pediatrician members of the American Academy of Pediatrics who appreciate knowing what's hot and the brand that is helping them keep up with their patients.

A number of pharmaceutical companies have also designed public relations programs to reach specific users of their products. SmithKline Beecham published a quarterly newsletter called *Gut Reactions* to a list of 200,000 over-the-counter antacid users. The newsletter consisted of health-care–related articles and insights into causes of and cures for heartburn and tips on how to prevent it. Enclosed were coupons for SmithKline's Gaviscon over-the-counter antacid. One issue featured a send-away booklet of Southwestern recipes including chili and Cajun dishes that presumably would be no problem for Gaviscon users to digest. The news was mailed to a database of names generated by a Carol Wright direct-mail consumer survey. The database was supplemented by names captured through a toll-free telephone number promoted on point-of-purchase displays. This newsletter followed the company's success with *Calcium Communiqué* launched in 1991 and mailed to a targeted database of 900,000 women over thirty-five in behalf of its calcium supplement Os-Cal.

Mead Johnson Nutritionals targets a very specific audience—mothers in the last trimester of pregnancy through the first two months after birth—with a program designed to create an ongoing relationship between the company, the customer, and the physician. The company, which markets Enfamil infant formula, produces a series of mailings, each timed to various first-year life stages. They include informational newsletters for mothers, personal letters, offers, premiums, and other interactive opportunities. The program serves a precise public relations objective—to build highly personal relationships by positioning the product as a "service."

Another innovative use of databases by public relations is to turn satisfied consumers into advocates. Upjohn Company used its database of users of Rogaine to attack a public relations problem. The product was introduced in 1988. By 1990, it was old news and articles on hair loss categorized it as an expensive, sometimes ineffective, product. But research indicated that users who had success with Rogaine were universally enthusiastic about it. They spoke about the self-esteem and self-confidence they gained after they discovered they could control hair loss. Upjohn's public relations firm, Manning, Selvage & Lee, compiled an extensive profile of Rogaine users by conducting a database search. A total of 5,000 questionnaires were sent to Rogaine users. Based on the responses and follow-up telephone and personal interviews with promising prospects, Rogaine identified role models in nineteen selected markets who had both attained success with the product and achieved their personal or professional goals. The Rogaine Recognition Program for Personal Achievement turned satisfied users into spokespersons for the brand. They were booked for extensive media interviews in their markets that focused on messages about the effectiveness of Rogaine, which at the time was available only by prescription and couldn't be advertised.

Going One-on-One with Influencers

Many public relations programs are designed to target influencers rather than consumers. The influencer may be an authority figure such as a teacher, a doctor, or a pharmacist. But it could be someone that has a different kind of one-on-one relationship with the consumer—someone like a beautician or a bartender.

A few years ago, Southern Comfort, a spirits brand with near universal bar penetration, identified twenty regions that offered the best opportunities for on-premise sales. Brokers in these regions were asked for a list of owners and managers of bars. In all, a database of 28,000 bar owner/managers was compiled.

They received a series of personalized mailings from celebrity spokespersons such as Woody Harrelson who played the bartender on the long-running

TV show *Cheers*. The mailings featured bartender tips, Southern Comfort recipes, celebrity shot glasses, and personally autographed photographs. A bartender recipe contest netted 3,500 entries and other interactive devices produced an active database of 15,000 bartenders. PR man George Drucker, who masterminded the campaign for Edelman Public Relations Worldwide, says that Southern Comfort registered increases during each of the five years of the campaign. That's especially important for a brand that generates nearly 40 percent of its sales in bars.

Database development and telemarketing are increasingly being used to support business-to-business marketing public relations programs as well. One leading public relations firm, Fleishman-Hillard, has established its own stand-alone service to provide clients with direct marketing services. The unit has worked with its clients to build targeted databases to generate greater return on direct mail for seminars; to build support for sales development and community relations programs; to generate vendor participation in client programs and promotions; and to build greater attendance at client-sponsored events.

Lessons Learned

- Use databases to create a "buzz" among trendsetters before the ads break.
- Identify VIPs and invite them to preview your product.
- Unite core consumers in a product fan club.
- Use direct mail to provide heavy users with important new information.
- Keep your brand top-of-mind by providing customers with news of what's in and what's out.
- Segment consumers by how they use your product.
- Use names and data generated by PR programs to make special offers.
- Use databases to identify satisfied customers and turn them into advocates.
- Find creative ways to influence the influencers.
- Use databases to keep in touch with satisfied (and dissatisfied) customers who write or call.
- Compile database information about key reporters, how they work, and what they want.
- If you aren't a database expert, subcontract or form a strategic alliance with somebody who is.

CHAPTER 15

Building Person-to-Person Relationships with Customers

WORLD-CLASS MARKETING GURU PHILIP KOTLER BELIEVES THAT THE VERY DEFINITION of marketing has changed and that we are moving from transaction-based marketing where the exchange or sale is the end, to relationship-based marketing where the goal is to create a lifetime customer.

The reason is clear. It is more cost-effective to keep an old customer than to create a new one. In the financial-services field, it is believed that it costs five times as much to create a new customer than to keep an old one. In packaged-goods marketing, the rule of thumb is four to one.

Consultant Larry Light points out that in category after category, a small share of loyal brand users account for an extraordinary share of a brand's profits. He says that a loyal customer can be nine times as profitable as a disloyal one who switches brands.[1]

The growing focus on relationship marketing was articulated by Silicon Valley marketing guru Regis McKenna in his influential 1991 book *Relationship Marketing*. McKenna believes that the new relationship between company and customer represents a fundamental shift in the role and purpose of marketing from selling and telling to communicating and trading knowledge.

In many ways, the concept of relationship marketing is a new expression for public relations. The very name *public relations* means relationships with the public, or as traditional public relations would have it "publics," whose understanding and support is needed by an organization or business. The segmenting of the public into "publics" is one of the great contributions of public relations to communications theory. In recent years, the terminology has changed, but the process is the same. Public relations people are increasingly using the term *stakeholders* in place of *publics* to describe all those audiences who have a stake in the organization. These stakeholders include employees, shareholders, neighbors, suppliers, and customers.

Integrated marketing takes that one step further, moving from customers to individuals or in public relations terms from publics to people. This thinking has been facilitated by the increasing sophisticated use of databases to identify customers whose loyalty companies want to maintain or specific prospective customers qualified by their previous buying or lifestyle behavior.

The Pillsbury Bake-Off:
The Super Bowl of Cooking

There is no better example of creating person-to-person relationships with consumers than the Pillsbury Bake-Off, the grand dame of all public relations events. Since the first Bake-Off was created in 1949 to promote the company's flour and other baking products, the Bake-Off has become an important part of many people's lives. Many enter time after time. Pillsbury research reveals that nearly 80 percent of consumers are aware of the contest.

In announcing the 1996 event, Paul Walsh, Pillsbury's CEO, said that "the Pillsbury Bake-Off was getting the biggest make-over in its history." He said that the changes in the contest reflected the changes in consumer lifestyles and cooking patterns. It also reflected the expanded line of Pillsbury products by including representative products from subsidiaries Green Giant, Hungry Jack, Old El Paso, and Progresso, in addition to products bearing the Pillsbury brand. The updated Bake-Off had more new recipe categories, more ways for consumers to become involved, and more consumer input in judging the final recipes. Most important, Pillsbury raised the stakes by awarding a grand prize of $1 million, the largest in any consumer cooking competition.

The theme of the thirty-seventh Bake-Off was "The Way America Cooks Today." Its updated categories, reflecting changing lifestyles, included thirty-minute main dishes, quick treats and snacks, special side dishes, and simple breads, in addition to the traditional favorite—special occasion desserts.

In addition to the multitude of bakers and cooks who enter the contest, Pillsbury invited all consumers to participate in the event by entering a sweepstakes to win trips to the Bake-Off to enjoy the fun and sample the recipes. Consumers were also invited to participate in a call-in voting sweepstakes during the nationally televised Bake-Off Awards program with a $10,000 Sears Kitchen Makeover as top prize.

All eligible recipes were reviewed by home economists of an independent judging agency, who selected those that best met the judging criteria. These recipes were sent to the Pillsbury test kitchens for further screening and kitchen testing. One hundred winning Bake-Off recipes were chosen and the winners, ninety women and ten men, were invited to prepare them in minikitchens set up in a Dallas hotel. Their recipes were judged by a panel of twelve judges, including magazine and newspaper food editors, and restaurant and supermarket experts.

The expanded thirty-seventh Pillsbury Bake-Off recognized the power of a public relations idea. By upping the ante from $50,000 to $1 million, Pillsbury assured both maximum consumer participation and optimum media coverage.

The event was structured to meet the new realities of the marketplace and the new prominence of the retail trade to brand marketing success. Underscoring the importance of supermarkets to the success of the Bake-Off was the fact that the contest was announced for the first time at the Food Marketing Institute (FMI) national convention, the largest meeting of the supermarket trade.

CEO Walsh was joined by Alex Trebek, host of TV's popular *Jeopardy* quiz show. Trebek followed the long tradition of Bake-Off celebrity spokespersons beginning with Arthur Godfrey and including Art Linkletter, Bob Barker, and Willard Scott. Trebek would promote the Bake-Off on a satellite media tour of major television markets and appear at the Bake-Off to present the grand prize.

The retail extensions of the Bake-Off included the use of in-store demonstrators to distribute coupon books and entry forms for both the contest and consumer sweepstakes. A program of local market television advertising supporting the Bake-Off was personalized for participating retailers. Retailers who built a qualifying retail display, earned a Pillsbury Doughboy collectible. Point-of-sale displays were used to distribute entry forms and other Bake-Off merchandising tools. Special point-of-sale material was created for stores in largely African-American and Hispanic neighborhoods.

Pillsbury also ran national freestanding inserts incorporating product coupons and sweepstakes entry forms and announcing the televised awards program.

The interlocking public relations, merchandising, and advertising elements made this Bake-Off a truly integrated marketing program. But, as in the past, the event was driven principally by public relations.

The Bake-Off announcement was covered by food editors assigned to the FMI show and network television, and the event itself was attended by more than 100 media guests. Newspaper food editors participated in seminars on leading-edge food developments and grocery trade editors were updated on the latest in merchandising methods.

Kurt Wait mixing up his Macadamia Fudge Torte at the Pillsbury Bake-Off contest. Wait was the first male grand prize winner. He took home $1 million, the largest prize ever awarded in any consumer cooking competition. (Courtesy of the Pillsbury Bake-Off Contest)

The announcement of the grand prize winner was a major public relations coup, enhanced not only by the $1 million prize money but by the fact that it was won, for the first time, by a man. Even the *New York Times* found "$1 Million Bake-Off Winner Is a He" news fit to print. Californian Kurt Wait and his Macadamia Fudge Torte made a clean sweep of the network morning shows and the Peter Jennings, Tom Brokaw, and Dan Rather network nightly newscasts. Wait was even given a guest shot on NBC's *Tonight Show* with host Jay Leno. On ABC's *Good Morning America*, host Joan Lunden tasted the torte and enthusiastically endorsed it. "Mmm. Mmm. Mmm. Mmm. That's definitely a winner."

Video footage of Alex Trebek introducing the winner was satellited to hundreds of local stations.

When the winning recipe appeared in newspapers, there was a run on Pillsbury Moist Supreme Devil's Food Cake Mix, the principal ingredient in the torte. As in the past, the product used in the winning recipe met its annual projections within weeks following the Bake-Off.

Stories about the three other semifinalists who each won $10,000 and many of the other finalists appeared in their hometown media, further extending the reach of the coverage and adding to the human-interest element.

The success of the Bake-Off can also be measured by sales of the scores of Pillsbury company products eligible for use in contest recipes. The company will not reveal the number of recipes submitted but says they are in the tens of thousands. That means sales of hundreds of thousands of packages of Pillsbury products were used to develop the contestants' very best recipes. Grand prize winner Kurt Wait said he practiced making his torte at least twenty-five times.

Terry Thompson, Pillsbury's Vice President of Public Relations, says that the Bake-Off fulfills all four criteria the company believes special events should accomplish. They are to: (1) be organic and grow from the business; (2) reward consumers and (trade) customers; (3) be newsworthy; and (4) be integrated and revolve around the company's core disciplines.[2]

Lessons Learned

- Go with a winner. Nurture a classic. Take a fresh look and it won't wear out.
- Move with the times by recognizing changing consumer lifestyles.
- A $1 million prize buys many millions of dollars' worth of publicity.
- Capture names of past contestants and keep them involved by sending them entry forms.
- Tell them to tell their friends. Generate word of mouth.
- Dramatize the event by employing a well-known and well-liked celebrity in the announcement and the event.
- Get the CEO behind the effort. When he or she takes ownership, money follows.
- Build in programs that involve not only contestants but all consumers.
- Get the trade involved. Your customers can multiply the effectiveness of everything you do.
- There is no better place to be visible than at the point of sale. Everybody eats. Everybody shops.
- Find a great partner that enhances your event. Food is made in kitchens.

- Involve the media from the outset. Build up their anticipation and that of their readers, listeners, and viewers.
- Plan educational programs for those attending the event.
- Invite editors to participate in the judging.
- All finalists are big news where they live. Don't forget local newspapers and radio.
- Look beyond the expected media. Behind every great food story there's an appealing human-interest story.

CHAPTER 16

Involving People
with Products

WHILE THE USE OF PUBLIC RELATIONS IN DRAMATIZING NEW PRODUCTS IS universally recognized, its use in maintaining high visibility for mature products may well be more important to marketers. This is especially true for flagship products, those cash cows that most impact the bottom line and generate the capital needed for new product development—such products as Tide detergent, Campbell's soups, M&M's chocolate candies, and Flintstones vitamins.

Keeping old-line favorite products such as these top-of-mind presents a challenge to creativity. One way to involve consumers with these products is to invite them to participate in brand-sponsored contests that are fun and offer winners the chance to win not only great prizes but also fame for a day. At their best, these contests are designed to generate media coverage that reminds consumers of the importance of these products in their everyday lives.

Tide at Fifty

Introduced as the "washday miracle" in 1946, Tide remains to this day America's bestselling family detergent. That's a marketing miracle in itself. Procter & Gamble used the fiftieth anniversary of Tide to celebrate the brand that built the company and one of the bestselling of all brands of any kind in the United States.

To mark the milestone and remind consumers of the history of the most-popular laundry product in America, Tide mounted a yearlong public relations program with Burson-Marsteller. It was designed to capitalize on the nostalgia associated with the product and to showcase what Tide still does best—clean clothes.

A broadside publicity campaign announced the fiftieth with P&G Chief Archivist Ed Rider serving as spokesperson. The major anniversary public relations effort was a contest to find the "Dirtiest Kid in America." The contest was intended to deliver the message that Tide knows kids have fun getting dirty and Tide knows how to get their clothes clean.

Key media received a press kit in a collector's commemorative Tide box with the original bull's-eye design on one side and the current version on the other. The kit included stories and pictures about Tide's history, information about new product formulations that prove that "the revolution in a box is better than ever," and the announcement of Tide's "Dirtiest Kid in America" contest. Also included was a 3-D View Master with a reel of a half-dozen historical pictures. They included vintage photographs of excited 1940s homemakers declaring Tide a "washday miracle," early elaborate store displays testifying to Tide's popularity, and Tide boxes that came free with washing machines of the 1950s.

Parents were invited to send in their favorite photo of their dirty kid, age five to twelve, along with a message on "How my kid came clean with Tide." The contest was supported by publicity, in-store pads, and a freestanding insert.

Ten finalists were selected and their winning photographs featured in an ad in *People* magazine. Consumers were invited to "Help Tide Celebrate 50 Years of Keeping Families Clean" by voting for the "Dirtiest Kid in America." Readers could vote by calling 1-800-TIDEKID toll-free. Partnering with *People Weekly* worked extremely well in reaching the target audience. Up to 10,000 calls on the toll-free number were received in two days. To generate additional media coverage, publicity was placed in the finalists' hometown media.

The final phase of the program brought the finalists and their families to New York City to participate in a giant "Stain-a-Thon" in Central Park. The giant, gooey, messy obstacle course was designed to smear the lucky finalists and their bright orange Tide jumpsuits with stains from head to toe. Events included a giant ramp slathered with peanut butter on one side and jelly on the other; a giant inflatable hamburger loaded with catsup and a massive twenty-eight-foot mountain of chocolate pudding and whipped cream. At the event, Monique Eldred, a kindergartner from Olive Branch, Mississippi, was crowned the "Dirtiest Kid in America" and awarded a Florida trip for her family and a "much-needed year's supply of Tide."

Tide added a cause-related element that made the contest more than just fun and games. For every entry received, Tide donated fifty cents to Give Kids

Readers could call a toll-free number to vote for one of these finalists in Tide's "Dirtiest Kid in America contest." (Courtesy of Procter & Gamble)

the World, a nonprofit organization that provides vacations to children with life-threatening illnesses and their families. A donation of $10,000 was presented to Give Kids the World during the Stain-a-Thon event.

The Tide fiftieth anniversary program also provided an ideal platform for the introduction of Tide Ultra 2, a new formulation that delivers improved product performance. The program was effectively integrated at the tactical level, assuring its success. In addition to publicity that yielded an advertising equivalency of $1.3 million, the elements included an in-store display contest with *Progressive Grocer*, a leading grocery trade publication, in-store tear-off pads, limited edition packaging, an FSI drop/contest entry form, and promotion on Tide's Web site. These elements worked together to build momentum with all audiences, including consumers, trade, P&G employees, sales, and media.

The Art of Soup

Not only has the Campbell soup can been a family favorite for generations, but it became, in the 1960s, a pop-art icon. The legendary pop artist Andy Warhol created his first Campbell soup can painting in 1962 and over the years painted more than 100 renderings, each new series altering the colors, size, and imagery of the can.

If the Campbell soup can had an impact on Warhol, Warhol had an impact on Campbell. In 1985, at the suggestion of its public relations firm, Golin/Harris, Campbell commissioned Warhol to paint his impression of the box for its new line of dry soups. The paintings were unveiled at New York's Whitney Museum, home of several Andy Warhol works, where the artist personally autographed posters of the box art.

It was only natural that Campbell create an "Art of Soup" contest to bring attention to the most comprehensive label redesign in the company's history in 1994. The new label put photos of the product front and center for the first time. Campbell wanted to generate widespread awareness and consumer support of the new design in a way that built on the integrity of the original red and white label. The company enlisted Golin/Harris to help generate considerably more than fifteen minutes of fame for the new label.

Billed as "the search for the next Andy Warhol," the contest was designed to recognize artists of the 1990s. It called for entries in youth, amateur, and professional categories. The contest was announced at a press conference at the Campbell Museum in the company's headquarters in Camden, New Jersey, and was transmitted to TV stations via video news release. A toll-free number that artists could call for official entry forms was publicized.

Entry forms were also incorporated in a freestanding insert that appeared in newspapers two weeks after the newsbreak.

More than 10,000 entries were received, 3,000 of them generated by the public relations alone.

Phase two of the public relations program was the announcement of the contest winner at the Whitney Museum. Four finalists and their artwork plus

The Campbell Soup Company annual report was inspired by the public relations "Art of Soup" contest. This red-and-white lighthouse appeared on the cover and winning art appeared throughout the report. (Courtesy of Campbell Soup Company)

200 additional pieces of soup art from the thousands submitted to the contest were displayed at the event. The late Andy Warhol was represented by his brother, Paul Warhola, and pop artist Peter Max. A private gallery in the museum displayed thousands of pieces of artwork entered in the contest.

Eleven-year-old Matthew Balestrieri won his fifteen minutes of fame as the next Warhol for his Egyptian hieroglyph painting "from the tomb of Isip Soop."

A video B-roll package and press kit highlighting the winner were transmitted from the event to broadcast and print media, resulting in network TV coverage, wire service and syndicated features and photographs, and national radio coverage. Media coverage of Campbell's "Art of Soup" contest was sustained for more than a year, reaching an audience of 200 million readers, radio listeners, and TV viewers through unpaid media with an advertising equivalence of $1.8 million.

Content analysis of the "Art of Soup" contest publicity found that 95 percent of the coverage of the contest announcement and 75 percent of the winner coverage mentioned the label change.

It was a contest only Campbell could have pulled off. *Brandweek* called it "brilliant on several levels. It plays beautifully off of the cult standing Warhol brought to the brand and it perks continued interest in and awareness of the redesign, which in itself was a good move for Campbell."[1]

The powers that be at Campbell were so impressed with the contest that they themed the company's annual report "The Art of Winning," ran a red-and-white Campbell's lighthouse painting on the cover, and illustrated it throughout with other winning art.

M&M's Color Campaign

M&M/Mars involved people with America's favorite chocolate candies when it gave them an unprecedented chance to vote for a new candy color in "M&M Chocolate Candies Color Campaign 1995." It was the first time since the product's creation in 1941 that consumers were asked to vote for a new color. Their choice was to keep tan or switch to blue, pink, or purple.

Like Campbell soup and Tide, M&M's is a longtime American favorite. The company said it was giving America the chance to interact with an American icon it had grown to love.

The campaign was kicked off at a giant party for children at a Los Angeles children's hospital that was covered by news and lifestyle TV programs.

To create consumer affinity, the company made costumed M&M characters a highly visible part of every media event from the kickoff throughout the three-month campaign. Blue, purple, and pink candidate characters traveled the country. They appeared at more than 100 campaign events in twenty-three cities at malls, colleges, and other venues where the target twenty-four-and-under crowd hung out. They appeared at such high-traffic venues as the Super Bowl, danced at the New Orleans Mardi Gras, and cheered on runners at the Los Angeles Marathon.

Ballots were offered by publicity and at retail. During the last two weeks, television spots kicked in urging consumers to get out the vote. Stories about M&M Chocolate Candies Color Campaign 1995 ran in nearly 1,000 newspapers and on more than 200 television stations, including segments of ABC's *Good Morning America* and *Entertainment Tonight*. The public relations–driven integrated campaign caused 10.2 million people to call, write, or fax in their votes for their favorite colors. Call-in response was so high that telephone line capacity had to be tripled to handle the increased volume.

The three color candidates concluded their whirlwind national tour at a press conference atop New York's Empire State Building. There the election results were announced and the building lit with the winning color—blue! Blue captured 54 percent of the vote, winning by a large margin over purple and pink. The wisdom of the color change was confirmed when "no change" received only 4 percent of the vote.

Even after the election results were announced, the campaign achieved a life of its own, as consumers searched out the first packages with the new color.

The integrated campaign continued when commercials introducing the M&M blue character began to run. The new spots gained the highest levels of recall and intent-to-purchase scores ever recorded in the category.

The color campaign hit the media again when a giant M&M blue balloon appeared on national television with the telecast of the Macy's Thanksgiving Day Parade.

M&M's color campaign is regarded by the company as one of the most successful public relations campaigns in its history. The campaign that began with the announcement of the consumer poll and culminated with the coverage of the announcement of the winner and the lighting of the Empire State Building generated more than one billion consumer impressions according to Warner, Bicking, Morris & Partners, M&M's public relations firm.

Time declared M&M/Mars a "winner." The item in the magazine's "Winners and Losers" column stated "Candy company hits public relations jackpot with ultrahyped election of M&M blue." *Tonight* host Jay Leno kiddingly proclaimed the voting for blue M&M's one of the most important elections held in 1995. And the popular comic strip "Sally Forth," syndicated to 500 newspapers, devoted an entire week of comics to how Sally and her family were voting in the M&M's color campaign. The campaign also made "Best of the Year" lists in *Life, Us, Business Week,* and the "Year in Review" segments on ABC's *World News Tonight* and CNN.

The M&M Chocolate Candies Color Campaign produced strong and sustainable sales results for the entire year, growing its number one share position 6.5 percent.

Lessons Learned

- People love contests.
- People especially love talent contests that offer the promise of fifteen minutes of fame.

- Build the contest around a brand benefit.
- If there is no product news, focus on the package.
- Integrate on the package, in print, on the Net, and at the store level.
- Extend media exposure by picking multiwinners in target market categories.
- Media loves kids. If your product is used by or for kids, make sure you have kid winners.
- TV cameras love company spokescharacters. Have them on hand for every event.
- There is no better way to involve consumers than by asking them to pick their favorite color or flavor.
- Build media anticipation of the results.
- Sustain the news over a period of time by staging a series of local and national events.
- Find a dramatic way to announce the winners.
- If there are lights and action, you'll get the cameras.
- Shameless stunts work. And they don't have to break the bank.

Should Betty Be a Vitamin?

Rosie O'Donnell brought the subject into the open. During an interview on CBS-TV's *Eye to Eye*, Rosie, who played Betty Rubble in the live-action film *The Flintstones*, revealed the shocking fact that Betty was not a Flintstone vitamin. "There's Fred . . . Barney . . . and Wilma," she exclaimed, holding up each vitamin. "Even Dino . . . but no Betty! Hand me the phone. I need to call my agent."

Seizing the opportunity to capitalize on Betty's plight, the Flintstones vitamins brand group at Bayer Corporation and its promotion company, advertising agency, and public relations firm Manning, Selvage & Lee, collaborated on a truly integrated marketing effort called "Here's Betty."

The centerpiece of the promotion was putting Betty icons in special packages of Flintstones vitamins and offering prizes to lucky consumers who found them. By interviewing longtime company employees, Manning, Selvage & Lee uncovered two possible reasons why Betty didn't make the cut. First, in an effort to make the vitamin true to form, the designers gave Betty an extra-thin waist that kept breaking during production. Second, manufacturers back in the late 1960s had a tough time distinguishing the Betty vitamin from Wilma, so Betty was nixed in favor of Fred's more popular wife.

Further Manning, Selvage & Lee research uncovered a *SPY* magazine exposé that blew the whistle on the missing Betty, located a rock group in Atlanta that had named itself Betty's Not a Vitamin, and found a 100-strong Betty Club of

Grants Pass, Oregon, who were circulating a petition to give Betty her rightful place in the vitamin bottle. The agency recruited both the band and the club to join the public relations effort.

They recommended a public relations program targeted to the brand's market, mothers of children two to twelve. The stated objectives were to use Betty to remind mothers about Flintstone vitamins and, mirroring the title of this chapter, "to involve moms and kids with Flintstones vitamins."

The strategy was to let the public decide Betty's fate through a national referendum. A boulder-like prehistoric voting booth was created where voters could cast "Yes" or "No" using stones as ballots. Parents and their kids voted in high-traffic regional shopping malls in Los Angeles, Chicago, New York, New Jersey, Atlanta, and Dallas. Preevent signage was posted in the selected malls and tie-ins arranged with mall kids clubs. A costumed Betty character oversaw the voting and attracted attention to the booth. Locally, there was preevent publicity at each mall event. The results of the local vote attracted additional media coverage.

Betty's fate was not decided by the mall shoppers only. Manning, Selvage & Lee set up an 800 number where everyone else could cast their votes. Publicity alerted the public to the poll and the 800 number. A "Should Betty Be a Vitamin?" video was produced showing voters in action at the kickoff event in Los Angeles and included actual Betty footage from the classic original Flintstone cartoons.

Three waves of publicity were planned: the national announcement of the referendum (and 800 number), the local publicity coverage of mall events, and the announcement of the results of the poll.

The campaign culminated with the announcement of the vote and the brand's decision to include Betty as a Flintstone vitamin. More than 3,000 kids and their moms cast stones at voting booths in five markets and more than 17,000 calls were logged to the 800 number with 91 percent in favor of adding Betty to the bottle.

In its "Cheers 'N' Jeers" column, *TV Guide* applauded the decision and asked "Who made up the other 9 percent? Probably fans of the Flintmobile, which is being deleted, and fans of a Georgia band called Betty's Not a Vitamin, which now needs a new name."

The lead of the *Chicago Tribune* wire story was "The maker of Flintstones vitamins has decided to reunite Barney and Betty. Twenty-five years after the children's supplement based on *The Flintstones* cartoon series was introduced, Bayer Corporation is adding a Betty Rubble vitamin to the chewable crew from Bedrock. But to make room for Betty, the company had to lose one of the other vitamins—Fred, Wilma, Barney, Dino, Pebbles, Bam-Bam, or the Flintmobile. 'We decided to bag the car,' said Karen Lazan, product manager."[2]

As a result of the three-stage effort, Betty publicity appeared in more than 1,000 print and broadcast stories generating more than 175 million impressions.

The result of the integrated program was a market share increase from 31 to 34 percent at the climax of public relations activities.

Lessons Learned

- Do your homework. There's no telling what secrets lurk in the company's archives.
- Talk to retired employees who were there.
- Awaken the nostalgia vote with archival footage.
- Find some unlikely allies, maybe even a fan club or a rock group bearing your product's name.
- Ask a good question and get a good answer.
- Get target moms and kids involved in person.
- Meet them at the mall. Tie in with their kids clubs.
- Create a nifty booth and bring your costumed character along.
- Let the country vote using an 800 number.
- When the voters have spoken, announce the results and what you are doing about it.

CHAPTER 17

Cultivating a Core
Consumer Base

TODAY'S MARKETERS ARE BEGINNING TO RECOGNIZE THAT THERE IS SOMETHING MORE important than making a sale. It is what we might call making a friend. A friend not only can become a loyal lifetime customer but the most effective surrogate salesperson a company can have.

All manner of products can inspire dedicated fans, but especially those of the wheeled variety. Ford Mustang fans are legendary in their devotion to the original pony car of 1964. Ford went all out to make the car's thirtieth anniversary a red-letter occasion to turn the spotlight on the 1994 state-of-the-art Mustang. To build excitement, the company put new Mustangs on display at high-traffic venues such as Knott's Berry Farm in California and car lovers' meccas such as the Indianapolis Motor Speedway and the Charlotte Motor Speedway.

Charlotte played host to 3,000 Mustang owners from twenty countries, including an owner of a 1967 blue-gray Mustang convertible: Bill Clinton. The president of the United States was surprised when his car was transported from an Arkansas museum to Charlotte for a presidential spin around the track. "I never dreamed I'd be invited here to this event and given a chance to drive my car," the president exclaimed, "nobody lets me drive anymore." The president's appearance was widely covered on television and in newspapers across the country. It made the nation's news agenda and gave many car fans their first look at the new Mustang that was to be named by *Motor Trend* as "Car of the Year."

Saturn's Homecoming

From the beginning, Saturn Corporation was positioned as "a different kind of company" that made "a different kind of car."

It was natural then that Saturn would stage a different kind of event to reinforce its relationships with its car owners. When the company invited all of its 700,000 owners to come to its Spring Hill, Tennessee, plant for a little get-together, it learned how special the bond was between company and customer.

In February of 1994, every Saturn owner received an invitation to attend the Saturn homecoming that summer. Sue Jordan of Saturn said, "We thought it would be a good idea to foster the feeling of family among our Saturn owners, team members, and retailers. We also wanted to thank the people who took a chance on Saturn in its early days when very few people knew who we were or what we were all about."[1]

The company was astounded when 43,398 Saturn owners accepted the invitation and showed up at Spring Hill the weekend of June 23 to 25. They drove their Saturns from every state in the United States and almost every province in Canada to Tennessee to feast on fried chicken, burgers, roasted corn, and cinnamon buns, and celebrate Saturn.

The company figured that one of the first things most owners would want to do in Spring Hill was to see where their cars were made and meet the people who made them. There were plant tours, of course, but some of the more intriguing parts of the Saturn were taken outdoors where it was less noisy and crowded and where team members could answer questions and engage in conversation with owners.

A tented area called Team Town was set up across from the plant. It contained an array of interesting automotive demonstrations and displays. For serious car buffs, Saturn provided a vintage vehicle display and contest. To add to the hometown flavor of the occasion, local arts and crafts were displayed and sold and continuous entertainment was provided. Camp Saturn was set up for the kids, and teens were invited to participate in a special version of Saturn's "Excel" course where they helped each other climb ropes, jump from platforms, and in the process learn how Saturn team building works.

Saturn owners were invited to visit the Opryland Theme Park in nearby Nashville on homecoming weekend. Back in Spring Hill, Saturn hosted its own big show featuring headliners Wynonna Judd and Olympic medalist Dan Jansen.

Meanwhile, Saturn dealers participated by hosting a variety of homecoming events in their local communities.

The 7,000 team members and 2,000 local volunteers made the visitors feel right at home in Spring Hill. Even though a rainstorm and a windstorm ended the weekend early, the owners were pleased to have made the special trip to the reunion part of their summer vacations. When asked why they came, many owners answered "because I love my Saturn and the people that built it."

The unique relationship that Saturn has created with its customers was expressed this way in a company-produced homecoming film documentary. "They came to see what this thing was that they all bought into. To see how Saturns were made and meet the people that make them. As much as anything people came here to be a part of something that was part of them. Which is what Saturn is all about. Pretty much just the values we grew up with and want to believe in. That somehow got lost between efficiency experts and work rules and sheet metal. We had all been away but in a funny kind of way it seems we were finally coming home."

The event successfully demonstrated Saturn's five basic values: (1) commitment to customer enthusiasm, (2) excellence, (3) teamwork, (4) trust and respect for the individual, and (5) continuous improvement.

Relationships with owners based on these company values are maintained and nurtured through the *Saturn Magazine,* which is also available on the company's Web site, along with Saturn's "Extended Family Database," which provides owners and prospects with information on Saturn models, how-to-order brochures, and how to locate the nearest Saturn dealer.

Going Hog-Wild in Milwaukee

All roads led to Milwaukee when more than 60,000 riders rolled into town in 1993 to celebrate the ninetieth anniversary reunion of America's only surviving motorcycle manufacturer, Harley-Davidson Motor Co., Inc.

A crowd of more than 100,000 onlookers lined the highways and parade grounds where the reunion was held. A parade of bands entertained and more than thirty restaurants operated on the festival grounds. There was even a double wedding on stage. The high point of the celebration was a birthday ceremony emceed by Jay Leno, host of NBC's *Tonight Show* and a Harley enthusiast. Leno, clad in a cyclist's leather jacket, motored onstage on his gray-and-red Harley. The ceremony was followed by a ZZ Top concert.

To make their visitors feel right at home, Harley published a *Bikers' Guide to Milwaukee* that featured Milwaukee's attractions, events, eateries, night spots, and neighborhood crawls. For those looking for something more sedate, the Milwaukee Public Museum offered an extensive anniversary exhibit of Harleys, including cycles owned by Malcolm Forbes and Elvis Presley.

The event had a charitable aspect as well. Riders participating in the Muscular Dystrophy Association (MDA) Reunion Ride traveled ten separate designated routes to Milwaukee from all parts of the country. Executives from Harley-Davidson hosted each leg of the ride, leading the cyclists cross-country to the reunion celebration. Riders were urged to sign up friends to make per-mile pledges to the MDA, H-D's corporate charity and the beneficiary of the ninetieth anniversary fundraising activities. Harley's Milwaukee neighbor, Miller Brewing Company, contributed an additional twenty-five cents to MDA for every case of sixteen-ounce Miller Genuine Draft ninetieth anniversary commemorative cans sold during the celebration.

The media were out in force. Harley's communications department and agency, Bozell Public Relations, saw to it that the picturesque event was omnipresent on weekend network newscasts. "Road to Hog Heaven" was a *USA Today* cover story. Even that most respectable medium *National Public Radio* ran a business feature on the company's comeback and the special place it holds in the hearts of Harley owners.

Putting Customers First

Harley-Davidson survived tough times in the 1980s but thanks to new managers who went back to the basics, the company had come roaring back in the 1990s to become the undisputed champion of heavyweight motorcycles. Its product is so sought after that by 1997 there was a one-year waiting list to buy a new Harley. A new plant is being built in Kansas City to satisfy the demand both in the United States and in Europe where cyclists can't wait to get high off the hog.

Harley-Davidson's comeback is directly attributable not only to advanced management and manufacturing technologies but also to the company's success in cultivating its core consumer base. The ninetieth anniversary celebration coincided with the tenth anniversary of the Harley Owners Group. HOG was established by the company in 1983 as a means of getting Harley-Davidson owners more involved in the sport of motorcycling. A decade later, there were more than 235,000 HOG members and 800 chapters worldwide.

Members share their enthusiasm for motorcycling with each other through various chapter functions as well as regional and national rallies. In the United States alone, there are as many as forty-five state rallies every year, attracting up to 5,000 participants and national rallies attracting 20,000. Members receive a bimonthly magazine called *Hog Tales*, pins, patches, touring handbooks, emergency road service, and fly-and-ride programs that allow members to rent motorcycles at locations throughout the world. But according to *Reputation Management* magazine, "the most important benefit is the opportunity to hang out with other Harley enthusiasts, to immerse oneself in the Harley lifestyle."

Another important benefit is a voice with the company. Harley-Davidson executives are themselves motorcycle enthusiasts and regularly attend HOG functions to interact with members. It is their best way to stay "close to the customer," and to let the customers know that their opinions and suggestions will be heard.

According to *Reputation Management,* "the bond between Harley-Davidson and its customers is deep and almost mystical." Chairman of the Board Richard F. Teerlink says "Harley-Davidson doesn't sell transportation. We sell transformation. We sell excitement, a way of life. We give people a way to transform themselves."[2]

The company says that the typical Harley-Davidson rider is a salesperson, physician, mechanic, chef, CEO, lawyer, teacher, or housewife. It points out that while motorcycling continues to be a male-dominated activity, women make up one of the fastest-growing segments of Harley riders.

Nonowners can live vicariously by wearing a catalog full of Harley motor clothes, from leather jackets to T-shirts sold at Harley Designer Stores, and dropping in at Harley watering holes that are popping up in high-visibility locations such as New York's Fifth Avenue. The company also does a nice business in accessories and collectibles.

Harley-Davidson does virtually no advertising, and most of its marketing efforts are spent interfacing with customers, which the company calls "public relations in its purest form."

Lessons Learned

- Use public relations to build relationships that turn customers into boosters.
- Stay in touch with customers and let them know you care.
- Give customers a forum for talking back. Listen and learn.
- Build camaraderie by organizing customers into owner organizations or fan clubs.
- Create a package of exclusive membership benefits.
- Seed, stimulate, and support their events.
- Sponsor local and regional events that bring together your biggest enthusiasts.
- Mark milestones such as big birthdays with big doings.
- Make it fun for all.
- Bring on the celebrity endorsers.
- Use the occasion to help a worthy cause.
- Look for tie-ins with companies with similar target markets.
- Invite the media to join in the fun.

CHAPTER 18

Providing a Value-Added Customer Service

THE NAME OF THIS BOOK REFERS TO THE USES OF PUBLIC RELATIONS TO HELP consumers make better-informed purchasing decisions. It also refers to ways in which companies ensure brand loyalty by maintaining contact with and continuing to provide useful information to customers.

Publicity may or may not be part of the process. A plant tour that shows consumers how products are made, a museum exhibit that demonstrates how products work, a video that shows why they work, all provide a value-added service to clients that does not depend on publicity.

Consumer service departments traditionally answer letters and telephone calls (and now fax mail and e-mail) about products and how to use them. The 800 consumer service number is an important way to engender personal relationships with consumers.

Butterball Turkey Talk-Line Saves the Day

The mother of all 800 numbers is the Butterball Turkey Talk-Line. This public relations initiative was created for Butterball in 1981 by Edelman Public Relations Worldwide and has been the brand's primary market vehicle ever since.

The Talk-Line (1-800-323-4848) was designed to keep the product top-of-mind at a time when there was a glut in the turkey market. The idea was to

145

establish a toll-free national number staffed by home economists ready to personally assist consumers to prepare their Thanksgiving dinners. In the first years, the Talk-Line succeeded in selling every available Butterball Turkey.

Since the Talk-Line was created, it has been supported annually by an extensive media relations campaign. By 1996, the Talk-Line had handled more than two million calls. The calls are answered by forty-eight professionally trained home economists and nutritionists who offer one-on-one assistance on any and all turkey-related questions from thawing to roasting to carving. This twenty-four-hour service runs for a two-month period from November through Christmas. It includes automated assistance after-hours. There is even a special 800 number for the hearing- and speech-impaired. On Thanksgiving Day alone, 8,000 calls are answered.

The Turkey Talk-Line press kits developed by Edelman typically include a behind-the-scenes look at the Talk-Line headquarters and staff members, a holiday turkey checklist, answers to frequently asked questions from previous years, suggested menus for Thanksgiving dinner, a customized holiday menu plan that shows how much to prepare for the number of guests attending, and even quick and easy low-fat leftover serving suggestions.

In 1996, 210,000 calls were received during November and December. A total of 1.7 billion impressions were generated for the Talk-Line, including network and local radio and television and stories in virtually every food and

In 1995 the Butterball Turkey Talk-Line took on a new look, reflecting the launch of a year-round Web site. The Talk-Line, a public relations initiative, created in 1981, has become the company's primary marketing vehicle. (Courtesy of Butterball Turkey Company)

women's magazine and newspaper food section as well as Hispanic and African-American media.

NBC's *Today Show* has featured turkey preparation segments with host Katie Couric and Butterball's Sarah Chase. CNN *Headline News* has reported live from a turkey farm and interviewed Jean Schnelle, Director of the Butterball Talk-Line. For many years, CBS has covered the story live from Talk-Line headquarters in Downer's Grove, Illinois, with Schnelle demonstrating how to carve a picture-perfect Butterball Turkey.

Typical print media commentary: "S.O.S. for turkey traumas. . . . Do you have thawing issues? A roasting quandary? Where does that darn meat thermometer go, anyway? Nutritionists and home economists at Butterball's Turkey Talk-Line have answered nearly two million queries since 1981. . . ." (*Self Magazine*) and "It is the mother of all 1-800 talk lines. Manned by forty-eight unflappable pros—all of them women with solid cooking experience—the BTL fields 8,000 calls on Thanksgiving day alone" (*Chicago Tribune Magazine*).

Butterball now launches its expertise in cyberspace with a home page on the World Wide Web (http://www.butterball.com). In the first year, the interactive Web site generated 1.4 million hits. In the second year, the Butterball home page was an even greater success, receiving more than 4.4 million hits. This represents more than 600,000 consumers who tapped into Butterball for online turkey advice during the 1996 holiday season. Consumer use of the Web site is expected to increase greatly in future years.

Butterball offers every caller and Web site visitor a set of five recipe cards that feature important turkey preparation techniques and recipes for year-round turkey enjoyment plus $5 in coupons. Consumers can also receive a five-minute video *Preparing a Picture-Perfect Butterball Turkey* (in either English or Spanish) for a small postage and handling charge.

To celebrate its two-millionth call in 1996, the lucky caller was awarded a fully prepared Butterball Turkey dinner and a trip for two to Colonial Williamsburg, a milestone that was covered by media across the United States.

Dinner on a Disk

Consumer education has long been one of the principal marketing functions of trade associations. This is especially true in the food industry. While few food trade groups and advisory boards can afford to run national advertising campaigns, most of them sponsor public relations information and education programs. Traditional tools include recipe development, recipe cards, recipe books, food page publicity, and special programs directed to home economists, nutritionists, dietitians, and consumer affairs directors of the grocery chains.

The National Potato Promotion Board, created in 1971, was one of the first commodity groups to promote its product generically. In recent years, the

Potato Board has been a pioneer in developing cutting-edge technology to modernize the image of potatoes and bring useful product information directly to consumers as a value-added service.

The Potato Board and Ketchum Public Relations working together with technology suppliers have created some innovative high-tech tools that make meal planning easier, spur impulse sales of potatoes, and serve as a hook to gain national media attention for potatoes. These tools include interactive Potato Board recipe kiosks in supermarkets, meal planning/recipe software, satellite media tours, and a World Wide Web site.

To determine if the target audience would order and use menu-planning software or use an interactive kiosk in a supermarket, Ketchum conducted research that revealed that more than 40 percent of all working women use computers and more than seven million women use computers at home. They were positive about software as long as it was easy to use. The agency also conducted focus groups in which consumers said they would use an interactive kiosk to obtain new and interesting recipes.

The result was the development of user-friendly software that was easy to install, fits on one disk, and was so simple to use that a manual was not needed. Called "Ready, Set, Dinner," the software offers consumers a library of forty main dish recipes, makes a weekly menu, and creates a shopping list. The software has lively graphics, music, and animation. It also allows users to personalize the meal planner by adding their own recipes and typing in their own notations.

The software was offered free to consumers who paid only a small postage and handling charge.

The supermarket kiosk has a touch-screen computer and offers shoppers five potato-based recipe categories: Last Minute Wonders, Kid Pleasers, American Favorites, Dinners for Two, and Around the World. Shoppers could also specify if they want recipes for chicken, fish, beef, vegetarian, pork, seafood, soup, or salad. They could then print out recipes they would like to take home.

The Potato Board was lauded by food journalists and supermarket produce managers who saw the kiosk increase potato sales. Exit interviews revealed that kiosk users would buy the recipe ingredients, including potatoes, during their shopping trip that day and prepare one of the recipes that night.

To capitalize on the media interest in practical uses for high-technology tools, Ketchum conducted a twenty-station satellite media tour featuring Jonathan Taylor Thomas of *Home Improvement*. A child star was selected because children are increasingly computer-literate and could help mom with meal planning.

The public relations program succeeded in repositioning potatoes as a contemporary solution to the dinnertime dilemma by focusing on quick cooking strategies in the context of cutting-edge technology. Media coverage positioned

potatoes as easy or quick to prepare, helping to overcome perceptions that potatoes were not contemporary and that they were too time-consuming to prepare.

Lessons Learned

- Value-added consumer services separate you from the pack.
- They build relationships, brand equity, and store traffic.
- Test your program before taking it national.
- Programs can be ongoing or repeated annually to focus media and con-
sumer attention.
- Use traditional and new media to deliver the message to target markets.
- Make it personal with a hot line where consumers can meet the experts.
- Consider using Web sites, interactive kiosks, and computer software to
deliver the message to consumers one-on-one.
- Join with government agencies, advocacy organizations, and opinion
leaders.
- Create a national event to bring attention to the program.
- Stage local events that support the national effort.
- Know the difference between a value-added service and a self-serving
promotion.
- If you aren't prepared to make a long-term commitment, forget it.

CHAPTER 19

Bringing a Brand to Life

BRAND EQUITY IS ONE OF A COMPANY'S GREATEST ASSETS. IT IS IMMEASURABLY enhanced when the company can be humanized through real or fictional spokespersons. Real figures such as Frank Perdue, Orville Redenbacher, and Colonel Harlan Sanders are known and loved by consumers everywhere. The trouble is, they die. Lately, an actor portraying Colonel Sanders has popped up in KFC commercials. The company may be just as happy. After the Colonel sold his company and continued on as its spokesperson, he sometimes embarrassed the new owners by commenting on how they had ruined his famous gravy.

Betty Crocker Gets a Make-Over

General Mills has no such problem. Betty Crocker is the greatest spokesperson who never lived. Even though she first appeared seventy-five years ago, Betty, like Orphan Annie, doesn't age. She just moves with the times. In fact, she goes through a make-over about once a decade.

Betty began life in 1921 when the ad manager for Gold Medal flour created her to personalize letters answering baking questions from thousands of consumers. Although she never was a real person, her name and identity have become synonymous with helpfulness, trustworthiness, and quality. She has survived the decades by providing consumers with food information and good products.

General Mills celebrated the seventy-fifth Betty Crocker anniversary with a yearlong consumer-involving "search" for an entirely new Betty. The new Betty would be the eighth since Betty materialized in her first portrait in 1936.

A three-step public relations program created by General Mills and its public relations firm, Shandwick USA, kept Betty in the news throughout the year. To kick off the program in September of 1995, the company announced a nationwide search for seventy-five women who best embodied Betty's characteristics. The company said that photographs of the seventy-five winners would be incorporated in a single computer-generated composite image that would help guide the creation of a new portrait to be painted by internationally known artist John Stuart Ingle.

Nominees could enter themselves or be nominated by someone else. They were asked to provide a photograph and a real-life anecdote or description of how the nominee reflected the characteristics "that make up the spirit of Betty Crocker"—that she enjoys cooking and baking, is committed to family and friends, is resourceful in handling everyday tasks, and is involved in her community. Entrants were also asked to include the name of either a favorite recipe from a Betty Crocker cookbook or the name of a favorite Betty Crocker product.

The announcement was so inherently newsworthy that no media event was held. A press release alone generated 150 million print and broadcast impressions. Thousands of nominations poured in from husbands, mothers, grandmothers, friends, and women nominating themselves.

In January of 1996, General Mills announced the names of the seventy-five winners chosen by a panel of independent judges from among thousands of entrants. The company said "nominees ranged from teenagers to ninetysomethings and included everyone from research scientists to homemakers, great-grandmothers, college students, and more." General Mills said that seven entrants were actually named Betty Crocker, and that one of them, a Salt Lake City homemaker was, like the famous Betty, celebrating her seventy-fifth birthday.

The company released excerpts from heartwarming winning entries and provided personalized releases to media in each of the seventy-five winners' hometowns. The result was a flood of hometown, as well as national, publicity.

In addition to achieving a place in history as one of the women chosen for the seventy-fifth anniversary Betty Crocker portrait, each of the seventy-five winners received a Betty Crocker Red Spoon diamond pin, a special copy of Betty's seventy-fifth anniversary cookbook, and a framed seventy-fifth anniversary portrait of the new Betty Crocker. The General Mills Foundation also made a $500 grant in each winner's name to a local elementary school. A shipment of Betty Crocker products was also donated on behalf of each winner to a food bank in her community.

Computer artistry was used by a software company to combine photographs of the seventy-five winners with the current Betty Crocker portrait. Using the computer-generated image and inspiration from the women's essays, artist Ingle painted the portrait of the new Betty to reflect contemporary women. It was unveiled at a press conference held in a New York hotel and broadcast live via satellite. The company announced that the new portrait would soon appear on some Betty Crocker products.

Betty's portrait appeared in newspapers and magazines, often with portraits of her seven predecessors. The unveiling was widely covered on television news as was a video news release of the morphing of Betty. Betty was, of course, excused from media appearances but her "seventy-fifth anniversary manager" appeared on many programs. She even was able to restage the portrait unveiling on ABC's *Good Morning America*.

The three-phased public relations program announcing the search, revealing the seventy-five women whose pictures would be incorporated in the new Betty, and the unveiling of the portrait kept Betty Crocker in the news for the

A new portrait of Betty Crocker was based on a computer-generated composite of seventy-five winners of a seventy-fifth anniversary search conducted by General Mills. She is the eighth Betty since 1936. (Courtesy of General Mills, Inc.)

entire anniversary year. It focused attention on the more than 200 products that General Mills markets under the Betty Crocker brand. Together these products represented total sales of $1.3 billion in 1996, the year of the new Betty.

George Lazarus, marketing columnist of the *Chicago Tribune,* commented that "the latest make-over of Betty Crocker, the eighth marking her seventy-fifth birthday, has given this American icon a new lease on life."

Later in the year, General Mills introduced a new line of Betty Crocker cereals backed by the largest consumer marketing campaign in the company's history. A General Mills marketing executive told *Advertising Age* that the Betty Crocker name represents "a huge franchise and equity for us."

The seventy-five women whose characteristics are incorporated in the new Betty became General Mills media ambassadors participating in the introduction of the cereals and other new products, product sampling programs, and special events.

The company employs the Betty Crocker name and persona in a number of other ways. There are at least thirty Betty Crocker cookbooks currently in print along with a monthly recipe magazine sold in supermarkets. In the Consumer Services Department, Betty now answers baking and meal-preparation questions from more than 600,000 consumers annually. Many callers to the company's 800 lines insist on speaking to Betty Crocker herself. She's either out of the office or away from her desk.

Lessons Learned

- Real spokespeople can die. Made-up ones have a shot at immortality.
- Your spokesperson may need a make-over.
- Involve consumers in a contest that gives them a chance to be a small part of history.
- Pick multiple winners. The more winners, the more local publicity.
- Play the human-interest card for all it's worth.
- Stretch the story over time. Make news at each step. Announce the search. Announce the winners. Present the prize.
- Tie the prize to the event. Create something special nobody else can get.
- Sometimes fiction is greater than fact. People want to communicate with famous friends, real or imagined. Santa gets more mail than anybody.
- If you can't appear on TV because you are unreal, send a stand-in.

Tony the Tiger: A Major-League Promotion

Many of our most-endearing spokescharacters are not humanoid at all. The Pillsbury Dough Boy, M&M characters, Chester the Cheetah, those Dancing

California Raisins, and Kellogg's G-R-R-R-EAT Frosted Flakes spokescharacter Tony the Tiger have emerged from their commercials to appear "live" at supermarket openings, event sponsorships, and high-visibility public relations stunts.

The Kellogg Company saw a natural fit between baseball and Kellogg cereals, for both are All-American favorites that have strong family appeal.

To maximize its involvement, the cereal sponsor of major league baseball, Kellogg Company, and its public relations firm, Porter/Novelli, created a season-long high-profile program featuring Tony.

Their strategy was to capture media attention and reach families by positioning Tony as the baseball mascot of all mascots. To launch the program, Tony hosted the first spring training camp for those wacky and much-loved major league mascots at the Philadelphia Phillies spring training camp in Clearwater, Florida. The event was timed to attract sportswriters and lifestyle media covering spring training in Florida.

The event was designed to provide irresistible photograph and video opportunities. Coverage ranged from an Associated Press photo of Tony leading baseball training exercises to coverage in media as diverse as *Sports Illustrated*, *Entertainment Tonight*, and ESPN's *Baseball Magazine*. *CBS This Morning* weatherman Mark McEwen even covered the event live.

A video news release played in more than 100 markets including a number where Tony was scheduled to make live appearances during the season. Wherever Tony appeared in twenty-four major league baseball stadiums across the country, fans could redeem vouchers from Kellogg product packages for free baseball tickets. A local public relations effort supported each of these "Tony Day" promotions. Before each special day, pictures of Tony and the local mascot taken at spring training blanketed the local media. Kid pages of local newspapers reached the kid market, while coverage on sports pages and sportscasts reached their parents.

At World Series time, the media received personalized and paw print–signed letters from Tony announcing Kellogg's plans to produce a limited-edition Frosted Flakes box celebrating the winning team. Within hours after the conclusion of the Series, commemorative boxes featuring Tony in a Minnesota Twins uniform were delivered to print and broadcast media in time for morning-after roundup stories.

The Tony program effectively enhanced all of Kellogg's other promotional tie-ins with major league baseball.

Lessons Learned

- Kids love critters.
- Kids love sports. Put them together for a winning combination.
- There is more room on sports pages and sportscasts than on cereal pages and cereal shows.

- Create an event with your character as the star attraction.
- Stage it where the media are already assembled.
- Pick a slow news day.
- Make sure there is plenty of action for the TV cameras.
- Produce your own video.
- Take your character off the box and put him on the road to meet the fans.
- While he's in town, take him to places that sell your products.

California Dancing Raisins Between the Ads

One of my earliest public relations assignments at Edelman Public Relations was to keep ice cream top-of-mind during the winter months, when ice cream consumption was lowest and advertising the least. We came up with a public relations and promotion program called "Ice Cream for the Holidays" and filled newspaper and magazine food pages with creative holiday dessert suggestions featuring ice cream.

Bringing the brand to life can be effectively used to maintain high visibility between advertising campaigns. Most advertisers who can't afford the high cost of buying broadcast time throughout the year run their commercials when sales potential is the most advantageous. Marketers can take advantage of the cost-efficiency of MPR to keep their products top-of-mind between advertising flights. One of the benefits of integrated marketing is that the various elements can be coordinated on a timetable that keeps a high level of exposure even when there is little or no advertising.

The ability of public relations to maintain high visibility between ad campaigns can be greatly enhanced by using advertising spokescharacters.

Take the famous California Dancing Raisins. From the beginning, their success was the result of the seamless integration of advertising and public relations. Before raisins could dance, they were thought of as a little old-fashioned. Research showed that consumers thought of them as tasty but decidedly dull and wimpy. So the California Raisin Advisory Board issued a challenge to its advertising agency, Foote, Cone & Belding, and its public relations firm, Ketchum. Make raisins cool. Make them fun. Make people want raisins.

Foote, Cone & Belding took the challenge to heart and created the lovable California Dancing Raisins. They appeared in their first commercial in 1986 and became celebrities virtually overnight. The spot instantly soared to the top of *Adweek's* top-ten list. The Dancing Raisins rendition of "I Heard It Through the Grapevine" sparked a mini-Motown revival.

Ketchum was asked to extend the reach and the life of the Dancing Raisins in ways unique to public relations. It worked hand in hand with Foote, Cone & Belding to extend the media dollars by obtaining news coverage of the ad campaign and bringing the characters to life. This strategy was critical to the success of the campaign since the first-year ad budget was a modest $6 million.

The public relations firm transformed the Claymation characters of the animated commercials into bigger-than-life-size costumed characters and picked the best spots for in-person appearances. They appeared live at a media event introducing their costar in a commercial, Ray Charles, and a satellite media tour featuring Michael Raisin, the Claymation counterpart of Michael Jackson who starred in another raisin spot.

Because advertising dollars were limited, the ad campaign was suspended for the summer of 1988. That is when public relations took over with a high-visibility campaign to keep the Dancing California Raisins top-of-mind. Billed as the "Vacation Across America" to help them recuperate from their instant stardom, the tour found the costumed California Dancing Raisins visiting twenty-seven U.S. cities. Local media covered them as they checked out landmarks, were greeted by mayors, gave away raisins at supermarkets, and visited children's hospitals.

The tour was an enormous success, generating media exposure at a fraction of what it would have cost to sustain the ad campaign during the summer months. The California Dancing Raisins were given celebrity treatment reserved for the biggest stars by the media, including more than 1,000 stories on TV and radio and in newspapers and magazines. The tour generated 110 million media impressions. The only dried fruit to have its own fan club signed up 3,000 new members.

Despite the absence of advertising, California raisin sales jumped 20 percent during the summer. There is no better example of how public relations can ring up sales between ad campaigns by bringing spokescharacters to life to interact with consumers.

Lessons Learned

- No product is so dull that it can't be made cool.
- MPR can stretch your ad dollars.
- It takes teamwork and a plan.
- Between ad campaigns, let PR take over.
- Give your spokescharacters the celebrity treatment.
- Take your show on the road.

- Invite mayors and governors to get into the act.
- Take them to meet kids and moms where they shop.
- Use their appearances to hand out free samples and branded mementos.
- Arrange radio trade-for-mention promotions when they are in town.
- Find time for them to cheer up shut-ins.
- Alert the media to their doings about town.

CHAPTER 20

Leveraging Event Sponsorships

EXPERIENCED MARKETERS RECOGNIZE THAT PAYING A BIG PRICE TAG TO BECOME A major event sponsor is only the beginning. They know they must be prepared to spend from two to five times that amount to assure high visibility. That is particularly true of mega-events with multiple sponsors. The mega of megas is, of course, the Olympic Games. In the summer of 1996 a handful of companies paid $40 million to be official sponsors.

The game is getting rougher. Sponsors not only have to devise ways to stand out from the other sponsors, increasingly they must duke it out with guerrilla marketers that wrap themselves in the mantle of the event without paying the whopping price of admission. The 1996 Olympic Games in Atlanta found Reebok, the official athletic shoe sponsor, left in the dust by the Nike marketing colossus. Through its Olympic-like TV commercials and Nike Park, a $3 million retail center and sports museum that opened near the official sponsorship village in Centennial Olympic Park, Nike gained higher visibility than most official sponsors.

The Coca-Cola Olympics

No one even tried to compete with Coca-Cola, the sponsor of sponsors of the Centennial Olympics at Atlanta.

Coke's promotion programs began a year before the Summer Games, and the company was identified by consumers as early as February as the top sponsor of the Olympics. For months leading up to the Olympics and during the Games themselves, there was "Always Coca-Cola."

Who would expect less with the world's largest sporting event in the backyard of the world's best-known brand.

Coke and the Olympics go back to 1928, when a freighter carrying the U.S. Olympic team and 1,000 cases of Coca-Cola arrived in Amsterdam. It was the start of the longest continuous corporate sponsorship in Olympic history.

Before the 1996 Olympics, Sergio Zyman, Coca-Cola Senior Vice President and Chief Marketing Officer, said, "This is a fantastic investment for us if we are willing to do three things. First, we want to enhance the fans' overall experience, not detract from it. That means being tasteful and strategic and doing things that only we can do to increase excitement while moving volume and increasing brand purchase intent. Second, we have to use the broad sponsorship as a local marketing property in all applicable markets. And finally, we have to realize that when the games hit Atlanta, this is not just a brand-building opportunity, but a volume-building opportunity as well."

He said that the company's efforts would "involve people in the specialness of the Olympics in a way that only Coca-Cola can."

The starting point was the 1996 Olympic Torch Relay. As the exclusive Relay sponsor, Coca-Cola gained high visibility in thousands of communities across America. It began with a "Who Would You Choose?" program to select 10,000 Americans to carry the Olympic flame. Nomination forms were made available throughout the United States at special Coca-Cola displays at participating retail outlets. Consumers were asked to submit the name of a person they believed worthy of the honor of carrying the Olympic flame.

Those selected carried torches on foot and by bicycle, horseback, steamboat, biplane, and a nineteen-car Union Pacific train on an eighty-four-day, forty-two-state, 15,000-mile journey across the country. The relay began on April 27 in Los Angeles and ended in Atlanta with the dramatic lighting of the Olympic Cauldron by Muhammad Ali during the Opening Ceremony that was watched by three billion TV viewers worldwide.

The *New York Times* reported that Coke's sponsorship was impossible to miss on the display route. "Wherever the torch goes, there are cars with Coke logos, trucks with Coke logos, vans with Coke logos."[1] There was always plenty of ice-cold Coca-Cola to drink and plenty of local publicity at every stop along the way because locals were carrying the torch. Human-interest stories by the carload appeared in local newspapers and on radio and TV.

Public Relations Tactics reported that "The Torch Relay was a megaspecial event that generated millions of media impressions nationwide. But the relay's real power was on the local level, where unsung community heroes nominated by local admirers ran with the torch, creating minicelebrations in small towns across America. Talk about a media relations coup. The Olympic Torch Relay was a story with legs."[2]

Ketchum Public Relations, who handled media relations for the Torch Relay, assigned a rotating team of staff members from all of the firm's U.S. offices to manage event issues and coordinate media logistics while an Atlanta-based team ensured around-the-clock media coverage.

To Coca-Cola, the $40 million Olympic sponsorship fee was just the beginning. In all, the company spent $350 million on its Olympic marketing programs. It also set a new record for Olympic ad spending by purchasing $62 million worth of airtime on NBC. A pre-Olympic "For the Fans" campaign was followed over the seventeen days of the Olympics by a rotation of 100 spots, old and new, designed to emphasize "the multidimensionality of Coke."

Coke's "Olympic City," together with AT&T's "Global Olympic Village," Anheuser-Busch's "Bud World," and General Motors' "Century of Motion" dominated Centennial Olympic Park, the official site of the Corporate Olympics near downtown Atlanta that attracted 100,000 visitors a day before and after the unfortunate bomb blast that closed the park for a few days.

Visitors to Coca-Cola Olympic City were greeted by a towering 165-foot Coca-Cola bottle. The venue was designed to make fans feel what it is like to be an Olympian. Fans were able to challenge the world's greatest athletes through a wide variety of interactive experiences: sprinting against Jackie Joyner-Kersee in an interactive 100-meter dash; shooting hoops with U.S. Dream Team member Grant Hill; walking the balance beam with Olympic medalist Shannon Miller; pitching and hitting against Olympic baseball stars; careening down a treacherous Olympic-style mountain biking course; and competing in a wheelchair race. They could even be awarded a gold medal and be able to take home a picture of themselves on the victory stand. For the kids, there was an outdoor obstacle course, batting cages, and daily visits from that famous Coca-Cola partner, Ronald McDonald.

Coca-Cola Olympic City was also home to an 800-seat World Record Theater where guests were entertained several times daily by a troop of thirty "Coca-Cola Olympic City Kids."

A strictly public relations initiative designed to enhance Coca-Cola as a world brand was the "Coca-Cola Olympics Salute to Folk Art." Legendary Georgia folk artist Howard Finster, who had used Coca-Cola bottles in his work since the 1970s, was commissioned by the company to create a bottle for the exhibition as an inspiration to artists all over the world.

Artists from six continents were invited to submit a work that incorporated their vision of the famous Coca-Cola contour bottle. They were asked to use indigenous materials that expressed the traditions, culture, and heritage of their native lands. The work of artists from fifty-three countries was accepted to be exhibited in the historic Georgia Freight Depot in downtown Atlanta.

Publicity about the artists as well as the athletes represented at the Olympics appeared in media throughout the world. The coverage in the United States included a feature on the exhibit on NBC's *Today Show*. Al Roker did his weather report standing next to a ten-foot contour bottle from the Philippines transformed to look like a native hut with a thatched roof tied together with rattan strips and covered with ground coconut shell.

The company estimates that twenty million servings of Coca-Cola products were consumed at the official venues of the Atlanta Olympics by athletes, officials, spectators, and members of the media. What better way to quench your thirst in an Atlanta July with temperatures often in the nineties?

At the conclusion of the Atlanta games, Juan Antonio Samaranch, President of the International Olympic Committee, said that "commercialism must be controlled," but he acknowledged that it would be impossible to organize the games without corporate sponsorship. Coca-Cola's research showed that consumers didn't think that Coke had overcommercialized the Games.

Was it worth it? Coca-Cola answered resoundingly in the affirmative by signing immediately with the International Olympic Committee to be a worldwide sponsor of the Summer and Winter Olympics through 2008, the lengthiest sponsorship deal in Olympic history.

Before the Olympics, Coca-Cola shareholders were told, "As with all of our sponsorships, our goal is a very simple one: to drive profitable volume increases, the key to our long-term success."[3] The company has no doubt that its Olympic sponsorship was highly successful in doing that.

After the Olympics, Coke Chairman and CEO Roberto Goizueta reported to shareholders that "strengthening our connection with consumers" is the company's top priority. He wrote: "We continue to become smarter about using our sports and other marketing sponsorships to connect with consumers in unique, compelling ways. And we've immediately begun applying the knowledge we gained from sponsoring the Olympic Games and other premier events to every other activity we sponsor."[4]

Lesa Ukman, editor of *IEG Sponsorship Report*, said of Coca-Cola's sponsorship, "They spent a lot and sold a lot. It was a huge platform globally."[5]

Olympic Winners and Losers

Another Olympic sponsor did not come off so well. *USA Today* reported that "IBM, which had touted itself as provider of the best technology ever used at an Olympics, suffered glitches which made headlines in *USA Today*, the *New York Times*, and newspapers around the world." The *Wall Street Journal* reported "at issue

Georgia folk artist Howard Finster with his rendition of the Coke bottle at the "Coca-Cola Olympics Salute to Folk Art" exhibit in Atlanta. The work of artists from fifty-three countries was displayed. (Courtesy of the Coca-Cola Company)

for IBM was its elaborate Olympic information system, intended to showcase the computer maker's technology, providing instant scores, athlete profiles, and other information to reporters as well as fans through computer screens, kiosks, and an Internet site. But for days, it spewed out wrong information, bizarre responses, or no data at all. Newspapers and other media outlets that had to scramble to devise backup systems have been chronicling the snafus since the beginning of the Olympics."

To make things worse, IBM continued to run a series of upbeat commercials bragging about its technological prowess at the Olympics while the world watched the product fail.

IBM's public relations problem was so pervasive that on the final weekend of the Olympics, *USA Today* ran a cover story on "IBM's frenzied race to save face in Atlanta." The paper, which was given an exclusive behind-the-scenes look at what went wrong and how the IBM team scrambled to recover, concluded "No one knows if IBM will lose business because of the publicity but IBM's own research says not to worry."[6]

A clear winner in the publicity Olympics was nonsponsor General Mills. As the Games progressed, the media speculated which Olympians would be the big winners of marketing gold. Corporate sponsors and their agents seeking to cash in on Olympic celebrity were looking for newly minted world-class athletes to endorse their products. First out of the box or rather onto the box was General Mills Wheaties, Breakfast of Champions. Wheaties made the most of its tradition of instantly producing a special box with its choice of Olympic champions. The company skillfully built interest in its choice throughout the Olympics before announcing it as the games concluded. The story was mentioned throughout the network coverage of the Games and was the cause of speculation in countless television, radio, and newspaper stories. The selection had become so much a part of the Games that media treated it as being as noncommercial as the selection of the most valuable player.

Chicago Sun-Times columnist Richard Roeper wrote:

> It's always a big deal when an athlete is given the honor of appearing on a box of Wheaties. The event is treated not as a marketing gimmick but as a legitimate news story. Witness all the hoo-ha devoted to the announcement from General Mills that there will be five red, white, and blue Wheaties boxes on the shelves within a week or so, featuring U.S. Olympic champions Michael Johnson, Dan O'Brien, Amy Van Dyken, Tom Dolan, and the women's gymnastic team. More than 1,000 people attended the ersatz ceremony, hosted by Bruce Jenner and Mary Lou Retton. The crowd cheered wildly as each of the athletes was introduced, pep rally–style. Surely getting your own Wheaties box has to be a thrill, whether you're Michael Jordan or an Olympic star. Everyone understands that a reference to "appearing on a box of Wheaties" is pop jargon for making it, big-time. There probably wasn't a newscast or telecast in the country that didn't go with

an item listing the new Wheaties stars after Sunday's announcement. "We've never had a reaction from the media like we've had
this time," a General Mills spokesperson told me Monday. Many
news organizations even ran stories in advance, speculating on
who would make the grade. More than 200 such stories ran in
papers nationwide. Little wonder then that Wheaties didn't buy
any television advertising time on NBC. Why bother? No other
cereal promotion, perhaps no other consumer product gimmick,
has become such a part of the American landscape.[7]

Another media-generating Wheaties box was the subject of a front-page
story in the *Wall Street Journal*. "OLD FASHIONED PR GIVES GENERAL MILLS
ADVERTISING BARGAINS" reported how the company garnered lots of publicity
for Wheaties by dispatching its publicists to the 1997 Super Bowl armed with
boxes featuring both the Green Bay Packers and New England Patriots. When
it was clear that Green Bay would be the winner, the company delivered the
Packers package to TV news crews covering the game, enabling Wheaties to be
featured on the Fox game telecast as well as on CNN, ESPN, and countless local
stations. The *Journal* observed that while Super Bowl commercials that year cost
$1.2 million per thirty-second spot, "the Wheaties caper cost only a few thou-
sand dollars, the cost of a couple of round-trip airline tickets."[8]

Lessons Learned

- If you are putting big bucks into a major event, be prepared to spend
  several times that amount to leverage your investment.
- Use sponsorships both to build the brand and to drive volume.
- Plan far ahead. Begin breaking promotions months before the event.
- Wrap yourself in the event so consumers will know you were there.
- Whip up enthusiasm and participation within your entire organization.
- Motivate wholesalers and retailers with special incentives.
- Go all-out in entertaining them on-site and off.
- Find ways to engage consumers in preevent events.
- Put your show on the road. Attract attention. Call out the media.
- If you are a national company, create an event that makes hometown
  publicity.
- If you are a world company, create an event that makes home country
  publicity.

- Keep your focus on the product, the logo, the package.
- Don't forget the kids. Make it fun for the family.
- Make your product part of the story by signing the stars.
- Don't use the event to demonstrate your product to the world unless you are sure it will work.
- Nice guys sometimes finish last. Watch for guerrillas.

CHAPTER 21

Target Marketing Public Relations

PUBLIC RELATIONS HAS LONG RECOGNIZED THE IMPORTANCE OF COMMUNICATION with key audiences. Consumer audiences may be defined demographically, psychographically, geographically, or ethnically. In traditional public relations terminology, these discrete audiences are called *publics*. In marketing parlance, they are *target markets*. Increasing competitive pressures have caused marketers to look beyond the mainstream population and to use public relations to deliver specific messages to specific target market audiences.

An entire book could be devoted to target marketing public relations. For this chapter, we have selected several noteworthy MPR programs specifically directed to target youth, Generation X, over-forty, and minority markets.

The Disney Magic

Talk about knowing your market. Nobody knows what will appeal to families with small children better than the Walt Disney Company. The company fashions its products and its marketing communications to appeal to kids and their parents not just in the United States but all over the world. For the Disney marketers, *It's a Small World* indeed.

The great Disney animation renaissance that began with *The Little Mermaid* was followed by an amazing string of films that were both artistically and commercially successful and became instant classics. In successive order came such blockbuster hits as *Beauty and the Beast* (which found later success on ice and the Broadway stage), *Aladdin*, and *The Lion King*.

The creative genius of the filmmakers was matched by the ability of the company's marketing wizards and master publicists to generate excitement about each of these films with its target family audience.

They had their work cut out for them with *Pocahontas*. The Disney version of the epic romantic legend of the Indian princess and the English adventurer Captain John Smith followed *The Lion King*, a film that was not only the box-office king of 1994 but one of the top-grossing films of all time. To build interest in *Pocahontas*, Disney included a sneak preview of one of the songs from the new film with the successful theatrical rerelease of *The Lion King*, a technique it repeated with *The Lion King* home video, the top-selling video of the year.

Four months before *Pocahontas* opened, Disney presented a free mall show, *The Pocahontas Animation Discovery Adventure,* in twenty-three cities, the first-ever for a new film. The press release stated that this unique touring attraction was "designed to give mallgoers an early, exclusive sneak peek at the process of creating an animated film by focusing on the story, background, and characters of *Pocahontas*, this show combines a wide variety of elements that are both entertaining and informative at the same time." Kids could climb aboard a twenty-six-foot replica of Captain John Smith's ship, try their hands and voices at electronic animation, and hear Powhatan tales told by a Native American animator who worked on the film. The mall show attracted big family audiences in the hundreds of thousands and garnered great local publicity in every city it visited from February through June.

Disney CEO Michael Eisner, one of the world's best-known business executives, pitched in personally when he and New York Mayor Rudolph Guiliani invited all New Yorkers to participate in a free lottery for tickets to a mass *Pocahontas* preview in Central Park. Eisner billed the event as "a family Woodstock."

From 500,000 people from fifty states who entered a lottery for free tickets, 100,000 lucky first-nighters won the opportunity to see the legendary Indian princess save Captain Smith on four 120-foot screens. Of course, they were also able to buy all manner of blankets, dolls, T-shirts, and other Pocahontas merchandise as mementos of the occasion.

New York was only the beginning. Disney staged state-of-the-art sound and light shows featuring favorite Disney characters in seven big American cities. A live twenty-minute stage extravaganza, "Disney's Magic Moments," was presented as the opening act of the "Pocahontas Summer Spectacular," an event that featured, along with an exclusive preview of the film, such sideshows as an interactive animation kiosk, a video wall of memorable Disney-animated classics, and a forest maze where kids could enter an enchanted environment of the film and meet Pocahontas's animal pals. Onstage, costumed actors lip-synched and a troupe of dancers danced to a program of Disney movie songs. The theater darkened, an unseen voice proclaimed "Let the magic continue" as the curtains parted, and Pocahontas appeared on-screen.

Disney followed its own successful formula of producing a "making of" television special. The Pocahontas special called *The Legend Comes to Life* was first aired on the company's own cable TV channel, the Disney Channel, which was guaranteed to reach a mass family audience of Disney enthusiasts. Irene Bedard, the voice of Pocahontas, gave viewers a behind-the-scenes look at the artists, animators, and cast, including Mel Gibson, the voice of Captain Smith. Russell Means, the Native American activist who is the voice of Powhatan, described the film as "the single finest work ever done about American Indians by Hollywood."

A *Chicago Tribune* reviewer said the TV special "is more hype for Disney's newest blockbuster, but it offers a sense of history and helps kids and adults feel the passion that goes into making a movie like this."[1]

Yet another network TV special, *Disney's Pocahontas—the Musical Tradition Continues,* appeared on the ABC network a few nights later. It featured the music from Disney films sung by recording artists, including Jon Secada, Shanice Wilson, and Vanessa Williams who introduced "If I Ever Knew You" and "Colors of the Wind" from the soon-to-be-released film.

A new weapon, the Disney marketing armada, could be found online at http:/www.disney.com., the *Pocahontas* site on the World Wide Web.

Integral to the success of all the marketing events and activities was the leave-no-stone-unturned efforts of the Disney publicists. *Newsweek* proclaimed that "Pocahontas got the kind of media attention advertising dollars can't buy."

Toy Story *Comes to Life*

Disney followed *Pocahontas* with one of the studio's greatest artistic and commercial successes, *Toy Story*. *Pocahontas* was to have been the company's major merchandising effort of 1995, but *Toy Story*, which was released at the end of the year, was the runaway winner.

The fact that *Toy Story* was the first animated feature to be created entirely using computer graphics afforded the Disney publicists a golden opportunity. That the story was so endearing and the characters so lovable to kids and their parents alike made the film much more than a successful technoevent.

Disney's publicity department issued a sixty-eight-page press information package describing *Toy Story* as "a delightfully irreverent new animated comedy-adventure." Included in the kit was a portfolio of a dozen stills tracing the adventures of Woody, the pull-string cowboy whose position as a little boy's favorite toy was challenged by the arrival of Buzz Lightyear, a flashy spaceman action figure who doesn't know that he is a toy.

The comprehensive kit contained information about the cast, writers, animators, technical artists, artists, production people, computer engineers, musicians, and songs.

The press kit included an invitation to visit "Toy Story Online" at www.toystory.com. At the Web site, interactive kids and their parents could find out everything in the press kit and much more. They could hear Tom Hanks and Tim Allen, the voices of Woody and Buzz, and such supporting players as comedian Don Rickles, a.k.a Mister Potato Head. Features on the site included a database where you could find the movie houses nearest you showing *Toy*

This still from the Toy Story *press kit introduced Woody, a traditional cowboy doll, and Buzz Lightyear, a brash new space-ranger action figure, who starred in Walt Disney Pictures' animated comedy adventure.*

(©Disney Enterprises, Inc.)

Story and where you could buy the plethora of *Toy Story* merchandise, including toys, books, games, and soundtrack CDs. By clicking on the hypertext and buttons you could find material on the hot new 3-D video game, read all about the musical score, or take a quick tour of "The Incredible Totally Toy Store."

That's the name given to an instant theme park Disney set up at the restored El Capitan movie palace in Hollywood, where parents and grandparents could take the kiddies not only to see the movie but to enjoy a three-and-a-half-hour entertainment experience in a 30,000-square-foot Toy Story Funhouse in an adjacent convention hall.

The *Chicago Tribune* reported that "The attractions in the three-story, seven-room complex pick up where the movie leaves off. The toys still talk but now they're life-size as well. Costumed entertainers assume the roles of the cartoon characters. They perform in several musical revues and, among other things, guide children into simulated space-capsule rides and colorful playrooms based on scenes from the movie. Inevitably, all paths led to the souvenir shop. Logos and brand name tie-ins totally dominate the Funhouse—from Etch-a-Sketches in Mr. Potato Head's Playroom to the Sega and Nintendo Toy Story games in the Totally Interactive Room."

The reporter commented that the attempt to recapture some of the old Hollywood glamour at the El Capitan takes older patrons on a trip down memory lane and that parents who drop in Mr. Potato Head's Playroom so their children can draw pictures and enjoy dexterity improving toys "will be delighted to see that the floor has been constructed out of old board games, including Chutes & Ladders, Sorry!, Candyland, and Ouija."[2]

Kids could also join a *Toy Story* fan club and get *Toy Story* premiums for providing information about themselves to be stored in the Disney database for future promotional use.

The *Toy Story* Web site also promoted the now standard "making of" special, *To Infinity and Beyond,* on the Disney Channel. Computer fans could also find a lengthy list of *Toy Story* promotional partners, including Frito-Lay, Minute Maid, Nestlé candy bars, Payless Shoes, and Burger King. The Disney deal makers left no stone unturned in obtaining high visibility for the film on TV, in grocery displays, and on snack packages leading up to the release of the film. The synergy with Burger King was especially effective (so much so that within the year McDonald's had signed a long-term agreement to be Disney's exclusive fast-food partner). Burger King offered six different action figures from the film, including Buzz and Woody with all Kids' Club Meals. Burger King also plugged the film in its Kids Club newsletter and offered a series of four collector plush puppets.

Before running out, Burger King had given away some thirty-five million action figures, run out of puppets, and added to the massive media exposure leading up to the all-important weekend release of the film.

Back from cyberspace, the Disney marketeers staged a series of high-visibility events to promote the film in major markets.

Disney publicists did their usual excellent job of covering all the media bases. *USA Today* and scores of newspapers ran four-color, behind-the-scenes stories on the making of *Toy Story*.

Toy Story was an instantaneous hit and the top-grossing film of the holiday season and the year. Investors responded by driving Disney stock to a new high for the year. Pixar Inc., the digital animation studio, leaped into the stock market with its initial public offering (IPO), closing its first day of trading 77 percent above the asking price. Record sales were achieved not only for Woody and Buzz dolls but for classic toys featured in the film such as Mister Potato Head, Slinky, Bucket of Soldiers, and Etch-a-Sketch. *Newsweek* sent "Condolences to G.I. Joe and Barbie, whose manufacturers denied them permission to appear in the movie. It could turn out to be as bad a career move as holding M&M's back from *E.T.*"

Lessons Learned

- When everything depends on one make-or-break weekend, do whatever it takes to grab attention.
- Pull out all the media stops. Orchestrate plenty of exclusive angles and pictures for publications
- Find a promotional partner who will buy more TV time than you to build store traffic.
- Find other partners who will plug your product on their packages and in-store displays in stores where families shop.
- Package everything the media always wanted to know about your product in a press kit. Fill it with pictures, features, facts, and fun.
- To reach computer-literate kids directly and interactively, put the press kit and much more on the Internet.
- Stage big newsmaking, audience-involving events in the biggest markets.
- Bring out your big guns. Let the mayor share the spotlight and take credit for something you are paying for.
- Take your show on the road. Find creative ways to get kids involved.
- Know your market. Create events that will appeal to kids, moms, and dads. Grandparents, too.
- Get local media to cover the event by providing interesting traveling spokespersons.
- Use your current product to preview your next one.
- It helps to have your own stores and TV channel.

Pizza Hut's National Reading Incentive Program

One of the most enduring marketing public relations programs directed to young children offers the product as a reward. Pizza Hut/BOOK IT! has become America's most successful reading incentive program.

Pizza Hut targets the youngest consumers because children spend nearly $7 billion of their own money each year and directly influence another $130 billion of their parents' buying decisions. Pizza Hut/BOOK IT! National Reading Incentive Program targets parents and children from kindergarten through sixth grade attending public, parochial, and private schools.

The program was created by Pizza Hut in 1985 to encourage early reading habits.

It grew from a Library of Congress report that identified reading as a major problem area in our schools and nation. It also suggested ways that the problem could be solved. A report on children's eating habits showed that pizza was kids' favorite food. Pizza Hut saw a connection and decided to establish a national program that would reward students with free pizza for reading above and beyond their normal assignments.

From the beginning the program struck a responsive chord with teachers, superintendents, and school board presidents. In the first year, seven million students in 233,000 classrooms enrolled in the program. They were signed up by teachers who assigned them individual reading goals according to each child's ability and reading level. Students who signed up for the program on a classroom wall chart provided by Pizza Hut were required to submit written or oral book reports. Parents were sent letters and verification forms and urged to become involved with the program.

Students reaching monthly goals received immediate positive reinforcement in the form of Pizza Hut award certificates. When they went to their local Pizza Hut restaurant, they were given BOOK IT! buttons with their free pizzas. Pizza Hut owners and managers were trained to treat BOOK IT! as a public-service program and not a promotion. They were urged to treat each award as a miniawards banquet. If all the students reached their goals, the entire class received a free pizza party.

Millions of children participated in the program during its first decade. Pizza Hut still uses the incentive of free pizza to help educators motivate students to read more. Because students must visit Pizza Hut to claim their pizza rewards, the program drives traffic into restaurants. They usually bring family and friends with them to celebrate their reading achievements. The result is that Pizza Hut achieves both sales and goodwill.

The program is not advertised and depends on public relations, telemarketing, and direct mail to principals and teachers. Pizza Hut and its public relations firm, Creamer Dickson Basford, created several program enhancements for the tenth anniversary of BOOK IT!

Store managers rewarded students who met their first monthly reading goals by lighting a birthday candle on their pizzas and presenting them with tenth-birthday buttons. Teachers were given "BOOK IT! Bunch" adventure story-books designed to bring the joy of reading to life and were offered a BOOK IT! Pictionary game, an educational and entertaining classroom game based on children's literature.

Other tenth-anniversary events included a 100 percent sweepstakes that encouraged principals to enroll all of their K–6 classrooms in the program. More than 32,000 principals entered with the sweepstakes winner receiving $10,000 for his or her school library. An anniversary classroom contest offering a school pizza party and contributions to the school library also boosted teacher and student interest.

Another anniversary event was the presentation of the first BOOK IT! Award to former First Lady Barbara Bush on behalf of her Foundation for Family Literacy.

The BOOK IT! program also cosponsors National Young Readers Day with the Center for the Book in the Library of Congress. The day is an annual celebration of the joy of reading. It is celebrated by children across the country who come to school dressed in costumes as their favorite book characters.

Through the years, BOOK IT! has been lauded by educators and parents. More than 22 million children now participate annually in the program, making it the country's longest-running and most-successful reading incentive program. BOOK IT! enrollment now exceeds 890,000 classrooms in 56,000 schools. It serves as a curriculum resource in 70 percent of all public, private, and parochial elementary schools in the United States.

In the classic public relations sense, it truly melds the public interest with the private interest by generating incremental sales at Pizza Hut restaurants. It is also a fine example of target marketing public relations.

Lessons Learned

- Get behind a cause that makes a difference.
- Make it relevant to your target market.
- Draw a line between public service and promotion.
- Look for long-range brand-building benefits, not short-term returns.
- Find ways to use the program to build store traffic.
- Make the product the reward.
- Make it fun.

- Gain the support of cause-related national and local organizations.
- Involve community leaders.
- Make your local manager the hero in his or her community.
- Test it with teachers and students before rolling it out.
- Be committed to the program.
- Find ways to keep it fresh.

Microsoft Imagines the Magic

Microsoft made imaginative use of marketing public relations to break through to what was at the time an entirely new target market—families with school-age children.

The "vehicle" for involving both consumers and the media with Microsoft CD-ROM software was the "ExplorasauraBus," a traveling "theater on wheels" ride experience created for the company by Edelman Public Relations Worldwide. The ExplorasauraBus was unveiled during an exclusive NBC *Today Show* interview and opened to other media and consumers in New York's Times Square. The big-time publicity assault resulted in stories on CBS and CNN and in *Entertainment Weekly, USA Today, Time,* and *Newsweek.*

The bus then hit the road to ten important retail markets in ten weeks. Participating stores in each market reported significant software sales increases during the ExplorasauraBus visit. The buyers were families who read about the bus in local newspapers or heard about it on local radio and TV.

The company also staged a creative press event called the Microsoft Home Exploration Expedition for long-lead magazines designed to move computer-shy consumers from "fear and intrigue to acceptance to purchase and habit."

Edelman also created an "Imagine the Magic" contest in which children in grades three to six could tell Microsoft in fifty words or less their ideas about what the "coolest" computers would do. The contest was a vehicle for children to creatively express how they imagine technology could impact their lives while motivating them and their teachers and parents to think about computers in a whole new way.

The next year, the bus no longer existed and the "Imagine the Magic" contest was developed into a stand-alone program. This time a program was created that would reach the entire United States, not just ten cities. Kids were encouraged to send drawings, projects, and cutouts as well as essays.

Strategic partnerships were formed with Cartoon Network and *Sports Illustrated for Kids* to help generate awareness with the target audience of kids six to eleven years old. To get the word out to the education community, tie-ins were arranged with *Instructor* and *Electronic Learning* magazines.

A special Web page was created that served as an additional entry-generating vehicle. The Web page allowed kids to enter their coolest computer ideas online. It also offered tips on creativity from the contest spokesperson, Dr. Lawrence Kutner, a teacher's guide, and a place for feedback and participation ("If you could ask Bill Gates anything, what would it be?").

All 22,000 entrants received an "Imagination Navigation" certificate signed by Bill Gates. Fifty semifinalists each won Microsoft software for themselves and their schools. Their names and entries were featured in local market publicity across the United States. The big payoff for six of America's most imaginative kids was an all-expense-paid trip to Microsoft headquarters in Redmond, Washington, where they met and shared their ideas with Bill Gates himself. They also got a behind-the-scenes look at the making of Microsoft magic and participated in a Kids' Technology Summit. Each winner received a Gateway Destination Mutimedia System and a Microsoft software library for their home and school. They also appeared on Cartoon Network's *Toon World News* and in a special Microsoft page in *Sports Illustrated for Kids*. Edelman produced a video news release package that included Bill Gates with the winning kids that was distributed by satellite the evening of the summit.

Microsoft Chairman and CEO Bill Gates meets six national prize–winning six-to eleven-year-olds who came up with "the coolest things a computer could do" in the Microsoft "Imagine the Magic" contest. (Courtesy of Microsoft Corp.)

The program succeeded in meeting Microsoft's objectives of increasing enthusiasm for home computing. A survey of the kids' entries revealed that they saw computers in their homes as friends, communication tools, and problem solvers.

The 215 million media impressions were heavily skewed toward kids and their families, including Kids Radio Network and Radio Ads for Kids.

Lessons Learned

- Create a bus and invite the kids in to play with your stuff.
- Pick the best show on TV and give it an exclusive ride.
- Take the bus on the road and offer it to key retailers as a traffic builder.
- Create a great contest for kids that allows them to write, draw, paint, or cut-and-paste.
- Wrap it in a kid-friendly logo.
- Find the best strategic partners that reach kids.
- Get teachers involved. Make it a classroom project.
- Create a Web site to get kids and teachers involved.
- Pick lots of winners. That translates into lots of local publicity.
- Give the top winners great prizes like their very own computers and software and a chance to be in pictures, on TV, and in magazines read by other kids.
- Grant them a private audience with the man himself.
- Capture it all in pictures and send it up and out on videotape.

Chrysler Meets Generation X

In the 1990s, marketers began to explore ways to identify, understand, and reach an elusive post–baby boomer audience between ages eighteen and twenty-nine labeled variously as busters, twentysomethings, and Gen Xers. They began to create products especially for and direct marketing communications especially to this market for everything from beverages to apparel to cars.

When Chrysler Corporation introduced the launch of the Neon in 1994, it wanted to give the new car a personality that would set it apart from other vehicles in the small-car market. It is well documented in the auto industry that small-car buyers are made up of boomers and busters. Chrysler research also revealed that older buyers—boomers age thirty to forty-five—tend to buy a younger person's car rather than the reverse. Therefore, marketing communications was targeted at busters.

The challenge was to create a car with a personality that would set it apart from all the other vehicles in the subcompact market, a market in which foreign automakers had established a foothold years before.

The public relations objectives were to create awareness of the Neon, to distinguish it from the competition, and to generate interest and excitement about the vehicle with its target audience.

To meet the objectives, a strategy was designed to bring the car to life by associating it with the major personality and lifestyle choices of Generation X consumers, their music, their clothes, their jobs, and their leisure pursuits. The Neon was differentiated from competitors by highlighting its fun-to-drive features.

Operating on the ancient Chinese proverb, "A picture is worth more than a thousand words," Chrysler commissioned four of the best automotive photographers in the world to interpret its vision of the Neon's personality and spirit for the introductory media kit. The company selected settings from Miami's hip South Beach to New York's neighborhoods to trendy Southern California to show off the car to target buyers.

The press material carefully avoided the potential turnoff trap of stereotyping Generation X buyers by covering all the bases. A news release was titled "Neon's new design and fun-to-drive nature create a winning personality." It states "ultimately, Neon's affordable, fun-to-drive personality, which exhibits thoughtful attention to safety and value, will appeal to a rapidly emerging new generation of buyers. Fundamentally, they all want the same characteristics in a small car—durability, reliability, value, price, safety. However, their lifestyles may be different. Some are less inhibited about expressing a need for styling and performance. Others are more rational: cars are basically just transportation. Neon's combination of styling, performance, and practicality will satisfy the emotional needs of some, and the rational economic conditions of others."

In keeping with the spirit and personality of the car, Chrysler's public relations staff and agency, Golin/Harris, designed a series of fun and offbeat programs to capture the attention of the buster market.

The Neon launch departed from Detroit's tradition of keeping new cars under wraps until they are unveiled in Motown. Instead, Chrysler borrowed a successful page from high-technology marketing by inviting key media to "backgrounders" on the car during its preproduction stages. Reporters were introduced to Neon's personality, later made famous by outdoor advertising with the smiling car saying "Hi!" They were made aware of the car's synergy with the lifestyles of the target youth market.

The Neon was unveiled not in Detroit but at the Frankfurt International Automobile Show, demonstrating that the Neon was a car designed for markets around the world. A news conference set was designed like a pinball machine to represent the new game in the small-car market. Simultaneous media events were held in eight U.S. markets with interactive satellite feeds from Frankfurt with Chrysler Chairman Bob Eaton and President Bob Lutz. Satellite transmission carried simultaneous interviews with Eaton on NBC's *Today Show* and with Lutz on ABC's *Good Morning America.* The Lutz interview also featured *Automobile Magazine* Deputy Editor Jean Lindamood who excitedly told viewers that "With the Neon, Chrysler is once again blowing them away." This explicit editorial endorsement doubly enhanced the third-party endorsement implied by its coverage on *Good Morning America.* Together with other network, cable, and local telecasts, television impressions totaled more than 130 million. An Associated Press photo of the car's unveiling ran in 90 percent of U.S. newspapers.

Other media events followed—one at Chrysler's Belvidere, Illinois, plant, where the first Neon rolled off the assembly line to be finished by Bob Eaton and Illinois Governor Jim Edgar. Chrysler revealed Neon's low base price of $8,975 at a media conference attended by more than 600 reporters from around the world at the domestic car industry's most important show, the North American International Auto Show in Detroit.

Finally, 200 international and domestic auto reporters and editors were given the opportunity to ride and drive Neon production models in Austin, Texas, and the surrounding Texas hill country. To further strengthen Neon's personality, the reporters were immersed in Generation X lifestyles, supplied with their favorite clothing such as Dr. Marten shoes, their music, and sports. Those so inclined were even given rollerblading lessons.

The integrated marketing program featured print ads and TV commercials in addition to outdoor advertising, and such promotions as a video catalog that came on-screen with a *Star Wars* video game, Neon kiosks in Bally Health Clubs, an Olympic mall tour, and sponsorship of Recording Artists Against Drunk Driving.

Chrysler's decision to bring in the automotive press during the preproduction phase led to Neon being named *Automobile Magazine*'s "Automobile of the Year," a first for a vehicle before it was produced.

John Baroody, Marketing Director of *Automobile Magazine,* said, "No one has ever totally quantified what it's worth in dollars or sales to have a publication like ours put a product on our front cover. But if you could ever get your hands around it, it would be an overwhelming number, I'm sure."[3]

Advertising Age pointed out the importance of the car-enthusiast magazines known in the industry as the buff books—"the other side of new-car marketing: using public relations to win the attention of the small population of people, who, in turn, have the attention of millions of readers across the country."[4]

Did the integrated marketing program reach its target market? *Advertising Age* reported that a month after greeting Generation X with a friendly "Hi!," Neon had captured students' attention nationwide. The ad trade book interviewed college students on ten campuses and found that 65 percent were aware of Neon and liked the car's looks and personality.[5]

Time magazine picked Neon not only as the automobile of the year but as the product of the year 1995, an editorial decision based on its sales and marketing success.

Lessons Learned

- Find out all you can about who buys what you are selling and why.
- Learn all you can about their lifestyles—their favorite sports, music, clothes.
- Learn but don't patronize. Nobody wants to be stereotyped and ripped off.
- Words aren't enough. Use visual imagery that appeals to the target market.
- Give your product a personality.
- Enlist your top brass to show the media and the public that you mean business.
- Invite key media to preview the product. Solicit their input and win their support.
- Create a long-lead event that's fun for the press. Involve them personally with the product. Your words can't compare to their hands-on experience.
- Break the mold. Do the unexpected. Defy conventional wisdom about where and how to launch your product.
- Dramatize the news to excite dealers. Let them in on the action via videoconferencing.
- Maintain media and consumer excitement by revealing the story over time. Create a series of events to keep the product in the news.
- Target media beyond the usual suspects. Know what your prospects read, watch, and listen to.
- Get people talking about the advertising and the promotions.
- Take the show on the road.

Advil Fitness Over Forty

An integral part of Advil's campaign to position the product as the over-the-counter pain reliever for all aches and pains is a program that specifically links Advil with the fitness and health of the age forty-plus population. The program grew from a growing body of research that pointed to the increasingly sedentary lifestyle of Americans over the age of forty and the inherent health risks associated with this lack of activity.

Advil's public relations firm, Edelman Public Relations Worldwide, recommended that the Advil Forum on Health Education join with the President's Council on Physical Fitness and Sports to create programs that would fill the over-forty exercise gap. The Advil Forum is a nonprofit organization that provides health-education programs and materials to health professionals and consumers.

To learn more about what was necessary to motivate Americans over the age of forty to get the exercise they need, Advil commissioned Yankelovich Partners to conduct a consumer survey. The Advil Fit Over-Forty Survey revealed that 37 percent of over-forty Americans never exercise and that half mistakenly believe that they need to work out for a minimum of thirty minutes at one time to gain health benefits.

Working with the Advil Forum, Edelman Medical Communications identified and interviewed twenty top physicians and experts in the fields of health and exercise. Their research-based studies confirmed that many of the physical effects associated with aging, such as decreased aerobic activity, loss of muscular strength, and declining flexibility, are probably more directly related to inactivity than to age. They concluded that while many people over forty want to be more active, they may not know where to begin or may try to do too much too soon, which can lead to frustration, quitting, and even injury.

As a result, the "Activity Made Easy for Forty-Plus Fitness" program was designed both to motivate the age forty-plus population to commit to physical activity and to dispel the misconception that exercise must be a grim and punishing experience.

To bring attention to the program, Advil called on baseball legend Nolan Ryan whose high level of fitness kept him pitching for twenty-seven years, and 1968 Olympic Gold Medalist Peggy Fleming to serve as "over-forty" role models.

A press conference was held in New York and Washington, D.C., to launch the program and release the results of the Yankelovich survey. James Rippe, M.D., noted cardiologist and exercise physiologist and the Director of the Center for Clinical and Lifestyle Research, moderated a panel including Nolan Ryan and Peggy Fleming.

A second press conference was held in Washington, D.C., to announce the second phase of the program. The location was chosen because of its proximity to health-care influentials and to highlight the impact that the alliance of government and the private sector can have on public health. The appearance of Donna Shalala, Secretary of Health and Human Services, as keynote speaker underscored the importance of the program. Dr. Shalala announced the three components of the Activity Made-Easy program: the Fit Over-Forty Standards, the *Nolan Ryan Fitness Guide,* and the Activity Made-Easy Workshops. She took advantage of the opportunity to urge the private sector to follow Advil's lead and team with the federal government on similar public-service initiatives.

The Advil Fit Over-Forty Standards resulted from a yearlong clinical study in Dr. Rippe's exercise laboratory. The study led to the establishment of the first-ever fitness guidelines for the age forty-plus population. The standards define average scores for fifteen fitness components and set up guidelines for maintaining and improving fitness scores.

The second program element is the *Nolan Ryan Fitness Guide*. The booklet offers encouragement and easy-to-follow tips on staying active. Its simple message is "get up and get active!" The guide lays out a fitness game plan and specifically discusses the importance of each of the primary fitness components: aerobics, weight training, and stretching. The guide was cosponsored by the President's Council on Physical Fitness and Sports and was made available to consumers free of charge.

Nolan Ryan was also enlisted to conduct workshops with Dr. Rippe and Tom McMillan, cochair of the President's Council on Physical Fitness and Sports. In the weeks following the press conference they initiated fitness workshops in five cities. Workshops followed at health clubs, senior centers, community clubs, and local health organizations nationwide.

The subject of the specific health needs of the forty-plus population had received little media attention prior to the program. However, Activity Made-Easy programs were covered extensively by the network television and radio and by the print media, registering 200 million media impressions.

USA Today ran two major features in 1994 on Nolan Ryan's role in the program. The first, "Ryan's pitch targets the over-forty crowd," included a picture of Ryan and Secretary Shalala introducing the fitness book at the Washington press conference. The lead was "Less than a year removed from his Hall of Fame–bound baseball career, Nolan Ryan is pitching the importance of healthy living to the over-forty generation." The second *USA Today* feature, "Nolan Ryan pitches commonsense approach to exercise," quotes Ryan and Dr. Rippe on how to accomplish fitness goals and summarizes the Fitness Guide recommendations. In February of 1996, *USA Today* ran yet another cover story, "Ryan's pitch to aging baby boomers: Get fit." It describes the former Texas Ranger pitcher as the "ideal pitchman for the antiaging message." Both stories credited Advil for creating the program and offered the guide free to readers.

Lessons Learned

- Focus your program on a target market that needs your help.
- Learn everything you can from the experts.
- Learn more by conducting primary research with the target consumer group.
- Release the findings and announce what you are going to do about it.
- Conduct further clinical studies that set standards.

- Partner with government departments and agencies.
- Pick a celebrity spokesperson target-market consumers know and love.
- He must practice what he preaches.
- Have him coauthor a book with a recognized expert.
- Get a presidential committee to cosponsor the book.
- A Washington, D.C., press conference says it's important.
- It's really important if you get a member of the president's cabinet to appear.
- Offer it free of charge to consumers.
- Take the experts and the celebrities on the road to run workshops.
- Publicize all of the above. You are ahead if the folks you want to reach can use this news.

Mary Kay Cosmetics Gets Down to Business with Black Women

Some companies have used marketing public relations not only to market their products to target audiences but to market their companies as good companies to do business with. Mary Kay Cosmetics does both effectively through a program directed to target the market of black women age twenty-five to fifty-four.

A company that has topped $1 billion in retail sales since 1991, Mary Kay is the best-selling brand of facial skin care and color cosmetics in the United States. More than twenty million U.S. consumers purchase approximately 150 million Mary Kay products every year. More than 475,000 independent Mary Kay Beauty Consultants operate their own Mary Kay businesses in twenty-five countries worldwide.

More than 45,000 black women have taken advantage of the Mary Kay career opportunity by starting their own businesses. As entrepreneurs, these women have enhanced their earning potential while receiving recognition for outstanding performance. They have also found fulfillment and security in a career in direct selling.

The company has demonstrated a commitment to black consumers for more than two decades. Still, many black women were not aware of Mary Kay products and the career opportunities that the company offered them. To reach the black consumer and bolster the black Mary Kay sales force, the company engaged Flowers Communication Group, a public relations company specializing in marketing to minorities.

With no budget for a broad-based advertising campaign, the Flowers Communication Group recommended a comprehensive media relations program that positioned Mary Kay products as quality products for black women and Mary Kay as a great company to represent.

Flowers interprets Mary Kay products in terms of its specific use by African-American women. A centerpiece of the program is *Shades of Perfection*, the first Mary Kay brochure created especially for the black consumer. News releases are tailored to the African-American consumer.

For example, the lead of a news release for Gentle Protection Sunblock SPF 20 was "African-Americans are just as susceptible to skin damage from harmful sunrays as any other race and therefore require adequate skin protection during the summer months. Mary Kay offers Gentle Protection Sunblock SPF 20 to provide all skin types, including highly sensitive skin, with the necessary protection from potentially damaging summer sun."

A story picked up by *Today's Black Woman* from a Mary Kay news release reports that "Black skin can often be plagued by skin blemishes, undereye shadows, uneven skin tones, or age spots. To cover these problems, Mary Kay Cosmetics offers Full Coverage Correcting Concealers." The story provides an 800 number to help readers locate a Mary Kay consultant in their area.

Rather than issue a traditional holiday release, Flowers prepared this story: "Mary Kay's 'Wishes' Color Collection has the answers to all your beauty needs and can provide you with essential beauty maintenance for Kwanza celebrations, tree-trimming get-togethers, and Afrocentric holiday parties." Kwanza is a weeklong African-American holiday celebrated between Christmas and New Year's. Each day is devoted to a facet of African-American life—Unity, Self-Determination, Collective Work and Responsibility, Cooperative Economics, Purpose, Creativity, and Faith.

Many releases offer tips for skin care, summer protection, hair care, and other subjects of interest to African-American women from the Black Women's Advisory Committee (BWAC) of Mary Kay. BWAC is an organization of top black independent sales directors from across the company.

The purpose of BWAC is to guide, direct, and solicit input on programs, products, and policies relating to the black sales force and its customers. It created *Shades of Perfection*, the first Mary Kay brochure created especially for black consumers. Flowers came up with "Getting Down to Business," a tag line that black women could easily identify with. The "Getting Down to Business" press kit quotes members of the committee on subjects such as making it as an entrepreneur and moving up the ladder of success. Members of BWAC also serve personally as effective media spokespersons.

A new image of success and financial independence for today's black woman was communicated to both internal and external audiences. Flowers created the first press kits especially for local and national black media, with easy reference information on Mary Kay career opportunities and products. Media tours to New York and Washington were conducted to meet with editors of key black publications such as *Black Elegance, Essence, Black Enterprise, Black Hair Care,* and Black Entertainment Television. The Mary Kay story was reported in a ten-minute feature on the nationally syndicated public affairs television show *Minority Business Report*. An article featuring each member of the Mary Kay BWAC that appeared in *Blac-Tress*, a national black hair and beauty publication, was reprinted and used as a recruitment tool by Mary Kay sales force members.

The first Mary Kay Cosmetics Black Women's Scholarship Fund was created and three high school seniors were selected to receive $10,000 toward their college educations. The scholarship winners were announced on more than 200 stations of the American Urban Radio Network.

The result of this marketing public relations effort was a 15 percent increase in the number of black sales force members, bringing it to more than 37,000 or 10 percent of the total Mary Kay worldwide sales force.

Lessons Learned

- MPR can be used to market career opportunities as well as products.
- Minority marketing requires in-depth knowledge of the consumer.
- You must know the special editorial requirements of minority media.
- Package the program with an identifiable tag line that your audience can relate to.
- Create media and sales materials especially for the target audience.
- Success breeds success. Use successful salespeople to sell your story.
- Take the story to key media in key markets.
- Don't forget the power of radio to reach target audiences.
- Underwrite a scholarship program for deserving minority students.
- Support minority recruitment with publicity reprints.

CHAPTER 22

Targeting Secondary Markets

ONE OF THE MOST COMMON MISTAKES MARKETERS MAKE IS TO DEFINE TARGET markets so narrowly that all efforts are pinpointed solely on that market. The advent of database marketing has led some marketers to target only those individual consumers whose buying patterns identify them as best prospects. The rationale is that reaching less-than-best prospects is wasteful. That is, it costs too much to reach them through paid media or direct mail.

This narrow-casting approach is grounded in the notion that the ever-higher cost of time, space, and mass mailing has made reaching next-best prospects prohibitive.

The problem is that secondary markets that may represent significant sales potential are excluded. The solution may be to use marketing public relations to reach important identifiable secondary markets at a very affordable cost.

Ocean Spray's Good Health News

There is no better example than the experience of Ocean Spray Cranberries, Inc., the leading producer of canned and bottled fruit drinks in North America.

In 1994, the *Journal of the American Medical Association* reported the results of a large-scale study funded by Ocean Spray demonstrating that regular use of cranberry juice reduces bacterial growth in the human bladder.

During the six-month study, older women daily drank either ten ounces of Ocean Spray Cranberry Juice Cocktail or a specially prepared placebo beverage that looked and tasted exactly like cranberry juice cocktail but did not contain any cranberry juice. After the trial, the group drinking the authentic cranberry beverage had a much lower frequency of bacteria and white blood cells in their urine than those drinking the placebo. Those drinking the placebo were four times more likely to have their urine remain infected from one month to the next than those drinking cranberry juice cocktail.

Despite the tremendous business opportunity represented by this good news about the benefits of its products, Ocean Spray adapted a conservative public relations strategy that was more responsive than proactive. A week prior to the JAMA article, it sent out a few hundred press kits to medical reporters containing a press release, a backgrounder on urinary tract infection (UTI), and a biographical sketch of the doctor who headed the project.

Media coverage capitalized on news of a scientific survey that confirmed an old wives' tale. For years, women had suspected that cranberry juice could help protect against urinary tract infection. The media was convinced of the validity of the survey because it was conducted by the Harvard Medical School and reported in JAMA, a double endorsement from respected sources.

Despite Ocean Spray's deliberately low-key public relations approach, the total reach of the coverage of newspapers, television, and radio exceeded 500 million consumers. The fact that the study was underwritten by Ocean Spray clearly did not detract from the widespread national coverage of the story in print and broadcast media. In fact, CNN and many other media reports pointed out that while Ocean Spray funded the study, it had no role in its design, analysis, or interpretation.

The endorsement implied by coverage of the story in the news media multiplied the endorsement of the study by the American Medical Association and Harvard Medical School. This endorsement to the third power is arguably far more credible than any other marketing communication vehicle for the same message could have been. Ocean Spray did not, in fact, include this information on the Cranberry Juice Cocktail package or in its advertising specifically because it believed this would jeopardize the credibility of the study.

Impact on Sales

The impact of the publicity on sales was reported by Ocean Spray in its annual report to its more than 900 grower members as follows:

> 66 News that regular use of cranberry juice cocktail reduces bacteria which cause UTI reached hundreds of millions of people worldwide. Sales increased by the highest percentage on weekly and monthly tracking bases since Ocean Spray began gathering sales data in 1986 through the InfoScan information system. 99

The effects of publicity on the study continued to exert a very significant effect on sales the following year. In a letter to members in the 1995 annual report, Ocean Spray's chairman and president wrote:

> **❝** One of the highlights of fiscal 1995 was the performance of the Cranberry Division. Revenues were $981 million, up 10 percent from a year ago. Ocean Spray Cranberry Juice Cocktail set sales records almost every month from the beginning of the year through spring as we continued to benefit from favorable urinary tract infection publicity generated by the *Journal of the American Medical Association* article published in May 1994.[1] **❞**

The results of the study were so positive that Ocean Spray is funding further research to determine whether younger women with symptoms of recurrent tract infections can reduce their frequency of infection by regular use of cranberry juice cocktail. Positive results from such a survey would surely be treated by the media as another significant news story.

PR Wave Reaches Primary Market

The significance of this public relations–driven achievement is that it was directed to a secondary market that proved to be a very significant source of incremental sales. The company's advertising campaign, "Crave the Wave," running concurrently and specifically targeted to the primary market of younger consumers, positioned the product as a refreshing, flavorful alternative to soft drinks, other juices, and water.

Public relations was also used to supplement this ad campaign to the youth market. A Women's Voice of Encouragement (WAVE) program generated millions of positive impressions for Ocean Spray's support of young women's participation in high school sports.

The program, created with Ocean Spray's longtime public relations firm, Creamer Dickson Basford, consists of grants, awards, and scholarships designed to get young women off the sidelines and into the games. The centerpiece is a competition for awards to schools that have effective programs to get more high school women to compete in sports. Grants are made to schools that need funding and scholarships awarded to outstanding young women athletes nominated by their coaches for being the best role models for getting others involved. Ocean Spray sends Olympic gold medalists such as Summer Sanders to visit high schools and encourage young women to get into sports. WAVE materials distributed to students discuss the role of fruit juice beverages in an athlete's diet, strongly identifying the Ocean Spray product with its primary target market.

Ocean Spray's success in conducting simultaneous public relations programs that communicate relevant messages to its primary youth market and an important secondary market of older women is an effective demonstration of public relations segmentation in action.

Lessons Learned

- Scientific research may produce a marketing silver bullet.
- Use it to find new benefits for old products.
- Funding such research is a small price to pay if results are positive.
- If they aren't, who says you have to publicize them?
- Your research will be more credible if it's conducted by a respected researcher from a prestigious institution.
- The better the source, the more likely it is to be published.
- The better the journal, the greater the attention that will be paid by news media.
- Less may be more if the news is good enough. There are times when reactivity beats proactivity.
- Overcommercialization can cancel out the benefits of good news coverage.
- Don't underestimate the power potential of secondary markets on sales success.
- Don't underestimate the power of positive public relations to tap this potential.

Chapter 23

Influencing the Influentials

ONE OF THE TENETS OF TRADITIONAL MARKETING IS TO DEFINE TARGET MARKETS as precisely as possible. Most marketing plans define target consumers demographically by age, sex, income, and education. Some superimpose psychographics to draw a more precise customer lifestyle profile. Database marketers are focused on reaching individual consumers rather than what they call "faceless markets." They are gathering scads of data about the interests, possessions, and purchasing behavior of individuals so that they can shape their marketing messages specifically to them.

One critical element far too often overlooked by both traditional and integrated marketers is the role that influentials play in affecting purchase behavior. Call them influentials, influencers, opinion leaders, opinion makers, they are the people that the rest of us look to to help us pick the products we buy, the places we visit, the movies we see, the candidates we vote for.

A 1995 Roper Starch Survey reported in *American Demographics* concludes that influentials are "marketing multipliers" who are much more likely than average to dispense advice about things such as vacations, restaurants, TV shows, software, cars, clothing, consumer electronics, investments, retail stores, office equipment, and alcoholic beverages.[1]

Experts believe that 10 percent who are the most influential spread the message to the other 90 percent. That is why influencing the influentials is exceptionally important. Public relations has long recognized the importance of reaching influentials through word of mouth and word of media.

The influential may be a doctor. My orthopedist recently recommended that I take Aleve twice a day. I told him that would make my friends at Procter & Gamble very happy. Most of us look to our pharmacist to recommend an over-the-counter cough medicine or cold pill. Teachers, especially consumer-education and home economics teachers, introduce students to an array of products, new and old. We look to our techie friends to help us pick a computer and tell us what software we need. We might ask another friend about stereo components and another about what golf clubs to buy or what microbeer to try. Our well-traveled friends can help us plan our itinerary for a foreign trip.

Many of these folks get their information online and from reading professional journals, the trade media, and so-called buff books. That is where the mainstream consumer media get a great many story ideas.

The influence of the media, old and new, on consumers is a principal theme of this book. In this chapter, we will demonstrate how public relations influences the influentials who, in turn, exert a geometric influence on many consumers.

MPR Does Wonders for White Bread

Dietitians and nutritionists exert both a direct and an indirect influence on what we eat and what we don't. They influence what we are fed in schools, hospitals, offices, and plants. They also influence what foods we buy, serve, and consume at home.

The folks at Continental Baking Company, makers of Wonder Bread, knew that dietitians could have a tremendous influence on how we perceive good-old store-bought white bread. While national bread consumption was on the rise, and whole grains and variety breads were increasing, white bread consumption was losing ground.

That's why the company whose brand name has been synonymous with white bread since 1921, funded a scientific study on the benefits of eating white bread and revealed the results to the 4,500 members of the American Dietetic Association attending the 1992 ADA Annual Meeting in Washington, D.C.

The study conducted for Continental by the Cooper Institute for Aerobic Research in Dallas helps dispel the myth that bread is fattening and suggests that adding bread, including white bread, to a daily eating plan helps people improve the quality of their diets.

Research to the Rescue

The Cooper Institute for Aerobic Research, a Dallas-based nonprofit research and education center, is widely acclaimed for its work in advancing and understanding the relationship between living habits and health. Despite the fact that the study was funded by Continental, the credibility of the Cooper Institute among health-care professionals and the media negated possible "research for hire" skepticism.

The study, "Improving Dietary Quality by Increasing Bread Consumption," was designed to determine the effects of eating different amounts and types of bread on nutrient intake levels, body weight, and body composition. The eight-week study looked at the effect of adding four to eight slices of bread to the diet of overweight, inactive men and women. At the end of the study period, not only had the participants experienced no significant weight gain but they had also improved the quality of their diets by increasing their intake of carbohydrates, dietary fiber, calcium, and iron.

The findings were on target with both the USDA Food Guide Pyramid recommendations and the "Healthy People 2000" report of the U.S. Department of Health and Human Services. The USDA guidelines suggest that a healthy diet should include six to eleven daily servings of breads, grains, and cereals. Healthy People 2000 also recommends adding carbohydrates, fiber, iron, and calcium to the daily diet and decreasing fat intake.

The study had extraordinary strategic importance to the marketing of Wonder Bread by substantiating the product's long-standing claim that it is good-tasting and good for you.

The Wonder Bread marketing public relations effort helped close the marketing credibility gap by documenting the case for white bread to consumers directly, and to the nation's dietitians who exert an important influence on what we buy and eat.

Continental blended the results of the Cooper Institute study with the recently released dietary guidelines recommended by the USDA to convince consumers that Wonder Bread increases complex carbohydrate and iron intake while decreasing fat intake, and that it provides a convenient source of fiber and calcium.

Thumbs Up for White Bread

Having presented its findings to the dietitians in a scientific session, Continental wanted to dramatically increase consumer awareness of the brand and the nutrition study. It wanted to stage an event that would make Wonder Bread the talk of the ADA meeting and, even more importantly, that would catapult the brand and study into the national spotlight through publicity.

Continental's public relations firm, Cohn & Wolfe, identified the following creative considerations its strategy should encompass:

- Give consumers and dietitians permission to believe the Wonder Bread message.
- Don't denigrate the brand.
- Don't overstate product/research claims.
- Don't cannibalize variety breads.
- Be brand-specific wherever possible.
- Have fun.

The vehicle Cohn & Wolfe came up with was a political-style rally for white bread lovers that would create excitement at the show and extend awareness of the Wonder Bread nutrition message via publicity.

An oversize postcard invitation was sent to all dietitians preregistered for the convention. Another card was placed under every attendee's hotel room door as a reminder of the rally. Finally, 10,000 copies of a good-natured tabloid newspaper spoof called *The Washington Toast* was widely distributed. It covered the research findings, recommended tips to add bread to the diet from Continental's own registered dietitians, and promoted the rally.

Mount Vernon Square, across the street from the Washington Convention Center, was transformed into "Thumbs Up for White Bread" rally headquarters, complete with soundstage and a Dixieland band. Hundreds of balloons in Wonder Bread red, yellow, and blue filled the sky, and rally signs appeared with messages such as "Rise Up for Bread," "Bread Lovers Unite," and "White Bread Is Right Bread." Dietitians and passersby attending the rally were provided with "Thumbs Up" buttons and miniloaves of Wonder Bread and were rallied to the white bread cause by comedian Elayne Boosler.

On-site media carried the story to millions of consumers. I was one of them. I was intrigued by a report from the rally by National Public Radio, coverage that money can't buy, and by reports I saw on CBS's *This Morning* and CNN, and read about in the *Chicago Tribune* under the four-column head "White bread not healthy? 'Baloney,' says Wonder's maker."

In reporting the results of the study, Charles Osgood, host of CBS radio's *The Osgood File*, said the study concludes that "White bread is not bad for you, which is saying quite a lot considering the bad-mouthing of white bread that's been going on." Osgood noted that it was Continental that introduced the first commercial sliced bread in 1930 so "If they say something is the best thing since sliced bread, they know whereof they speak."

Lessons Learned

- Company-sponsored research is credible if it is conducted by a respected scientific organization.

- Peer review and acceptance are key. Present the findings to professional audiences in accepted scientific format.

- Avoid exaggerated conclusions and claims. This is not the place to sell.

- Reveal your findings at a prestigious national forum that's covered by national news media.

- Take your story to media that don't cover the show.

- It helps if the media grew up with your product.

- Don't forget to spread the news to your customers in the trade.

- News in the trade press keeps your customers sold.

- Find an attention-getting way to tell the story to consumers.

- Think visually.

- Don't take your product or yourself too seriously. Have some fun, even if your product takes a lot of kidding.

Making Valvoline Number One

The importance of influencing the influentials is the key to a successful marketing public relations program for Valvoline motor oil.

Valvoline research showed that mechanics are the professionals whom consumers are most likely to consult for recommendations of a motor oil brand. Twenty-three percent of consumers said that they consult a mechanic about what brand to choose. Consumers participating in focus groups said they think of their mechanics as people they can trust and believe in.

The company recognized the marketing value of identifying Valvoline as the motor oil brand preferred by professional mechanics, particularly certified master technicians, the most highly regarded mechanics. The problem was that Valvoline, while regarded as a quality product, was not the top choice of professional mechanics. The challenge faced by the company and its public relations firm, Fleishman-Hillard, was to make Valvoline the clear number-one brand with this important audience of influentials.

The first priority was to define the target. The U.S. Bureau of Labor Statistics estimates that there are 757,000 automotive mechanics in the country but there is no national membership organization for mechanics. It was determined that the best avenue for reaching them was through the National Institute for Automotive Service Excellence (ASE), which conducts certification tests for mechanics and has certified more than 300,000 automotive mechanics. About 67,000 elite technicians have earned master certification by passing all automotive tests.

Focus groups with certified mechanics revealed two overriding needs among auto-service professionals: (1) the need for more technical information, particularly about motor oil, and (2) the need for recognition and support for their profession.

The Automotive Service Association (ASA) provided another avenue for reaching mechanics. The ASA represents 11,000 independent shop owners, many of whom are working mechanics who generally employ several mechanics.

The program created by Fleishman-Hillard was designed:

- To provide technical information on lubricants and other industry information to mechanics.

- To give much-needed recognition to the auto-service profession; to help elevate the role of mechanics in the minds of consumers.

- To create opportunities to associate Valvoline with mechanics in publicity aimed at general consumer and industry audiences.

To reach mechanics, the agency created a high-quality newspaper called *The Driving Force*. This eight-page, full-color publication features technical information and lifestyle stories of interest to professional technicians. It also includes an insert on auto racing, a favorite sport of mechanics. Because the imprimaturs of ASA and ASE are important to mechanics, these groups are featured in every issue. They help distribute the newspaper to 100,000 mechanics.

A survey of ASE-certified master technicians was designed for publicity purposes. It revealed their views on today's cars and automotive service and helped establish them as experts on the state of the industry.

The results of the 1996 Poll of the American Mechanic were announced at a news conference at the National Press Club in Washington, D.C. Some newsworthy key findings of the 1996 poll include:

- Technicians agreed that one of the primary reasons for the current popularity of sport utility vehicles is the ability to drive them in inclement weather.

- Half said they would place a lot of importance on the inclusion of passive restraint seat belts when purchasing a new automobile. They were cited as the best safety feature, followed by air bags and antilock brakes.

The most important finding for motor oil marketers like Valvoline was that nine out of ten mechanics polled strongly agreed that oil in auto engines should be changed every 3,000 miles.

Valvoline stepped up its participation in national, regional, and local meetings of the ASA. The company's field representatives were encouraged to "adopt a chapter" in their areas and were given suggestions for activities they could conduct with the ASA.

The company established the Valvoline Institute of Technology, a training program, and a speakers' bureau, and provided presentation materials to mechanics and automotive instructors for talks to interested groups in their communities.

Valvoline also leveraged its formidable presence in auto racing to help promote awareness of the ASE by placing the ASE logo on the front-running car at the Indianapolis 500 where it was seen during the race telecast. Finally, Valvoline placed ads in ASA magazines and other local mechanics' publications that spotlighted local mechanics.

Valvoline's primary objective was met through this public relations initiative. Valvoline became the number-one motor brand used by master technicians. A 1996 survey of master technicians revealed that 28 percent chose Valvoline. At the outset of the mechanics' initiative five years earlier, only 19 percent picked Valvoline.

The new status of Valvoline as the number-one pick was highlighted in national consumer advertising, an excellent example of the use of PR-driven advertising in an integrated marketing program.

Other positive results fulfilled Valvoline's secondary objective of enhancing consumer and trade identification of Valvoline with mechanics. *The Driving Force* identified in the masthead as "News for the Automotive Service Professional from Valvoline" has been enthusiastically received by readers and subscription requests have skyrocketed. All 100,000 subscribers are now on Valvoline's database for future communications.

The Valvoline/ASE Poll of the American Mechanic, now conducted and publicized annually, effectively positions ASE master technicians as knowledgeable industry authorities. ASE mails the poll results to all master technicians, further reinforcing Valvoline's concern for the profession. The results of the poll also appear in full-page ads in *USA Today*.

ASE's presence on Valvoline's Indy 500 car generates almost $1 million in equivalent advertising value during its exposure on the race telecast, bringing attention to the ASE logo and endearing Valvoline to the organization. The company's participation has not only been appreciated by members but has opened new sales opportunities for Valvoline representatives.

The overall result is that Valvoline has become the company that mechanics come to for information and professional support. It is now the first choice of mechanics, the consumers' most-asked professional source for motor oil recommendations.

Lessons Learned

- Use research to identify the most important influentials.
- Find out how to best reach these influentials.
- Support their professional organizations nationally.
- Participate actively in local chapters.
- If you find they "don't get no respect," design programs that help them get the recognition they deserve.
- Design a communication vehicle with news they can use to keep your brand top-of-mind.
- Maintain an up-to-date database to communicate between issues.
- Conduct a survey that projects influentials as experts.
- Measure the impact of your program periodically.
- Apply what you learn to make it better.
- Merchandise the endorsement of influentials in advertising, publicity, and promotion.

CHAPTER 24

Identifying Brands with Causes That People Care About

SINCE AMERICAN EXPRESS INTRODUCED THE CONCEPT AND GAVE IT A NAME, CAUSE-related marketing has become a strategic option for marketers. American Express continues to donate a percentage of every American Express card transaction to support a variety of local philanthropic causes and large-scale national initiatives.

Some other companies sponsor cause-related programs with an overt commercial element. That is, the company offers to contribute a percentage of sales of a particular product to a worthwhile cause during a specified promotional period. Others support worthwhile social causes on a continuing basis.

Recent research conducted by Roper Starch Worldwide for Cone Communications shows that 76 percent of Americans would be likely to switch to brands or retailers associated with a good cause, when price and quality are equal. The 1997 Cone/Roper Cause Related Marketing (CRM) Trend Report is based on a national survey of 2,000 adults. It found that receptivity to CRM is greatest among those most likely to make key purchasing decisions: women eighteen to forty-nine, parents of young children, and influentials. The study corroborates a 1993 benchmark survey that found influentials are more positive toward cause-related marketing, more likely than other consumers to purchase a product or service associated with a cause, and more likely to switch brands or retail stores based on a cause. The 1993 survey also revealed that a company's responsible business practices are a more important influence than a brand's advertising.

Roper Starch defines influentials primarily by their social activism and their role as opinion makers and group leaders. Supporting causes especially touches a responsive chord among the socially active customer segment. They have particularly rewarded socially active companies who demonstrate a continuing commitment to causes that doesn't start and stop with a promotional period.

Carol L. Cone, CEO of Cone Communications, sponsor of the survey, says that consumers now expect the makers of the products they buy and the businesses they patronize to get involved and stay involved in improving the quality of their lives. More than half of those surveyed want companies to become involved on the local level.

"Increasingly, companies are finding that their sincere, long-term efforts are being rewarded by deeper relationships and trust with consumers, enhanced image, improved brand equity, and increased sales," Cone says.[1]

Leading Fortune 500 companies are turning to cause-related marketing as a value-added differentiator following the lead of socially responsible smaller companies such as Ben & Jerry's and The Body Shop.

"Our comprehensive commitment to community development and youth-at-risk programs are as much a part of our strategy in growing our business as the products we select and carry," states Arthur Blank, CEO of Home Depot. "It provides a way to reach our customers and a critical competitive advantage to our company."[2]

"Cause-related marketing has become a critical component of Avon's marketing strategy, giving customers yet another compelling reason to choose Avon and providing enhanced personal connections between them and our sales representatives," says Joanne Mazurki, director of global communications of Avon Products, Inc. The company sponsors the Avon Worldwide Fund for Women's Health and Avon's Breast Cancer Awareness Crusade in the United States.[3]

In their 1992 book, *Doing Best by Doing Good*, Dr. Richard Steckel and Robin Simons offer an explanation of why forming alliances with nonprofit organizations benefits business:

> 66 People trust nonprofits. It's almost as simple as that. We tend to believe in what they do, and almost more importantly, in how they do it. They are tackling the most pressing problems of our time for reasons other than personal gain. For this we tend to grant them respect. We acknowledge their integrity. We give them our trust. Business is, of course, not so fortunate. We all know that business's bottom line is profit. No matter how altru-

istic a company may be, when push comes to shove what really counts is money. However, companies that associate closely with nonprofits—that genuinely adopt a nonprofit's cause, that measurably help its work—find that an interesting thing happens. The goodwill accorded the nonprofit rubs off on them. Supporters of the organization begin to look favorably on the company, even to buy its products if it will help the cause. The public at large may see the company in a different light—as one that cares about people as well as about profits. The company's self-centered image is softened; its appeal to consumers softens. Partnerships help a company stand out from the crowd. Today, as products become increasingly similar and as space becomes increasingly cluttered, partnerships can distinguish a company's products and services from the competition. Since partnerships often get a lot of press, they can give a company a marketing edge.[4]

More than 250 U.S. companies responded to the call to team up with nonprofits to help American youth at risk at the nonpartisan Presidents' Summit for America's Future in April 1997, chaired by General Colin Powell and attended by every living president. *Newsweek* explained, "The implicit deal is this: the corporations get most of the public recognition (and the marketing punch of looking concerned about kids) in exchange for providing much needed bodies and dollars to the nonprofits that know how to make use of them."[5]

The Glad Bag-A-Thon

The Glad Bag-A-Thon that started in 1986 is America's largest organized litter cleanup. Sponsored by First Brands Corporation, the makers of Glad Wrap and Glad Bags in partnership with Keep America Beautiful, Inc., America's premier litter-prevention and beautification organization, the Glad Bag-A-Thon is designed to educate the public through community action about litter prevention, encourage recycling, and emphasize the importance of reuse.

The program started in only five cities. Now the program is nationwide. In 1996, more than one million volunteers collected twenty-eight million pounds of litter and recyclables in communities across America. During its first decade, more than 178 million pounds of litter and recyclables were collected.

In 1997, the Glad Bag-A-Thon announced that "America's Largest Litter Cleanup Goes National." A news release said that the Bag-A-Thon was extending its hands-on litter cleanup and prevention efforts beyond its current 100-city base by issuing a nationwide invitation to keep America beautiful and a practical way to get involved.

For the first time, First Brands Corporation distributed four million boxes of Glad Handle-Tie Bags with the invitation on the front of the box to stores in virtually every community in the country. Inside each box was an educational brochure giving consumers easy-to-follow information about how to organize a litter cleanup, cleanup safety tips, a special decal, and a High Value coupon for Glad Handle-Tie Bags. The invitation also appeared in a freestanding insert in Sunday newspapers reaching fifty million households.

Glad also announced that it would donate fifty cents to Keep America Beautiful for each bag of litter collected by volunteers, who were given a special 800 number to report their bagged litter totals.

Glad products Marketing Manager Dennis Mullin echoed the core belief of cause-related marketing when he said, "We have always believed that we can do well by doing good. The Glad Bag-A-Thon has offered so much to so many of our nation's cities so long. Our new national program is a simple but powerful call to action to every single American—young or old, big or small. We've got the cleanup bags, we've got the know-how, and we've got the expertise of Keep America Beautiful. Now everyone can be a role model by picking up a piece of litter and putting it in its proper place."

Ruder-Finn, the firm that has conducted the massive public relations support program for the Glad Bag-A-Thon since its inception, helps organize cleanup efforts and obtains national and local publicity in the 100 participating communities.

Typical of the local news coverage is this from a Memphis newspaper:

> 66 The Memphis City Beautiful Commission needs 15,000 volunteers to participate in the 1996 Glad Bag-A-Thon cleanup and recycling program to be held April 8 to 22. Thousands of volunteers representing businesses, schools, churches, neighborhood associations, and civic groups will be trying to fill Memphis's largest trash container—the ten-foot-tall Superbasket—with litter from throughout the city. The annual Glad Bag-A-Thon is sponsored by the Memphis City Beautiful Commission (the Glad Bag-A-Thon local sponsor and Keep America Beautiful local affiliate). Black trash bags and clear recycling bags are provided by First Brands (makers of Glad Wrap and Glad Bags) and Keep America Beautiful, Inc. Volunteers will be throughout the city, picking up litter in area neighborhoods, parks, roadsides, and work sites. 99

Ruder-Finn also obtains proclamations, recognition, and acknowledgments of the Glad Bag-A-Thon from public officials. More than 200 mayors and fifty governors have officially endorsed the effort. They love this volunteer effort to clean up their cities and are more than pleased to lend their support and their presence to the event, often wearing Glad caps and T-shirts. Their endorsement enhances the event by capturing the attention of local media.

One such proclamation, dated March 31, 1988, declaring April "Keep America Beautiful Month" was signed by the governor of Arkansas, Bill Clinton. In 1997, a *USA Today* ad with pictures of governors from participating states invites Americans "to join us in support of the nation's largest organized litter cleanup—the Glad Bag-A-Thon."

Lessons Learned

- Fill a real community need.
- It works so much better if your products fit naturally into the program.
- It won't work without the active participation of an army of volunteers.
- Pick a nonprofit partner whose interests and yours converge.
- Make sure there is plenty of visual identification of your brand on the scene.
- Design caps and T-shirts that will show up well in print and on TV.
- Enlist the governor and mayor to endorse your effort. Make it an offer they can't resist.
- Invite them to the event and put them to work.
- Invite media types to pitch in.
- Integrate the program by promoting it on the package and in it, and at the point of sale, in the Sunday paper.
- You can't cover every market personally. Do what you can to activate volunteers to do it themselves.
- Motivate them with a cause-related donation.
- Organize, organize, organize.
- Start next year's planning while doing this year's program.

Ben & Jerry's Social Activism

Ben & Jerry's tops the list of companies consumers believe to be most socially responsible. The Vermont-based ice-cream company has become synonymous with social activism. In their book, *Ben & Jerry's Double-Dip*, founders Ben Cohen and Jerry Greenfield describe an alternative to the traditional business model, called "values-led business" this way:

> ❝ Values-led business is based on the idea that business has a responsibility to the people and the society that make its existence possible. More all-encompassing and therefore more effective than philanthropy alone, values-led business seeks to maximize its impact by integrating socially beneficial actions into as many of its day-to-day activities as possible. In order to do that, values must lead and be right up there in a company's mission statement, strategy, and operating plan."[6]
>
> Ben & Jerry believe that "A values-led company earns the kind of customer loyalty most corporations only dream of—because it appeals to its customers on the basis of more than a product. It offers them a way to connect with kindred spirits, to express their most deeply held values when they spend their money. Unlike most commercial transactions, buying a product from a company you believe in transcends the purchase. It touches your soul. Our customers don't just like our ice cream—they like what the company stands for. They like how doing business with us makes them feel. And that's really what companies that spend huge amounts of money on advertising are trying to do—make their customers feel good about them. But they do it on a superficial level, with sexy women and cool cars.[7] ❞

In 1988, the company created its three-part mission statement that has become the cornerstone of the company. The three parts are:

1. *Product Mission*—To make, distribute, and sell the finest-quality, all-natural ice cream and related products in a wide variety of innovative flavors made from Vermont dairy products.

2. *Social Mission*—To operate the company in a way that actively recognizes the central role that business plays in the structure of society by initiating innovative ways to improve the quality of life of a broad community—local, national, and international.

3. *Economic Mission*—To operate the company on a sound financial basis of profitable growth, increasing value for our shareholders and creating career opportunities and financial rewards for our employees.[8]

Ben & Jerry's built a $140 million business on quality products, innovative flavors, offbeat promotions, community relations, and publicity about all of these. They did it all without the benefit of national advertising.

When the *New York Times Magazine* asked Ben Cohen to define a socially responsible business, he said, "It's a business that seeks to use its power to improve the quality of life within society. It seeks profits and tries to integrate spiritual and social concerns into day-to-day activities. Typical businesses tend to do everything in terms of narrow self-interest. They want to maximize profitability and quality. We add a third factor: impact on the community, on the consumer, on our employees. We use suppliers such as Greyston Bakers that provides jobs for the previously unemployable. We buy our coffee from a rural cooperative in Mexico, helping to raise the standard of living there. We sell some of our ice cream through partner shops like Common Ground, which trains the previously unemployed. We give 7½ percent of our pretax profits to our foundation that, as far as we know, is the highest percentage of any publicly held company."[9]

The company has a history of matching causes with its products and flavors. A percentage of sales of Peace Pops ice cream bars goes to an organization that lobbies the Pentagon to give a percentage of its budget to support peace.

Ben & Jerry's Rainforest Crunch flavor benefits rain forest preservation. Sales of Wild Maine Blueberry help the Passamaquoddy Indians who grow the berries. The company buys peaches grown by African-American farmers in Georgia, nuts gathered by Indians from the Amazon rain forest, and brownies made by homeless bakery employees. Ben says that the company "consciously sources their ingredients—even though it might cost more than somewhere else—and ends up bringing about a more positive benefit than probably all the money we give away through the foundation."

It's marketing all right, but on Ben & Jerry's it looks good. Consumers know that social activism grows from the values on which the company was founded. Ben & Jerry's is unique and inimitable.

When Ben Cohen and Jerry Greenfield set out to make the best ice cream they could, they didn't advertise. They couldn't afford to. "Instead they turned to creating events that drew attention to their business while giving them a chance to celebrate with their customers," according to Fred "Chico" Lager, former Ben & Jerry's CEO and author of the book *Ben & Jerry's: The Inside Scoop.*

Events evolved from Free Ice Cream Days to the "One World, One Heart Festivals" of the 1990s that moved out from the company's annual meeting to Chicago's Navy Pier and San Francisco's Golden Gate Park. This was followed by a cross-country bus tour. At each stop, more than 100,000 people saw the shows featuring popular musicians, dyed their own tie-dyed T-shirts, sent postcards and video messages to their congressional representatives on what was on their minds, and consumed free ice cream.

The importance of events and public relations was pointed out by Lager:

> ❝ The company's strategy was referred to internally as relationship marketing—developing a connection with our customers that went beyond that achieved by traditional advertising and promotions. One of the first examples of how we'd done that successfully was the factory tours that had begun in 1986, the first year after the Waterbury plant was opened. By 1991 it was the largest tourist attraction in the state of Vermont, drawing more than 225,000 paid admissions for the year. The tours offered us incredible opportunities to create what we hoped would be customers for life. With paid advertising, we had ten seconds or a momentary scan of a page, in among the clutter of other ads and editorial content to capture a customer's attention and convince that person to buy our ice cream. On the tours, we had the rapt attention of our customers for more than an hour, which afforded us an unparalleled opportunity to educate visitors on our company's history, products, and business philosophy.
>
> There was an indirect benefit that went beyond those who had a firsthand experience with any of our marketing events. The offbeat nature of the promotions, combined with the fact that most had either a tangible social benefit or helped articulate the values of the company, helped to feed the word-of-mouth network. As a result they generated both tremendous goodwill among our customers and attention in the media that multiplied their impact many times over.[10] ❞

The company's irreverent style can be seen in its colorful "Chunk Mail," a colorful oversize newsletter that is chunk-full of stories about and pictures of Ben & Jerry's products, events, and social programs. It also contains an array of Ben & Jerry's gifts by mail, including such products with a purpose as Rainforest Crunch with all natural cashews, Brazil nuts from tropical rain forests ("as one small part of the larger effort to preserve rain forest vitality through economic incentive"), and "Food from the 'Hood," salad dressings made with products from the gardens of a high school student-owned natural-foods company in south central Los Angeles that funds its own scholarships from profits.

When the company famous for chunky flavors such as Cherry Garcia, Chunky Monkey, and Wavy Gravy introduced Ben & Jerry's Smooth Ice Cream, it decided to advertise nationally for the first time. But true to form, Ben & Jerry's created a campaign that was rarely seen but widely publicized. Ben designated himself Smooth team head coach and declared, "when the smooth get chunky, the chunky get smooth."

The print ads picture eight faintly familiar faces sampling the eight new flavors. Rather than use today's celebrities, Ben & Jerry's returned to their 1960s' roots, picking activists such as former Black Panther Bobby Seale, folk singer Pete Seeger, and Vietnam War protester Daniel Berrigan. None of these people were identified, but the ads offered a poster with information about them for ten dollars. As you would expect from Ben & Jerry's, the proceeds from posters sales were donated to the Children's Defense Fund. A Spike Lee TV commercial showed the unidentified activists enjoying ice cream in a café setting and talking about the cultural diversity of chocolate, vanilla, and coffee coexisting in a bowl. The spot was screened for reporters who carried the story far beyond the reach of the tiny media budget.

To demonstrate the smooth flavors in typical Ben & Jerry fashion, Ben and Jerry, dressed as samurai swordsmen, appeared on *Late Night with Conan O'Brien,* slicing open a quart of Vanilla Caramel Fudge to show how evenly distributed the caramel fudge was.

Ben & Jerry's knack for generating publicity reached its zenith when the company announced that it was looking for a new CEO to replace Ben who said he wanted to "focus on the fun stuff." The media couldn't resist the story and the photograph of Ben and Jerry in paper Uncle Sam hats unveiling a poster proclaiming, "We want you to be our CEO." Applicants were invited to send in a lid from their favorite flavor with a 100-word essay on "Why I Would Be a Great CEO for Ben & Jerry's." First prize would be the job but second was membership in the Ice Cream for Life Club. The company urged applicants to "go for this one, it's a better deal." Ben & Jerry's promised to send all losers a "rejection letter suitable for framing."

Newsweek proclaimed that "Even for a company with a sixteen-year history of populist promotions, the scheme was inspired."[11] The "Yo! I'm Your CEO" contest drew more than 22,000 applications. The company said it heard from senior citizens, classrooms of children, husband-wife teams, people nominating their pets, pets nominating their owners, mothers, fathers, grandparents, babies, and even prison inmates. Essays were accompanied by songs, poems, top-ten lists, posters, plaques, hand-painted wooden creations, and baked résumés.

It generated the single biggest public relations windfall in the company's history. Investors were reassured that the company was paying as much attention to the financial side of its two-part bottom line as to its famous social mission.

Reporters were fascinated by the outrageous announcement and followed the story throughout the selection process. Typical was a *USA Today* story "Ben & Jerry's Contestants Come in Many Flavors" with the picture of a corporate trainer who mailed in a Superman suit with fake kryptonite rocks and a lid from Ben & Jerry's Chocolate Peanut Butter Cookie Dough ice cream, a flavor he said counteracts the rock's harmful effects. A *New York Times* search story was titled

"Ice Cream Dream Job Is Tempting Thousands," and a *Chicago Tribune* story headlined "Weird and Assorted Flavors for Top Job."

Postscript: The new CEO was recruited by professional headhunters and served an 18-month term.

The Body Shop—A Cosmetic Company That Makes a Difference

Ben Cohen was influenced by his friends, Gordon and Anita Roddick, founders of The Body Shop. Anita Roddick believes that business should be values-led and uses everything from store windows, in-store displays, and trucks to promote social causes.

The first Body Shop opened in the United Kingdom in 1976, about the same time that Ben & Jerry's opened their first ice cream shop in the United States. Like Ben & Jerry's, "the Body Shop's personality has been shaped by the larger-than-life-image of Roddick and the publicity she encourages," according to *Advertising Age*. "An ex-hippie like Ben and Jerry, she is now one of the wealthiest and best-known women in England."[12]

In 1992, the *New York Times* reported that "the company eschews advertising: its success has been built largely on word-of-mouth endorsements and publicity about the causes of its founder, Anita Roddick, including Amnesty International and its 'Trade Not Aid' programs to buy ingredients from developing countries."[13]

At this time, there are more than 2,000 Body Shops in forty-five countries, 275 of them in the United States. A new one opens somewhere in the world every two-and-a-half days.

Body Shops make and sell skin- and hair-care preparations, based on natural ingredients and formulas. They also sell social activism.

Anita Roddick says, "We make and sell our own naturally based products that cleanse, polish, and protect the skin and hair. Our business concerns itself not just with skin and hair preparations but also with the community, the environment, and the big world beyond cosmetics."

Stores are festooned with slogans and messages. They are in the windows and on the trucks. Causes range from saving the whales to helping the homeless. The prominently displayed literature racks in Body Shops are loaded with folders for human-rights organizations such as Amnesty International and Cultural Survival and "Body Shop Approach" folders on such subjects as:

- "Trade Not Aid" ("The Body Shop believes trade, not aid, offers a positive solution to economic hardship in the developing world. Rather than giving handouts, we prefer to help communities acquire the tools and resources they need to support themselves.")

- "Animals in Danger" ("The Body Shop's range of 100 percent vegetable soaps are in the shape of endangered animals. They are all wonderful species, but did you realize how seriously they are threatened?")
- "Against Animal Testing" ("The Body Shop is against animal testing in the cosmetics industry. We believe that animals should not suffer for our vanity. It is neither right, necessary, nor scientifically accurate to test skin- and hair-care products on animals.")

In his book *Image Marketing*, Joe Marconi wrote:

> 66 Ms. Roddick is the subject of a good deal more media attention during a typical year than CEOs of companies that advertise in the traditional ways. The reason she is able to garner so much media interest is only passingly due to her heading up a company that purports to sell "all-natural products," from soaps to shampoos to facial cleansers, and accessories. She presents herself as a passionate environmentalist opposed to animal testing, who pours money earned in her business into her social causes. In virtually every story ever produced on The Body Shop, the phrases "sells natural products," "eschews animal testing," and "spends no money on advertising" appear with enough frequency to seem like a mantra.[14]   99

Because The Body Shop's company policy prohibits advertising, the U.S. launch provided a rare opportunity in which public relations could be isolated and evaluated from other communications functions. Larry Power, president of McGrath/Power, the public relations firm that handled the launch, told *O'Dwyer's PR Services Report* that "Body Shop's publicity effort had not only to saturate the beauty pages but also had to go beyond them and reach the public through wider editorial channels, both print and electronic. Its story was played as a news, business, environmental, and beauty piece."[15]

The company believes that many customers shop at The Body Shop because they share their values. *Advertising Age* says, "The typical customer is a twenty-nine-year-old female, likely to be interested in the retailer's philosophy and practices, its aversion to selling products tested on animals, its in-store petitions aimed at protecting endangered species, and its attempts to help developing companies through business partnerships."[16]

The Body Shop may not advertise, but Anita Roddick was the subject of a widely seen American Express "Do You Know Me?" commercial and print ad in which she expounded on the joys of taking the profit from the sale of bubble bath and doing something worthwhile with it. "Defending the environment.

Human rights. Trading honorably. Sounds a lot more interesting than just selling soap,"[17] she says.

Lessons Learned

- Consumers want to do business with companies that support causes they care about.
- There's nothing like a great plant tour to build customer relationships.
- There's nothing like giving away free ice cream to win new customers and keep old ones deliriously happy.
- Take your show on the road. Combine food, fun, and social action.
- Pick a cause that's right for your company. Give it a human face.
- If it's a good cause that's relevant to your business, so much the better.
- Spell out why you support a cause and what your customers can do to help.
- Sell posters and other stuff that benefit the cause.
- Find ways to stay in touch with your loyal customers.
- Encourage their calls and letters and answer them personally.
- Do it because you mean it. Don't do it unless you really care. The consumers will know.
- Social activism is a long-term commitment, not a short-term promotional opportunity.
- If you are for real, the media will follow.

Chapter 25

Allaying Consumer
Fears to Gain Market
Acceptance

IN MY 1991 BOOK, *THE MARKETER'S GUIDE TO PUBLIC RELATIONS*, I SUGGESTED THAT traditional "pull" and "pass" strategies were not enough to gain market entry in today's increasingly complex marketing environment. I said that a new marketing strategy was needed to overcome or neutralize opposition by a gathering army of societal gatekeepers. They include an array of consumer advocacy groups, government agencies, legislators, and political and religious groups. I named this "pass strategy" and said that the role of public relations was to recommend strategies and actions that enabled marketers to pass these gatekeepers and enter the marketplace unimpeded.

Companies are particularly vulnerable when opposition is centered around questions of product safety and efficacy. This can be critical when it involves the air we breathe, the water we drink, and the foods we eat.

Maintaining Consumer Demand for Milk

Sometime before the FDA announced its proposed policy on genetically modified foods, activist groups vehemently and vocally opposed the technology. They enlisted the media in their efforts to alert the public to the supposed dangers of genetically modified foods, claiming they would cause more harm than good.

Almost universally consumed, milk has long been a symbol for wholesomeness, goodness, and purity. It became the test case for public and retail acceptance of what opponents derisively called "Frankenfoods." In February of 1994, the FDA approved the use of a synthetic version of a naturally occurring protein, recombinant bovine somatotropin (rBST) that promised to boost milk production by up to 15 percent.

Public or retail rejection of this new technology would have had a devastating impact on the U.S. dairy industry. Even a short-term drop in consumption would put one-third of all dairy farmers into receivership. It would have also put other new types of food biotech products, including pestilent-resistant corn, squash, and longer-lasting tomatoes, in jeopardy.

The dairy industry had previously been damaged in 1989 when retailer boycotts had short-circuited the food distribution chain on the mere rumor of rBST approval.

Chemical giant Monsanto, the producer of rBST, faced the opposition of high-profile consumer activists Jeremy Rifkin of the Pure Food Campaign and Michael Hansen of the Consumers Union. They claimed that the product that they derisively called Bovine Growth Hormone or BGH was unsafe and posed a threat to personal and economic health. By provoking public fear and promising boycotts, they threatened individual retailers, grocers, and co-ops unless they signed pledges to ban milk from rBST-supplemented cows. Rifkin predicted a drop in consumption of 10 to 25 percent.

The industry and public relations firm Capitoline/MS&L formed an umbrella group called the "Dairy Coalition" to protect members from attack. The group did not advocate the use of rBST but focused on the safety and purity of milk.

To put the issue into perspective and to quantify the science surrounding the issue, the Dairy Coalition collected scientific articles, studies, and reports on rBST issues ranging from human health safety to the economic impact on dairy farmers. It also compiled a resource list of more than 100 scientists and medical experts available to reporters and others with questions about rBST and milk safety. Key third-party experts from organizations within the health and science community, including the American Medical Association and the American Academy of Pediatrics, were identified as spokespersons.

The Dairy Coalition knew how hard it would be to create a national boycott of a product as universally purchased, consumed, and loved as milk. Their strategy was to ensure that the milk industry did not overreact to the threats of rBST opponents and to limit the attention and credibility the industry and media gave them. They believed that resolving the safety issue would make rBST less newsworthy and of lower priority to the national news media.

Communications outreach to consumers was designed to limit the widespread misinformation campaigns. Media relations focused industry response on each story, limiting coverage to a single day.

The Dairy Coalition developed CEO-to-CEO letter campaigns to advise producers, co-ops, and retailers how to resist bullying tactics. Capitoline/MS&L established the Dairy Coalition Infoline as a resource for dairy farmers, processors, and retailers facing picket lines, milk dumpings, letter-writing campaigns, and negative media coverage. Industry callers received scientific information to provide to their communities and advice on how to respond to activist scare tactics and news media interviews. The public relations firm formed strong alliances with such community referral points as extension agents, nutritionists, school administrators, and academics, and provided them with milk-safety information to help them respond to their critics wherever the safety debate ensued.

Capitoline/MS&L created national and local news desks to work with reporters who cover health, biotechnology, and agriculture issues. Media covering the rBST subject were provided with materials, expert sources, spokespersons, video B-roll, and other information needed to balance their reports. Targeted reporters were also contacted when rBST-related events such as hearings, protests, school board forums, or news conferences took place. Broadcast fax media lists were used to update reporters regionally and nationally with Dairy Coalition statements and information. Letters to the editor were used to respond to misinformation appearing in print media.

Milk consumption news releases were issued monthly after rBST went into use. These releases used USDA data to document the fact that milk consumption remained level and to debunk activist claims that consumer anxiety about milk safety would cause people to stop drinking milk.

Alliances were also built with national school organizations such as the USDA School Food Lunch Program, the American School Food Service Association, and the National Association of School Boards. Their members in "hot spot" areas were sent educational materials. School administrators received rBST information kits and an educational videotape *Questions and Answers about rBST & Milk*, featuring former U.S. Surgeon General C. Everett Koop and dairy consultant C. Wayne Callaway. The videotape was seen by hundreds of school boards, PTA groups, school food-service seminars, and teacher workshops.

As a result of these public relations efforts, and despite a significant jump in consumer awareness of rBST, milk consumption did not decline and public confidence in the safety of milk remained strong. Content analysis of news coverage revealed that positive milk safety and health messages outweighed every other message in the rBST debate. The overwhelming majority of U.S. schools now accept milk from rBST-supplemented cows.

Lessons Learned

- Be prepared.
- Fight misinformation with science-based information.
- Collect all scientific studies and economic reports.
- Line up expert spokespersons.
- Accentuate the positive to eliminate the negative.
- Don't give credibility to opponents by overreacting.
- Keep the industry aware of its rights to fight boycotts, threats, and protests.
- Provide information to relevant opinion leaders.
- Form alliances with community supporters.
- Don't stir the publicity pot but provide complete information to media covering the story.
- Have an immediate response system to limit coverage and correct misinformation.
- Leverage contacts with national school organizations.
- Give them a video to show to parents and teachers.
- Recruit a respected third-party expert to star in your video. There's none better than the former surgeon general.

Enter the FLAVR SAVR Tomato

When Calgene Fresh developed the first genetically modified whole food, the FLAVR SAVR tomato, activist organizations made known their intention of preventing it from coming to market. Early analysis of media coverage by Calgene's public relations firm, Porter-Novelli, revealed that it often featured powerful attacks against food biotechnology and imagery of mad scientists in lab coats growing tomatoes in test tubes. The concept of a tomato that delivered better taste, thanks to genetic modification, was unfamiliar and for some downright scary. Prior to FDA authorization, messages such as "more science fiction than science," "not nice to fool with Mother Nature," "killer tomato," and, of course, "Frankenfood" appeared frequently in the media. A *New Yorker* cartoon showed a mad scientist addressing a crop of menacing-looking plants captioned "That's splendid news from the FDA, my pretties."

Porter-Novelli wanted to gauge how much effect negative press had on the public perception of food biotechnology so the firm conducted a national consumer study of more than 1,000 adults in February of 1993. Only a modest level (23 percent) of awareness of the issue existed. Forty-two percent reported neutral feelings toward genetically modified foods. Twenty-seven percent said their feelings were positive or positive with reservations.

Most important to the marketing of the FLAVR SAVR tomato, the survey revealed that increased levels of awareness of genetically modified foods would increase the acceptance of the first genetically modified tomato. Among those who had prior awareness of genetically modified foods, 54 percent reported positive feelings. This strongly recommended an aggressive public information and education campaign before the product came to market.

Further research was conducted to determine which consumers would be the most receptive to the FLAVR SAVR message and would be the most willing to try genetically modified foods. That survey yielded a clear demographic and psychographic profile of target market consumers. They were somewhat more highly educated with smaller households and slightly higher incomes, had a higher level of interest and involvement with nutritional issues and food in general, were information seekers in their buying behavior and their use of media, and were more likely to try new products. They were more concerned about environmental issues and tended to be opinion leaders who were likely to have wider social networks for sharing information.

The MPR strategy was to communicate to consumers that the FLAVR SAVR tomato delivers "Summertime Taste Year-Round" and the role of food biotechnology in delivering it. At the same time, it was necessary to continuously monitor and manage all issues with the potential to affect consumer acceptance of genetically modified foods.

Of equal importance was the need to educate health and diet professionals to gain their endorsement.

Because consumers look to them for information about food issues, Porter-Novelli booked more than forty speaking engagements for Calgene executives and spokespersons. They presented the case for the FLAVR SAVR tomato to diverse groups representing dietitians, physicians, chefs and culinary experts, food retailers, and produce industry executives.

To shift the focus of media attention from the laboratory to the kitchen table, Porter-Novelli created press materials that described how FLAVR SAVR tomatoes are able to spend more time on the vine where they can fully develop their natural flavor and how this was made possible by Calgene's discovery of a way to slow down the rate at which tomatoes soften. This was contrasted to current tomato-growing practices that make it difficult to deliver good-tasting tomatoes throughout the year. Most of the fresh tomato crop is picked while the tomatoes are still green, prior to reaching full flavor potential, so that growers have enough time to get their products to market. The contrast was convincingly demonstrated in a video of FLAVR SAVR tomatoes being grown, ripened, and harvested in the field. For print media, there were photographs of ripe, branded tomatoes headed for the store and a simple graphic illustration of the growing process.

A proactive one-on-one media relations program led to significant coverage of Calgene Fresh and the FLAVR SAVR tomato months before the product appeared in grocery stores. The story of the tomato appeared on news agenda-setting media from the NBC *Nightly News* to National Public Radio. Media attention grew as FLAVR SAVR tomatoes grew in the fields awaiting FDA approval.

A crisis communication plan was drafted to manage incidents arising from the increasing scope and volatility of the issue. A Chicago labeling ordinance was defeated, and consumerist demonstrations and calls for boycotts were managed.

The Food Advisory Committee of the FDA held an extensive review in April and declared the FLAVR SAVR tomato safe. When the FDA announced its favorable review, Porter-Novelli was ready to release an arsenal of media materials developed months earlier, including video B-roll, radio actualities, and press kits. The Calgene video that showed the tomatoes ripening in the fields before being picked and shipped to supermarkets reached an audience of more than 100 million. It was the most-watched video since the development of video monitoring.

To mitigate the potential for activist demonstrations when the tomatoes were first sold to consumers, the initial distribution was limited to independent grocery stores in two markets, Chicago, and Davis, California. Local media enthusiasm was reflected in a *Chicago Sun-Times* story headlined "Altered Tomatoes a Smash Hit at Market."

Most of the more than one billion media impressions generated by the authorization and introduction of the FLAVR SAVR tomato featured the positive taste benefit of the product. The tomato was featured in media ranging from a live tasting on NBC's *Today Show* to articles in major newspaper food sections.

The FLAVR SAVR public relations campaign was so successful that some retailers had to ration quantities for their customers because of a limited supply. Activist opposition declined and Calgene became regarded as a responsible agricultural biotechnology partner. Rather than fighting for retail grocery shelf space, the product was demanded by the nation's top food retailers.

As Porter-Novelli says, "It didn't happen by accident."

Lessons Learned

- Recognize the need to build consumer trust.
- Monitor all opposition activities.
- Analyze the content of the media coverage.
- Conduct consumer research to assess the damage.
- Design a strategy to correct misconceptions and regain consumer acceptance.
- Emphasize benefits that are most important to consumers.

- Educate influentials to gain their approval.
- Turn approval into endorsement by joint media appearances with federal regulators.
- Build consumer demand by building interest and anticipation.
- Use both words and pictures, moving and still, to tell your story.
- Involve the media with the product to gain implied endorsement.

CHAPTER 26

Defending Products at Risk and Giving People Permission to Buy

LEST THE READER BY NOW HAS THE IMPRESSION THAT MARKETING PUBLIC RELATIONS is all fun and games, please be advised that it ain't so. While much of this book supports the notion that MPR plays a unique role in the IMC planning process, it should be noted by marketing and public relations executives one and all that at times the best-laid marketing plans, integrated or otherwise, go awry. When, as a onetime automobile executive turned crisis communications counselor put it, "it hits the fan."

Bad Guys

The public relations literature is replete with contemporary examples. The bad guys are usually represented by Exxon's "duck and see" policy when the oil spill from their tanker *Valdez* despoiled Port William Sound, inflicting near complete carnage on anything and everything that walked in, swam in, or flew above these pristine waters. You will recall that Exxon's top management absented themselves from the situation and when finally pressed by the media, responded too little and too late, minimizing the damage, the company's responsibility, and the effect of the disaster not only on the wildlife but on the economy and the curtailment of tourism.

Harlan Teller, U.S. Executive Managing Director of Hill & Knowlton, says that the Exxon corporate brand became a lightning rod. The public's perception of slow, insensitive reaction to the crisis precipitated both marketing and corporate problems from boycotts and tearing up credit cards to institutional shareholder activism.

Good Guys

The good guys most often cited are the folks from Johnson & Johnson and their public relations firm, Burson-Marsteller, for their handling of what were widely known as the Tylenol murders. By following the classic public relations model of taking action and then communicating, Tylenol survived two crises that might well have destroyed the product. The actions taken by Tylenol were immediately pulling its product off the shelves, reintroducing it in tamper-resistant packaging, and offering to replace capsules with solid-form caplets. The company communicated openly, honestly, and frequently to all of its major stakeholders—consumers, trade customers, doctors, hospitals, and employees, directly and through the media. By leveraging Johnson & Johnson's equity and reputation with all of these internal and external audiences, Tylenol was able to rebuild its brand in the aftermath of these crises.

More recently, the good guy white hat must be awarded to the management and public relations people of the Pepsi-Cola Company. The issue was again product tampering—alleged product tampering, that is.

The Pepsi Hoax: A Bizarre Chapter in Corporate History

That's what Craig Weatherup, President and CEO of Pepsi-Cola North America, called the drama that began on June 12, 1993, when an eighty-two-year-old Tacoma, Washington, man claimed that he found a syringe in a Diet Pepsi can. Twelve hours later, a similar report of a syringe found in another can of Diet Pepsi surfaced, prompting the FDA to issue a consumer advisory recommending that consumers take the precaution of pouring Diet Pepsi into a glass before drinking it. The warning was issued to consumers in areas supplied by Pepsi's franchise bottler in Washington State, Oregon, Hawaii, Alaska, and Guam.

For the next four days, the "Pepsi Scare" was America's biggest news story. With new reports of syringe sightings coming in from different parts of the country, Pepsi's national crisis team mobilized to manage the scare. Team members focused on the most critical needs: responding to the press, coordinating with regulatory officials, and giving trade customers, consumers, and employees the facts.

Vice President of Public Affairs Rebecca Madeira directed the crisis team's actions to ensure that Pepsi spoke with a single voice both inside and outside of the company. She later told the *Public Relations Journal* that "it wasn't like a standard public relations strategy where you come up with a plan and implement it. This wasn't a public relations crisis. This was a media problem. The more you saw of the can and the syringe, the greater the concern became."[1]

The key groups on the Pepsi crisis team were:

- Public affairs. A press team prepared to handle hundreds of media inquiries and interviews. A production team was formed to write and produce what would prove to be critical media materials, including video news releases, audiotapes, press releases, product line flow charts, and photographs.

- Consumer relations. Two dozen specialists manned a toll-free telephone line around the clock to allay consumer fears and assess public attitudes. The team handled nearly 10,000 calls the week that the syringe story dominated the nation's news agenda. They tracked consumer reactions to how Pepsi was handling the issue daily.

- Scientific and regulatory affairs. Technical and product safety experts tracked each complaint and served as the link with the FDA's Office of Criminal Investigation.

- Sales and marketing. Relayed the facts to Pepsi's customers, including supermarkets, convenience stores, and restaurants.

- Manufacturing experts assisted in local FDA investigations and developed effective explanations of the production and quality-control process for the press and the public.

- The law department coached the crisis team on communications and reporting issues.

Updated information was channeled through a clearinghouse before being communicated to Pepsi bottlers, the company's 50,000 employees, and hundreds of thousands of Pepsi customers.

Pepsi's company-owned and franchised bottlers were continually fed updated information and coached during the crisis on how to report tampering claims to the FDA, how to address media questions, and how to reassure customers to keep Pepsi products on the shelves.

At the outset, Pepsi conducted a thorough internal investigation to assure themselves that there was no health risk, no possibility that syringes could get into cans at bottling plants, and no possibility of nationwide sabotage.

Manufacturing procedures were exhaustively inspected by the FDA, employee records checked, shipping and customer inventories reviewed, and complainants interviewed. Because of the high speed and integrity of Pepsi's production line, internal tampering was ruled out and it was determined that whatever was found in Pepsi cans was put there after the cans were opened. There was no correlation whatsoever between the growing number of complaints from various parts of the country and where and when they were made.

Assured that there was no health risk, no injuries, and no confirmed tampering, and backed by the FDA, Pepsi determined that a product recall would not end the crisis and that it would send the wrong signal to the public focused on the media crisis.

Rebecca Madeira told the *Public Relations Journal* that "this was the only case I knew of where there was a crisis without a recall. If you are not going to recall the product, you have to reassure the public that this was absolutely the right move."[2] To back its claim that "a can is the most tamperproof packaging in the food supply," Pepsi produced video footage that dramatically documented how safe the Pepsi canning process is. The video, shot inside a Pepsi canning facility, shows how high-speed, high-tech equipment turns each can upside down, cleans it with a powerful jet of air or water, then fills and closes it, all within nine tenths of a second.

The video was satellited to the hundreds of TV stations across the country. Three hundred million viewers saw Pepsi cans whirling by at a rate of 1,200 cans per minute. To those like me, who saw this video, there could be little doubt that internal tampering was a virtual impossibility.

Pepsi President Weatherup appeared personally on a dozen TV network news shows, *The McNeil Lehrer News Hour,* and *Larry King Live.* The *New York Times,* which itself ran a photo feature showing five steps of "How Soda Gets Into the Can," courtesy of Pepsi-Cola Company, commented that "Pepsi pulled out all the stops to reassure the soda public, with its chief executive, Craig Weatherup, turning up so often—on late news, early news, on *Nightline,* and *Larry King Live*—that he seemed to be running for president."[3] Other designated Pepsi spokespersons conducted more than 2,000 interviews with newspaper, magazine, TV, and radio reporters.

Within a few days, FDA Commissioner David Kessler called a news conference to announce arrests and reassure the public that "on the basis of information we have so far, the notion that there has been a nationwide tampering of Pepsi-Cola is unfounded."

To illustrate the FDA's conclusion, Pepsi instantly released another videotape, this one of an in-store surveillance camera filming a shopper caught in the act of slipping a syringe into an open Diet Pepsi can while the cashier's back was turned.

The crisis was over, the company completely exonerated. To celebrate the end of the crisis, Pepsi created an ad that ran in newspapers across the country. It was headlined "Pepsi is Pleased to Announce . . . Nothing."

The copy read "As America now knows, those stories about Diet Pepsi were a hoax. Plain and simple, not true. Hundreds of investigators have found no evidence to support a single claim. There's not much more that we can say. Except that most important, we won't let this hoax change our plans for the summer."[4]

America knew it because of deft public relations handling. There was truly not much more to say than what had already been transmitted to the consumer through every news medium.

A meeting of 1,200 employees was held at Pepsi headquarters to announce the end of the Pepsi hoax. The ad and an open statement to the American public was transmitted to all employees at 400 Pepsi facilities around the country. Reassured, the employees were able to spread their company's good news.

Marketing Rebound

A grass-roots marketing campaign called "Thanks, America!" was quickly devised to convey the company's gratitude to customers. Included were ads in major newspapers and dollar-off coupons on cases of Pepsi products. All 50,000 Pepsi employees hit neighborhood streets sporting "Thanks, America!" buttons and distributing dollar-off coupons to friends and neighbors. Pepsi bottlers also created local events to thank consumers.

The week of the hoax, Pepsi lost $25 million in sales from worried customers. The crisis ended only a few days before the important July 4 sales week, but when the hoax was exposed, sales rebounded strongly and Pepsi actually experienced its strongest sales week of the year.

In a story headlined "Scare fails to flatten Pepsi sales," *USA Today* reported, "Credit PepsiCo's intensive public relations effort and the Food and Drug Administration for limiting PepsiCo's losses." *Advertising Age* called it "a textbook case of how to come through a PR crisis."

MPR Lessons Learned

- Have a crisis response team in place.
- Define all audiences affected by the crisis.
- Design a communications effort to reach them that addresses their concerns and fears.
- Have technology in place to reach them quickly and often.
- Speak with one voice during a crisis.
- Practice good media relations at all times. Know and stay in touch with key media. It pays dividends in times of crisis.

Media Relations Lessons Learned

In a booklet documenting how Pepsi handled the crisis called *The Pepsi Hoax: What Went Right*, the company's public affairs department points out that "one advantage Pepsi had going into the syringe hoax was the company's broad experience working with the media on everything from new advertising and marketing efforts to financial and environmental issues." Pepsi has a half dozen PR managers that work daily with editors and reporters.

The company identified these seven media relations tactics that were effectively employed during the syringe crisis:

- Assess the problem through the public's eyes. Take responsibility for getting the facts in a clear, reasonable way. Demonstrate that trust in you is well placed.

- Speak with one voice. Don't comment off-the-cuff. Be certain there is a single, unified voice. State the facts when you know them and be definitive.

- Communicate quickly. Be fresh and provide information as soon as it's available. When the issue is resolved, tell the public it's over.

- Keep the message simple. Too many facts can be overwhelming, especially when crammed into TV sound bites. Also, think visually. Show as well as tell. Video is one of the top news-making tools today.

- Choose the right spokesperson. Pepsi President Craig Weatherup considered addressing the public during the syringe crisis as "part of my job." During a crisis, consumers want to see where the buck stops.

- Use formats reporters use. Distribute media-friendly tools. Make spokespersons accessible around-the-clock because news happens in real time. It interrupts programs or lands as a teaser for the 11 P.M. news. Use tools media can use: video, diagrams, photographs. If you give the media tools they can use, you stand a much better chance of getting your message out than if you just issue a statement and let them fill in the blanks.

- Present the people, not the company. Nobody loves a company. They love products and people. The more you can personalize and involve people, the better.

Crisis Coordinator Rebecca Madeira said, "We concentrated on what consumers care about, the can of Pepsi in their hands, not some kind of assault on Pepsi's national name. We also gave them as many opportunities as we could to see real people solving real problems."[5]

Crisis Update: The Odwalla *E. Coli* Scare

Madeira's good counsel on giving the media—and the consumer—tools they can use has been updated with the advent of the World Wide Web. The Web barely existed in 1993 when the Pepsi tampering hoax occurred, but more than thirty million users were on the Web when in October of 1996, Odwalla, Inc., a California new-age juice maker, was alerted to the possible link between Odwalla apple juice and an *E. coli* outbreak. Odwalla immediately recalled all apple juice and apple juice blends from 4,600 retail outlets in seven states. The company cooperated fully with health authorities and began an investigation into the cause of the contamination.

Odwalla asked Edelman Public Relations Worldwide to establish a news bureau that processed media calls immediately, issued news releases daily, and made company executives available for every media request. Vehicles, including an around-the-clock 800 number, were established to communicate to all important audiences—consumers, the media, retail trade partners, salespeople, employees, health departments, and the FDA.

Edelman created a Web site within a day. It was necessary because the company needed a way to broadcast the story to the media all at once aside from holding press conferences, faxing press releases, and taking out newspaper ads. Misinformation was spreading quickly across the Internet about Odwalla and a vehicle was needed to relay factual information. The site address was included on all press materials and messages were posted to relevant newsgroups to alert people to the newly created Web site and link to the site from the newsgroup. The site received more than 20,000 hits in the first forty-eight hours of its existence and continued for several weeks at an average of approximately 3,000 hits a day.

At one point in the crisis situation, Odwalla had more than forty sites on the Web linked to its page, including the *Seattle Times* and the *New York Times* Syndicate. Dozens of stories and editorials praised the speed and thoroughness of the recall and company communications. Typical was this from the *San Francisco Examiner*, "I'm so happy to see people buying their orange juice and grapefruit juice. It's a good product and a good company."

The Web site was instrumental in assuring that Odwalla retained a high degree of consumer loyalty. America Online Bulletin Board conducted a survey and found that 87 percent of more than 900 respondents said they would continue drinking Odwalla beverages.

PART II

How to Write an
Integrated Marketing
Public Relations Plan

 Over the past decade, public relations has become more science than art. It's now a sophisticated marketing discipline that designs programs based on solid research and can show measurable results.

The Marketing Report, November 1993

CHAPTER 27

Step One: Reviewing the Situation

IN PART I, WE EXAMINED HOW THE TOP MARKETERS HAVE USED PUBLIC RELATIONS to add value to their integrated marketing programs. Now that you have seen how they did it, Part II will show you how you can do it. We will discuss each of the critical pieces needed to formulate a successful marketing public relations plan and how to integrate that plan into the overall marketing plan.

The following format is most commonly used for writing the MPR plan. The elements can be rearranged for presentation purposes, but each of them should be considered when writing a comprehensive plan.

It consists of five steps and an executive summary. The executive summary is a one- or two-page summary that states the problem/opportunity addressed by your plan. It sets forth your solution strategies and the expected results. Although it appears first, it must be written last. It should not be considered as an introduction. It is rather a conclusion that asks for the order. It should state the case for the plan so clearly and concisely that the ultimate marketing decision makers will have all they need to ask the right questions before giving final approval.

The five steps are situation analysis, objectives, strategies, tactics, and evaluation.

This chapter will examine the situation analysis. Subsequent chapters will address objectives, strategies, tactics, and evaluation.

What's Happening?

Traditional marketing (and public relations) planning begins with the situation analysis, which answers the question "What's happening?" It involves the collection of all the relevant facts and important information needed to understand the marketing problem and opportunity. This includes information about the product and the business environment, i.e., the marketplace and the consumer.

IMC programs begin by collecting information about the consumer.

Integrated marketing is the latest step in the evolution of the marketing concept that, in its simplest terms, decrees that we should make and market what the consumer needs or wants rather than sell what we make. So in a sense all marketing in the age of marketing begins with the consumer. IMC takes that a step further by saying that all planning should be "outside in" rather than "inside out." It should start by learning all that we can about the consumer, how he or she thinks and acts, as the late Ron Kaatz of Northwestern University put it, "as a real, living, breathing person rather than simply a demographic statistic."

Ron Kaatz suggested that we begin the process by finding the answers to these ten questions:

1. What is our product or service?
2. Who are our target prospects? What are their lifestyles? How do they think? How does our product or service fit into their lives?
3. What do our prospects want from us? What do they want to know about our products or service?
4. From where and from whom do they now receive their key brand contacts in the purchase decision-making process?
5. What are their main points of contact with us?
6. What needs do our prospects have for help in the decision-making process and how can we help them fulfill these needs?
7. What turns our prospects off?
8. What turns our prospects on? Who or what has a positive influence on them and who or what do they trust?
9. How can we connect with them and turn them on in a positive, trusting way?
10. What are the characteristics of an effective message delivery system that will best help us in accomplishing this?[1]

Uses of Consumer Research in IMC

Secondary research provides basic information about both the marketplace and the consumer. Of particular importance to marketers and their public relations counterparts is information about consumer lifestyles and media preferences. Lifestyle information is available from sources such as Simmons Market Research Data Bureau, Standard Rate & Data Service Lifestyle Analyst, The Conference Board, Roper, Gallup, and Yankovolich, and others. Government statistics can be very valuable in supplementing demographic information about target consumers.

This secondary data is usually supplemented with at least some primary research that examines consumer perceptions about the brand and the company. Especially critical to marketing is research that assesses the effectiveness and relevance of current brand positioning. Of particular value to public relations are additional perceptions of the company behind the brand, i.e., its corporate reputation.

Frequently used primary research tools include consumer surveys, personal in-depth interviews, and focus groups. Focus groups are frequently used by marketers because they are relatively inexpensive, because they may provide new insights, and because the input from focus groups can be obtained instantly and analyzed quickly. Researchers, however, warn that the results of focus groups are not projectable. It takes a skilled group leader to keep discussion on track and to prevent assertive members of the panel from dominating the discussion and influencing how others respond.

It should always be remembered that primary research, no matter how professionally planned or executed, may yield misleading information. The introduction of the so-called New Coke in 1985 is a case in point. Coca-Cola research indicated a greater preference for the sweeter taste of Pepsi-Cola so Coke took the unprecedented step of reformulating its product. The new formula was preferred in blind taste tests. But when New Coke (which was never called that—it was simply Coca-Cola with a new recipe) went to market, it was soundly rejected by legions of lovers of old Coke. The company's market research did not adequately assess the strong attachment of millions of lovers of the old Coke to the tried-and-true formula. The company recovered quickly, New Coke went away, and Coca-Cola returned as Classic Coca-Cola, enhancing its lead in the cola wars.

McDonald's likewise responded to consumers, nutritionists, and the media who were critical of the fat content of their burgers by creating a low-fat alternative called the McLean Deluxe. Introduced with much fanfare in 1990, the McLean Deluxe was a great public relations success. The healthy burger was featured prominently in the news media, including all major television network news shows. It was "news fit to print" on the front page in the *New York Times*. It interviewed and ran pictures of a half dozen consumers who pronounced it a winner.

The McLean Deluxe enjoyed good initial public trial, but consumers who said they wanted a low-fat burger had second thoughts and returned to their favorite Big Macs and Quarter Pounders. After five years of marginal performance, the McLean Deluxe was quietly removed from the menu. The Deluxe name was to return to the menu in 1996 with the Arch Deluxe, an all-beef burger with lettuce and tomato and a special sauce and a line of other adult-size sandwiches.

How Public Relations Uses Market Research

The emergence of public relations as a critical component of integrated marketing has further validated the importance of research in public relations planning. Virtually every public relations planning model begins and ends with research. Research is also frequently conducted during the program to track communications effectiveness and to assess the viability of alternative public relations approaches, materials, and spokespersons.

The 1996 Thomas L. Harris/Impulse Research Public Relations Agency Survey found that 86 percent of corporate public relations departments employ primary research and secondary research in program planning and a like percentage say they measure results of public relations programs. They report conducting these types of research both in-house and through their public relations firms.

In truly integrated marketing programs, up-front consumer research studies should be structured to accommodate public relations needs as well as those of brand management, advertising, and promotion. If this cannot be accomplished, public relations may need to conduct its own primary research to determine attitudes toward the company behind the brand and issues that impact the marketplace. Public relations may be interested in learning more about the media behavior and specific lifestyle activities not only of primary market consumers but also of secondary and specialized market consumers—how they think, live, and purchase. It is also vitally important to learn how attitudes toward companies impact attitudes about and loyalty to their branded products.

In addition to participating in integrated marketing research studies, public relations may have reason to conduct more expansive primary and secondary research that provides insights into how the industry and the company, as well as the brand, are perceived by consumers and other important audiences that influence consumers directly or indirectly. The importance of these influencers is sometimes overlooked by marketers despite their importance as "marketing multipliers" who expand the consumer base for products and services. Some experts believe that 10 percent who are most influential spread the news to the other 90 percent. *American Demographics* reports that about half of Americans often seek the advice of others before making a major purchasing decision. The importance of reaching influentials through public relations is that these "purveyors" are much more likely to read sophisticated magazines than the "receivers" they influence. Consider the influence of buffs who are dedicated readers of automotive or computer books on those that look to them for advice.

Public relations is uniquely sensitive to reaching influentials through both word of mouth and word of media—on paper, on the air, and online.[2]

The Public Relations Contact Point

IMC theory holds that brands are built, enhanced, maintained, and destroyed by information that consumers process about the brand from a wide variety of sources over the years. Professor Lisa-Fortini Campbell of the Medill School of Journalism at Northwestern University says that every contact consumers have with the brand has the potential to say something that can reinforce brand equity or undermine it. She points out that contact points are message delivery systems that influence the meaning of the brand.

Public relations contact points are particularly important because they enable the brand or the company behind the brand to communicate in a nonsales situation. When consumers become interested in a product they read about in a newspaper or magazine, see on television, or hear about on radio in an editorial context, the message sticks. If the integrated program is properly managed, the media-exposed consumer will be more receptive to advertising messages and promotional offers that follow. Likewise, a consumer who is involved in a community program, attends an event, enters a contest, participates in a seminar, or visits an exhibit sponsored by the brand or the company behind the brand will be predisposed to product messages received later in a frankly commercial context.

Media Research: Public Relations Style

Because public relations is the interface between the company and the media and because the media represents a vital contact point with consumers, it is important for public relations to assess how the company and how the brand is currently perceived by the media. This may include an analysis of the influence of particular reporters, reviewers, and commentators.

The first step is to conduct a media audit to determine not only the quantity of media coverage but also the quality—that is, to analyze the content of the editorial to determine how positive, negative, or neutral it is. This will provide a road map for building a media plan and suggest if the company should become more proactive. On a more finite level, it might determine which reporters are most important and need special attention. Secondary research of this nature is now made easier because of Lexis/Nexis, the online information services, and media Web sites on the Internet.

To gain greater in-depth insight into how the company is perceived by the media, public relations people may want to talk directly to key reporters. These reporters may include not only target reporters from the major business magazines and metropolitan newspapers but also trade editors. Trade books that cover an industry in-depth are often the primary sources for general business news media who look to them for insights and inside information. Through these "soft soundings," public relations people not only learn what reporters think about a company and its products, but also how helpful the company is in answering questions, providing additional information, and making top management available to the media.

Tracking Uncontrolled Contacts

In the best of all possible worlds, the entirety of a brand's communications can be managed. Contacts we can't control, however, can often communicate powerfully. Consider the effect of the surgeon general's reports on smoking, the warnings about fats in fast-food and movie popcorn issued by the Center for Science in the Public Interest, a consumer advocacy group, or the protests of animal-rights activists opposed to the fur industry.

Public relations plays a vital role in bringing to bear those factors in the business environment that could significantly impact marketing success or failure by identifying critical emerging social, cultural, and political issues. Marketers may be too close to their products and too focused on crunching the numbers to understand threats unrelated to products benefits and competitive positioning. Those who are guilty of this kind of marketing tunnel vision may be blindsided by attacks from the likes of consumerists; social advocates; religious activists; elected local, state, and national officials and legislators; and regulators and attention-seeking politicians. Public relations plays the key role in controlling the damage by communicating industry's side of the story and recommending short-range actions and long-range strategic options that may be required.

Public relations may find it necessary to conduct secondary research to assess political, environmental, and societal factors that could impact marketing. Secondary research findings could suggest primary research such as focus groups or one-on-one interviews. This would certainly be called for in newsbreaking situations. For example, how great a threat to Disney films, parks, and products is a religious boycott arising from the company's benefits programs for gay employees or how great the threat of a boycott of Texaco products by minority consumers as a result of racial discrimination charges against company executives.

The Business Environment Situation

Public relations is especially important when identifying emerging issues that have not yet appeared on the marketer's radar screen. These early warning signals might necessitate developing a proactive strategy that attacks the issue on the grass-roots or government level. The new knowledge may require a modification in marketing planning or product positioning to avoid potentially serious problems that can befall the otherwise best-laid marketing plans. It may mean correcting politically incorrect advertising that offends some consumers. Public relations people can help companies avoid errors of judgment that may cause irreparable damage or take years to repair. Skillful handling of the Diet Pepsi tampering hoax quickly dissipated a potentially devastating marketing threat, but the public has yet to forget the Exxon *Valdez* incident of 1989.

Forrest Anderson, Senior Vice President of Research at Golin/Harris Communications, uses this checklist to identify factors in the business environment that could impact marketing success. These factors should be considered when preparing the situation analysis:

- Natural green/ecological environment
- Social/cultural environment
- Technological environment
- Political/regulatory environment
- Economic environment

    Macroworld, U.S. economic performance

    Microindustry, competitive economic performance

- Events
- Trends
- Constituent demands

Putting It Together: Identifying SWOTs

The public relations strategic platform is built from both primary and secondary sources. It may connect new information with new insights gleaned from old knowledge. Existing information may be reorganized to address business environmental issues of particular concern to public relations.

A particularly valuable tool in analyzing the situation is a SWOT analysis. A model widely used in marketing, a SWOT analysis defines the company's (or brand's) Strengths and Weaknesses and its Opportunities and Threats.

Strengths are what a company does best in relation to its competitors. Weaknesses are restrictions to what can be accomplished. Opportunities are situations where the company's strengths and other external factors can be leveraged in addressing the problem stated in the public relations plan. Threats are situations that may adversely impact the company's ability to address the problem.

Primary and secondary research is used to identify competitive advantages by recognizing how to leverage Strengths, dampen Weaknesses, avoid the Threats and capture the Opportunities, according to Clarke Caywood, Chair of the IMC Department at Northwestern University. The particular strength of public relations and its opportunity to significantly impact marketing planning lies in its ability to assess external threats, particularly social, political, legal, and cultural threats that are quite distinct from internal strengths and weaknesses. Caywood flips the swot model into what he has labeled the tows model. This inverts the importance of Threats and Opportunities in keeping with the IMC principle of substituting "outside-in" thinking for "inside-out" thinking.

Prioritizing brand strengths and weaknesses and marketplace threats and opportunities is the first step to building an integrated strategy.

Developing an integrated strategy requires a restatement of integrated business goals and objectives. The IMC plan defines the role of all channels of communication in achieving these goals and objectives.

CHAPTER 28

Step Two: Setting MPR Objectives

MARKETING PUBLIC RELATIONS PLANS SHOULD ALWAYS BE CONSIDERED A PART OF the master integrated marketing plan. They must relate specifically to the achievement of marketing objectives.

Marketing objectives describe what needs to be done to reach sales goals. They are specific and measurable and address what will be accomplished.

Both trade and consumer audiences figure importantly in the development of marketing objectives.

If the product is sold at retail, the first and most important step of the marketing plan is to establish trade marketing objectives. Specific objectives for new and existing trade customers must be reached before consumer objectives can be achieved. The product must not only be in the store, but it must be displayed and merchandised to maximum advantage. In recent years, mass merchandisers, supermarket chains, and other large retailers have become increasingly dominant players in determining product success.

Consumer marketing objectives for introducing new products are expressed in terms of percent of trial (and, for low-ticket consumables, repeat sales) among the target audience over a given period of time, usually one year.

If the product is not new, consumer marketing objectives affecting both current users and new users should be considered. Typically, objectives for products in growth categories specify desired increase in usage by current users in the time period covered by the plan. In the case of mature products, the objectives may be to maintain usage or to prevent decline.

Marketing objectives may be stated in terms of percent of increased trial by new users (and in the case of consumables, maintaining an established level of repeat sales) for the plan period. Another objective may be to reach specified sales levels for defined secondary-market consumers.

Advertising and Public Relations Objectives: Similarities and Stumbling Blocks

Marketing public relations objectives are quite similar to advertising objectives in that both seek to build awareness of the product. In their book *How to Write a Successful Marketing Plan*, Roman Hiebing Jr., and Scott Cooper succinctly state the reason: "You must increase share of mind before you can increase share of market."[1]

Increasing awareness is the first step. But to be truly successful, communications must positively affect attitudes and cause consumers to act. Hiebing and Cooper point out that in the majority of situations, advertising alone cannot make the sale. (The exception is direct-response advertising, including direct mail, which is why some proponents of integrated marketing have become so enamored with database marketing.) Hiebing and Cooper believe that causing behavioral change, i.e., sales, should be stated as a marketing objective rather than as an advertising objective. It follows that sales should not be seen as a public relations objective.

While it may not be possible to state advertising or public relations objectives in sales terms, research can be used to measure increases in awareness and positive attitude formation.

As marketing campaigns become more integrated and seamless, however, these measures of the effectiveness of the various components of the marketing mix become more difficult to measure. Increased awareness and predisposition to buy may be influenced by a number of factors that include, but are not limited to, advertising or public relations.

Realistic expectations of advertising cited by Hiebing and Cooper that also apply to public relations are building recognition, creating a positive image, differentiating the product from the competition, building store traffic, introducing new products and product improvements, announcing promotions, and, in the case of business-to-business products, generating customer leads and opening doors for the sales force.

Because the objectives of advertising and public relations are so similar, it is often difficult to isolate their relative effectiveness. There may be more reluctance to conduct research that specifically measures public relations effectiveness for two reasons. One is that in a well-executed integrated program, it is near to impossible to determine where the public relations ends and the advertising begins and vice versa. The other is that marketers are more apt to spend on measuring the effects of advertising than public relations because of their relative budget allocations. Research might represent a small percent of total advertising expense while it may represent a disproportionate percent of total public relations expense.

Marketers, unfamiliar with public relations, who insist on knowing "how many cases did it move?" should be reminded that neither advertising nor PR can, in most cases, be measured in relation to the overall success or failure to reach marketing objectives and, in turn, sales goals.

Some cases exist, where advertising, public relations, or promotion are the only factors at work in the marketplace, but they are extremely rare. Overemphasis on the effectiveness of a single component in the marketing mix does not take into account key other-than-communications factors such as product quality, availability, and consumer satisfaction.

Public Relations Versus Publicity Objectives

While the seamlessness of IMC and the expense of measuring public relations results may make it difficult to quantify broad public relations objectives, quantifiable publicity objectives can more easily be established and measured. It should always be emphasized that publicity is one of a vast array of public relations tactics that can be employed in a marketing public relations program. But if generating exposure in the media is a high priority, as it is for many PR programs, publicity objectives can be established in lieu of or in addition to overall PR objectives.

Publicity objectives should take into account both the media through which the marketing message will be transmitted and the target audience reached by the media. The importance of "big hits" in mass media should not be underestimated, particularly for mass-marketed products. No matter how targeted the audience, chances are that it will be reached by the mass media, i.e., network news, news and general-interest magazines, and national newspapers. While "demassification" may be used by some as rationalization for moving away from mass-media advertising, the practical reason may be as simple as the high cost of buying time and space in mass media and the waste involved. On the other hand, cost is a minor factor in media relations and waste in reaching nontarget markets is no problem. Perhaps it may even be a plus, for significant numbers of nontarget consumers may become interested in buying products they read about or hear about in an editorial context.

Thus, publicity objectives may be more sharply focused on reaching consumers through specific media vehicles. When I managed agency public relations programs, for example, we often established both gross audience objectives and certain specified target audience objectives. For instance, one objective may have been to achieve positive media exposure for Campbell's soups in media with a total gross impressions of 200 million. Another objective may have been to place one or two stories about the nutritional value of soup in publications that are read by the most health-conscious consumers such as *Prevention, Self,* and *American Health.*

The relevance of reaching readers of these niche magazines is fourfold: (1) contribution to gross impressions, (2) direct reach to a specified lifestyle target audience, (3) reach to an audience of influentials whose expertise is sought by others, and (4) influence on the editorial agenda of general news and feature media who read the specialized books for story ideas and material.

Publicity objectives should match specific target markets assigned to public relations in the marketing plan. It may be determined, for example, that media exposure should be increased in certain key geographical markets. This might result in intensified local media placement efforts or the creation of local media events. Likewise, public relations may be assigned to specifically reach target ethnic markets that would otherwise be reached only through nonethnic specific general advertising. Likewise, public relations may be employed to extend the reach and credibility of ethnic advertising. In all cases, realistic publicity goals may be set, based not only on gross audience numbers but also on numbers of specifically targeted consumers reached.

CHAPTER 29

Step Three: Developing MPR Strategy

AFTER MARKETING OBJECTIVES ARE ESTABLISHED, IT IS TIME TO ADDRESS THE MOST critical and difficult element of the marketing planning process—the development of a marketing strategy. Strategies explain how quantifiable objectives will be reached. They should take into consideration target primary and/or secondary markets; national, regional, and local emphases; specific competitive situations; seasonal considerations; and timing.

These strategic considerations are critical in developing the advertising, promotion, and marketing public relations components of the marketing plan. Input from all these key players is, of course, important up front in establishing the overall strategy. Public relations people complain that they have often been left out of the strategic planning process. Because of the unique insight they bring about factors beyond demographics and psychographics that affect consumer attitudes and behavior, early input from PR can have important influence on marketing strategies.

One of the principles of integrated marketing is zero-based marketing planning. While advertising may well become the centerpiece of the plan, an advertising solution cannot be assumed. The question is how to most efficiently and effectively reach consumers (and the trade) and cause them to act. The answer may well be a communications mix with each of the principal components assigned the role that it is uniquely positioned to play.

Strategic development is the most basic and the most difficult step in the integrated communications process. It is much easier said than done. I have been reminded of this by my experience as a teacher of integrated marketing. Bright graduate students and marketing communications professionals alike often fail to draw the distinction between developing strategy and creating tactics. Inevitably, they want to cut to the chase and move directly into tactics.

The business of hammering out a strategy is hard work. But only after a clear strategy is developed is it possible to determine how the principal components such as advertising, promotion, direct marketing, and public relations will work together to achieve the objectives of the campaign. Only then can specific tasks be assigned to each of these disciplines so that their combined efforts are mutually reinforcing and so that all important audiences are reached most effectively.

The late Ron Kaatz, one of the most insightful communications authorities, referred to advertising, public relations, and the rest as "message delivery systems." He said that "as companies seek to maximize their marketing productivity, they must develop strategies that consider every media opportunity that can effectively maintain contact with their current customers and communicate with new prospects. These strategies must focus on both the traditional and nontraditional message delivery options. These strategies must also zero in on the time when, the place where, and the environment in which a brand can most effectively impact the consumer. An effective message delivery strategy gets into the mind of the consumer, is based on a solid set of predetermined planning criteria, and applies these criteria in evaluating every media possibility."[1]

Each message delivery system has its own strengths and weaknesses. Advertising allows you to choose your media and control your message. But consumers perceive it as self-serving. One of the earliest definitions of advertising is salesmanship in print. That was amended to salesmanship in print and broadcast when radio and then television became major advertising media. Now there is nothing wrong with salesmanship, but the antenna goes up when consumers know that somebody is trying to sell them something that they may or may not want to buy. Consumer skepticism has become a national pastime, and advertising messages are questioned, discounted, or ignored more than ever before. That includes messages delivered directly to consumers that our databases tell us should be most receptive. Direct-mail authorities admit that if you don't capture the consumer's attention within twelve seconds, you are dead. The same is true of database-qualified consumers reached via telemarketing. I would be wealthier than Bill Gates if I had a dollar for every time a consumer cuts off or hangs up on an unwanted call from a telemarketer trying to get him or her to change his or her long-distance service.

Publicity, like advertising, has its weaknesses. The principal one is that you cannot control the media or dictate the words and pictures. Media gatekeepers may not believe that your news is something their audience can use. On the other hand, when they decide to feature your product, the message is more credible precisely because they believe that your news will be of interest to their readers, listeners, or viewers. The appeal of publicity is that news stories and features seem more authentic to consumers than ads do.

Developing an IMC strategy requires a restatement of integrated business goals and objectives. The plan for how to achieve these goals and objectives defines the role of all channels of communication.

The role of public relations should be precisely defined and plotted on the marketing timetable. In the case of a new product introduction, for example, PR may be the initial trade and/or consumer contact point. The role of public relations in reaching influentials, including industry analysts, key media, and early adapters, should be detailed in the master marketing plan. Because media advertising budgets are often concentrated against narrowly defined target markets and database marketing against individual consumers, it may be decided to use public relations to reach specific target audiences that could not be reached cost-effectively through other marketing means. The special role assigned to PR may be to reach important secondary markets, defined demographically, psychographically, regionally, or ethnically. Special public relations efforts aimed at these markets can produce significant incremental sales beyond the target market. Women buy cars. Some men buy their own clothes. Ethnic audiences may be more brand loyal and therefore desirable to address with a specific PR effort to maintain their loyalty. Many seniors have more disposable income and time to shop and the desire to buy many of the same products as younger consumers do. That's an observation drawn from personal experience.

The MPR Strategy: Options and Opportunities

The marketing public relations strategy provides a broad, planned approach to addressing the marketing problem/opportunity identified in the situation analysis and to achieving marketing public relations objectives.

The strategic role of MPR in integrated marketing plans should be examined in terms of how to best:

- Design the marketing timetable so that opinion leaders, including professionals, industry analysts, trade audiences, and influential media, are reached well in advance of the public.

- Maximize the news value of new product introductions, new advertising campaigns, and event sponsorships.

- Time public relations events to reinforce advertising/promotion campaigns and/or to maintain high visibility between campaigns.

- Reach important secondary markets, defined demographically and/or psychographically, geographically, and ethnically, that might not be targeted by advertising or promotion.

I have identified three distinct kinds of MPR strategies. Let's consider each.

MPR Strategy I: Supplementary/Complementary

Public relations draws a distinction between the delivery of supplementary and complementary messages that is, on the surface, at odds with the integrated marketing theory. In their book, *Integrated Marketing Communications*, Don E. Schultz, Stanley Tannenbaum, and Robert R. Lauterborn emphatically state that IMC campaigns must be focused on one key benefit that can motivate the consumer to buy your product rather than the competitor's. That single benefit must solve a consumer problem or better the consumer's way of life and must be stated in a single sentence. ("Sanka tastes better than any other instant coffee"; "Holiday Inn gives you a better night's sleep than any other motel.")

Because public relations deals with information and education rather than salesmanship and sloganeering, a practical problem must be overcome for PR to be used effectively to supplement that specific consumer benefit. That is, PR will need to substantiate the claim with factual information. This might be accomplished, for example, by citing consumer research that found that a majority of consumers agreed with the proposition. Public relations events may be created that demonstrate the benefit and publicity may be generated that reference it. But it may not be realistic to expect media and other gatekeepers to use the same words expressed in the competitive claim, much less the advertising slogans through which it is communicated to the consumer.

McDonald's used a supplementary strategy in introducing its Arch Deluxe. The public relations–driven campaign found Ronald McDonald participating in various high-visibility national media events reaching the target adult audience. The PR effort supplemented the introductory commercials featuring Ronald but it was understood that the editorial side would not carry the "hamburger with the grown-up taste" ad copy verbatim.

One of the most important roles that public relations can play is to deliver complementary messages to different audiences. The key benefit to the target audience may not be the benefit that will attract secondary audiences to your product. The benefit of aspirin to the target audience may be to relieve headaches, but for older consumers it may be to prevent heart attacks and strokes.

MPR Strategy II: News/Borrowed-Interest Strategy

The news/borrowed-interest strategic option applies to publicity-centered public relations programs.

Public relations is uniquely capable of dramatizing product news. New product news represents the best and most-frequently used opportunity to use a news strategy but not the only one. A new feature of an old product, a new model of a favorite car, a new flavor of ice cream or soup, new bells and whistles of all sorts can make news. It should always be remembered that Windows 95 was basically a software upgrade. A newly discovered benefit of a familiar product may provide another optimal news opportunity, particularly if the benefit is health-related.

When there is really nothing new to say about a product or the product category is of very low interest, a borrowed-interest strategy is called for. There is not much new to say about Coca-Cola, but Coke's sponsorship of the Olympic Torch Relay was designed to generate high media visibility in local and national media. A low-interest news category such as mufflers can be made newsworthy when Midas sponsors a systemwide public service effort like Project Safe Baby. The Glad Bag-A-Thon year after year generates positive brand exposure for a low-interest product category—trash bags—in communities throughout the country.

MPR Strategy III: Push-Pull-Pass

Every marketer is familiar with push and pull strategies. As defined by Philip Kotler they are:

> A push strategy calls for using the sales force and trade promotion to push the product through the channels. The producer aggressively promotes the product to wholesalers; the wholesalers aggressively promote the product to consumers.
>
> A pull strategy calls for spending a lot of money on advertising and consumer promotion to build up consumer demand. If the strategy is effective, consumers will ask their retailers for the product, the retailers will ask their wholesalers for the product, and the wholesalers will ask producers for the product.

With retailers increasingly becoming the initiators as much as the recipients of manufacturer marketing programs, the distinctions are becoming blurred and now most marketing plans address both the consumer and the trade. Public relations is also increasingly playing a role in devising strategies to enlist dealer and wholesaler enthusiasm. Take the beer business, for example. With the proliferation of brands from the major breweries and scores of regional and microbreweries, the key to success is to grab distributor attention.

In my 1991 book, *The Marketer's Guide to Public Relations*, I coined the term *pass* to describe an option required by modern megamarketing. Success or failure in the marketplace may be determined by factors that have little to do with the quality of the product, the need or want it fills, or the effectiveness of the marketing communications campaign. There may be a need to win over or at least neutralize opposition to products from many quarters. These range from consumer watchdog groups, environmentalists, government regulators, religious-interest groups opposed to company policies, politicians trying to grab headlines and score points with voters by attacking well-known companies—and more. These societal gatekeepers are often aided by media looking for a story. The proliferation of *60 Minutes* type of newsmagazine shows on television may have a huge impact on marketing success. For example, as this is written, there have been a number of highly publicized attacks on clothing retailers and shoe marketers whose products are made overseas. Names make news and the Kathie Lee Gifford clothing line and the use of big-name spokespersons such as Nike's top celebrity endorser, Michael Jordan, feed the media.

The opposition of societal gatekeepers may block entry to or otherwise negatively impact the marketplace. These potential threats need to be identified in the situation analysis or as they arise unexpectedly during the plan year. Clearly they need to be addressed in the public relations strategic plan.

Choosing the Right Strategic Option or Combination of Options

Each of these three strategic options: Supplementary/Complementary; News/Borrowed-Interest; Push/Pull/Pass is concerned with a different dimension of the marketing plan, but they are not mutually exclusive. For example, a strategy may be supplementary if it reinforces the same marketing message to the same target market as the advertising and promotion. It may be based on news such as the introduction of a new product. And a "pull" public relations effort may be employed to build up consumer demand. On the other hand, the MPR campaign may employ more than one of the options. It may also be assigned to reach secondary markets with complementary messages, use special events to precede or follow a major news announcement, and employ strategies that reach the trade and inform employees and special-interest groups as well as consumers. The exercise of defining the strategic options is critical. All relevant options that address your public relations objectives should be considered.

CHAPTER 30

Step Four: Marketing Public Relations Tactics

TACTICS ARE THE METHODS, ACTIONS, AND ACTIVITIES USED TO ACHIEVE OBJECTIVES. They translate the directives of strategies into specific programs. When writing the marketing public relations plan, the tactics recommended should relate specifically to each strategy. The plan should specify what activities will take place, who will do them, when they will be done, and at what cost. The integrated marketing plan should incorporate the public relations timetable into an overall marketing planning calendar that details when which tactics will be executed in the marketplace. The budget needed to execute these tactics needs to be incorporated into the total marketing budget. The MPR program and budget must be an integral part of the marketing plan from day one rather than an afterthought requiring additional funding, or worse yet, moving funds from already allocated activities.

Tactics are the payoff of all the strategic planning that precedes them. The best strategic plans will succeed only if the tactics capture the attention of target market individuals. The importance of tactics cannot be overemphasized. All other things being equal, they make all the difference in the world. That is particularly true in this age of parity products. Advil was more effectively able to present its case for ibuprofen than Nuprin, an identical product introduced simultaneously. Nike's brilliant image advertising has made all the difference in the sneaker wars with Reebok. The company is selling not shoes but a lifestyle.

"Just Do It!" isn't about product benefits. It is about being the kind of person who wears Nikes.

Likewise, it is creativity that makes the best marketing public relations plans work. MPR tactics may not be so intrusive as commercials nor can they depend on pure imagery. The challenge to gain attention is even greater when the tactics are designed to generate media coverage or reach consumers directly.

As a former public relations agency principal, I have long been aware that clients, above all else, look to their public relations firm to come up with "the big idea." It was no surprise to me that clients participating in my annual public relations survey put creativity at the top of the list when asked what criteria they consider most important in selecting a new public relations firm. It's no wonder. With the exception of true breakthrough products, few products are able to command much media attention on their own. The world would have little noted nor long remembered most of the products discussed in this book if they had not utilized creative marketing public relations tactics.

Public relations offers the marketer more tactical options than any other component of the integrated marketing mix. Advertising, by definition, communicates through paid media. Its tactical options are limited to buying space for ads in print or outdoor media and time for commercials in broadcast media. The principal vehicles for direct-response advertising are direct mail and telemarketing. The creativity comes in the execution (and sometimes in the media selection).

Public relations, on the other hand, can be creative in the selection and use of a wide array of tactics to reach target audiences.

Opportunities in Cyberspace

Over the years, I have compiled a list of the tactics used in public relations programs. The list has more than doubled since I wrote "MPR Tactics—A to Z" in *The Marketer's Guide to Public Relations* in 1991. There are also new hybrid tactics that combine event marketing, promotion, and public relations. With integrated marketing, the distinctions are blurring.

One of the exciting things about public relations is that the list of tactics will continue to evolve, reflecting the creativity of its practitioners, new advances in technology, and new emphasis on reaching target individuals one-on-one as well as target groups through the media.

The advent of new technology has added a number of exciting new tactical options. The first scientific survey of the use of the Internet conducted late in 1995 by Nielsen Media Research revealed that thirty-seven million people, or 17 percent of the population of the United States and Canada, had access to the Net. On the average, those users spent nearly five-and-a-half hours a week online. Clearly that number will have increased geometrically by the time you read this.[1]

Use of the Internet and the World Wide Web for marketing purposes is, at this writing, in its infancy. It remains to be seen who will control content on the Net and how they will do it. The enormous potential of cyberspace has been recognized by both advertising agencies and public relations firms. Ad agencies see the Net as selling in space. Public relations firms see it as a way to communicate a vast amount of corporate and product information to target audiences. John Weckenmann, managing director for technology and telecommunications practice at Burson-Marsteller, the world's largest public relations firm, points out that "it's a medium that is custom-designed for PR because it is heavily oriented toward content." He told *Interactive PR* that "content is key and public relations professionals have always been content-driven as opposed to other marketing disciplines."[2]

The uses of marketing public relations in cyberspace are burgeoning. At this writing, literally hundreds of thousands of business Web sites exist, providing layer upon layer of product information directly to self-selected consumers and, importantly for public relations, to the media. Reporters, once dependent on clippings and microfilm, can now access all they need to trace a company story on the Internet from text of published articles and the company's file of press releases, past and present. They can also find out what competitors are doing by accessing their Web sites and what consumers are saying in newsgroups and chat rooms.

Live news conferences have been supplemented by teleconferences, video-conferences, and online interviews. "Media in Cyberspace," a 1996 study conducted by the Columbia University School of Journalism and Middleberg & Associates, found that almost one quarter of editors said that they or their staff use the Internet or online service daily. Seventy-one percent of newspaper reporters said they used online services at the time. The number continues to grow as young computer-savvy reporters replace old-school newspeople. They are using the Net to research articles, to contact sources by e-mail, to download data, and to read online publications, find new sources, check out newsgroups, and receive press releases.[3]

Time magazine points out how online information is changing the way we process news. "While journalists are in the communications business, that communication has been mostly one way: from the top down. Online media is about one person communicating to many—and many communicating back. It's about community building rather than simple 'publishing.'"[4]

MSNBC, the joint venture of Microsoft and NBC, offers a new kind of media outlet as do the cybereditions of traditional media including daily newspapers and newsmagazines. Virtually every major newspaper and news program now offers an online edition. At this writing, there were 700 American newspapers on the Net. In 1996, Microsoft began "publishing" *Slate,* the first online-only magazine.

A survey conducted for Creamer Dickson Basford, a leading public relations firm, as part of the 1995 Thomas L. Harris/Impulse Research Public Relations Agency Survey found that the three top ways public relations were using cyberspace were to access news wires, newspapers, and other news services; to communicate with members of the press who are online; and to release information directly to the public. More than 60 percent of PR professionals surveyed also indicated that they recognized the information-gathering and research potential of interactive information services: accessing marketing or competitive information; monitoring the online buzz about their company and products; and conducting surveys online.

Monita Buchwald, Managing Director of M/NET, the interactive public relations service of Manning, Selvage & Lee, predicts that the term *interactive communication* is going to become redundant because as companies become more comfortable with information technology, traditional one-way communication between business and customers will become a thing of the past.[5]

Larry Weber, CEO of the Weber Group, a public relations firm that specializes in high technology, predicted in 1996 that "the Web will change PR forever within the next ten years and will serve as the core of media relations." *Washington Post* reporter Kara Swisher told *O'Dwyer's PR Services Report* that the Internet will become as pervasive a medium as print, TV, and radio—and one day may surpass these traditional vehicles because "it mixes TV, radio, and print, all in one space and gives you instant interactivity."[6]

Looking into the future from Redmond, Washington, home of Microsoft, *New York Times* drama critic turned columnist Frank Rich comments, "For all the technological innovations of the explosive computer industry, it is the still-embryonic culture being dreamed up in our new Hollywoods, whether here or in Silicon Valley or downtown New York, that will transform American life as surely as the old Hollywood did with *The Jazz Singer* (the first "talkie") exactly seventy years ago."

But don't count on the early demise of traditional media. Rather than replacing traditional media, online media are more likely to become another, albeit particularly attractive media alternative, to at least some marketers. Radio didn't disappear when TV became the rage. It is still the medium of choice of drivers. At home, most Americans are still spending seven hours a day watching television and advertisers are spending more bucks than ever buying TV time. The number of cable channels continues to proliferate. Most cable-ready homes now receive up to fifty channels and those with the satellite dish receive many more. There is still talk of 500-channel TV.

The growth of cable has opened tremendous new opportunities for marketing public relations. The success of CNN and *Headline News* has led to another twenty-four-hour news network, Fox News Channel, as well as MSNBC. Two cable channels, CNBC and CNNfn, specialize in business news. Other MPR opportunities exist with networks as diverse as MTV (for youth-oriented products and attractions) and ESPN (for merchandise endorsed by sports stars) and such specialized channels as the Golf Channel and the Food Channel reaching niche audiences. An ever-widening array of magazines published for niche audiences feature product news.

In a 1996 critical appraisal of the Web as seen in the context of how earlier media achieved critical mass, the *New York Times* concluded that "the Web incorporates elements of the various print and electronic media that have preceded it. And yet, the Web is poised not to replace its predecessors but to take a place alongside them as a social, cultural, and economic force in its own right."[7]

MPR Tactical Alphabet

Let's review some of the tactics now being used in marketing public relations programs. Elsewhere in the book, you will find detailed accounts of how many of these tactics have been used in the most successful MPR programs of recent years.

Advertising. Advertising used as a public relations tactic to support special events or contests, announce or honor award winners, or support causes. Op-ed page advertising was created specifically to present the company or industry positions that impact marketing. Most important, public relations advertising can be used to reassure consumers about product safety and efficacy during a crisis situation.

Arts and Entertainment Sponsorships. Corporate or brand sponsorship of art exhibits and the performing arts are growing in prominence with the reduction of government support of the arts. They offer an opportunity to reach customers and influential business leaders in a noncommercial environment. Most major exhibitions and an increasing number of concert, dance, and theatrical series and events, as well as public television and radio productions, are now made possible by corporate grants. Prominent supporters of arts and entertainment include automotive companies, airlines, telecommunication companies, technology companies, financial-services companies, oil companies, and tobacco companies. Sponsorship of pop and rock concerts by youth-oriented product companies have proliferated since Jovan, a men's fragrance, broke the commercial barrier by sponsoring a Rolling Stones tour.

Awards. Brand-sponsored awards that support brand positioning and leadership. The perception is that the brand sponsoring the awards is the leader that preempts competition. Frequently used in such industries as apparel industry (best dressed) or health/beauty (most beautiful lips) but also used for broader public relations purposes honoring teachers, community service leaders, and heroes and heroines.

Example: Sara Lee Corporation's Front Runner Awards honor women in the arts, humanities, business, and government who have dramatically changed the world by donating $25,000 to a non-for-profit women's organization selected by each recipient.

Birthdays and Anniversaries. The use of significant brand birthdays to reinforce brand loyalty often can be used to announce product improvements, new sizes, new packaging, new flavors, or line extensions. Particularly effective with longtime favorite products. Opportunity to use archival advertising and nostalgia to gain media attention and consumer involvement.

Examples: Swanson's fortieth anniversary of the TV dinner, Tide's fiftieth birthday doings, and Crayola's ninetieth anniversary celebration as described in this book.

Booklets and Brochures. Brand-sponsored printed material that provides consumers with useful information as opposed to product sales literature. Information is usually but not always related to product use or the interests and lifestyles of target consumers.

Examples: Dirty Secrets and Clean Facts: The Wisk Laundry Guide. Numerous company-sponsored booklets feature recipes, nutrition information, freezing and food preparation, exercise and sports instruction, child care, pet care, and disease prevention and treatment.

Books. Publications that bring attention to companies, including authorized company histories and autobiographies of company leaders and their vision for the future. Also brand-titled references, how-to, or cookbooks that reinforce a company's expertise.

Examples: The Road Ahead (Bill Gates); *Ben & Jerry's: The Inside Scoop* (former president Fred "Chico" Lager); *Made in America: My Story* (Sam Walton); *Iacocca* (Lee Iacocca); *Grinding It Out* (Ray Kroc); Betty Crocker and Campbell soup cookbooks.

B-roll. Video supplementary or backup material. It is now standard practice to include B-roll with edited video news releases to give TV editors material to build their own stories. It might include file footage of production line and products in use; interviews with celebrity spokespersons and directors of new commercials; outtakes and "making of" commercials; company spokespersons and industry analysts commenting on new products as well as special-event coverage.

By-line Stories. Articles written by company executives in general business publications and trade books serving their industry. Also, newspaper op-ed pages offer opportunities to present company or industry points of view to influence public opinion or legislation impacting marketing.

Cause-Related Marketing. Corporate or brand support of causes based on product sales or transactions. May be either a marketing or public relations strategy or a combination with public relations identifying and working with the organization to be supported. Publicity support includes planning of media events, issuing sponsorship announcements, updates and results, and gaining editorial endorsement.

Example: Drackett's sponsorship of a program to clean and restore national monuments by donating a percentage of sales was supported by a publicity campaign with TV actor and outdoorsman Corbin Bernsen as spokesperson.

CD-ROM (Compact Disc, Read Only Memory). Optical discs and computer software are beginning to be used in place of or in addition to traditional printed public relations materials to communicate with both the media and consumers. The combination of text, graphics, video, and sound adds dimension and excitement to the kinds of material traditionally used in press kits, booklets, and brochures.

Example: Plank Road Brewing Company was among the first to distribute a supplementary CD-ROM press kit when it introduced Red Dog Beer in 1995. ABC television has replaced traditional paper press kits with CD-ROMs that contain all the information of press kits, photographs, bios, and press releases. Parent company Disney also now packages press information, video scenes, sound bites, and high-resolution photographs from its new films on CD-ROM.

Celebrity Endorsements. Use of celebrities as company spokespersons in media and personal appearances. To be credible as media spokespersons, celebrities must have some expertise or real experience with the product. Celebrity appearances are also frequently used to build retail traffic or celebrities appear at company-sponsored events.

Examples: Celebrity chef demonstrates how to prepare a recipe; supermodel who is a makeup or fashion expert; celeb whose name is linked with a sponsored event.

CEOs. The top executive should be the company's most effective media spokesperson and salesperson. The CEO may personally announce an important new product, especially one that could significantly impact the company's financial performance. Philip Kotler, of Northwestern Kellogg School of Management, says more and more CEOs are recognizing that they are their companies' CEOs of marketing. Past masters include Chrysler's Lee Iacocca, Disney's Michael Eisner, and Microsoft's Bill Gates, who has appeared on more magazine covers than most movie stars.

Chotchke. Term for merchandise that carries a brand logo. Originally inexpensive items such as pins, pens, and key chains were given away or sold at company stores. Early examples were Oscar Mayer weiner whistles and Heinz pickle pins. Merchandise for some brands has become so popular that it is licensed for use on a wide variety of merchandise. They include wearables from baseball caps to jackets, sweatshirts and T-shirts; posters, mugs, and stuffed animals. Some companies, ranging from Disney and Warner Brothers to Harley Davidson, have their own retail outlets, while others, such as Ben & Jerry's, do a thriving mail-order business in company merchandise.

Contests and Competitions. The terms can be used interchangeably in most cases. Sponsored events involving athletic skills are competitions rather than contests. Contest sponsorship remains one of the most popular and effective public relations tactics both in terms of consumer involvement and media interest. Contests are brand-specific and invite consumers to compete on the basis of their knowledge, creativity, skills, or talents.

Examples: Arts-and-crafts contests depicting products or packages (Campbell soup and Coca-Cola contests described in this book); recipe contests (Pillsbury Bake-Off; Ways to Serve Bay's English Muffins); Pamper's "Pamper Your Baby" photo contest; Visa's "Olympics of the Imagination," an international art challenge for children to depict their ideas of the Olympic Games.

Critters. Company spokescharacters personalize companies and brands. They are identifiable, likable links to the consumer. Critters not only refer to animals such as Kellogg's Tony the Tiger and Nine Lives' Morris the Cat but to advertising creations like the Pillsbury Doughboy, M&M's, and the California Dancing Raisins, and human characters like Ronald McDonald, the Campbell Kids, and Ernie, the Keebler Elf. Their appearances at company-sponsored events assure brand identification in television news coverage and pictures in print media. They are also used at retail events such as supermarket openings.

Demonstrations. Product demonstrations on television and in person attract consumer attention and involve audiences with the product. Demonstrations are also used to attract buyer attention at trade shows. Some companies have set up demonstration sites to show what their products can do.

Examples: Bill Gates personally demonstrated Windows 95 to network and closed-circuit TV audiences. Demonstrations at cooking equipment and department stores and on television talk shows were used effectively by Cuisinart to create demand for food processors. Automotive companies and even computer companies have set up "test-drive" programs to give target customers advanced hands-on experience in the driver's seat. Apple computers conducted a demonstration project to show how a personal computer network could benefit an entire business community.

Direct Mail. Growing sophistication of databases has enhanced person-to-person communications for public relations purposes. The line between direct response used to sell products and services and dissemination of useful product information by public relations to raise awareness and maintain brand loyalty is blurred. Typical public relations uses are newsletters that disseminate scientific information to users of prescription or over-the-counter drugs and recipes to cooks who are heavy users of certain branded food products and information about new improvements in household products. Public relations also uses direct mail to keep brands top-of-mind and to provide new information to important influencers, who may range from home economists and nutritionists to hairdressers, bartenders, and auto mechanics.

Exhibits. Many companies maintain historical exhibits from their industry and of their products and advertising at company headquarters. "The World of Coca-Cola" is one of the most-visited attractions in Atlanta. Other companies maintain and update exhibits at major museums such as the Museum of Science and Industry in Chicago and major tourist attractions such as Epcot Center. Others periodically mount traveling exhibits assembled from their own and other collections. These exhibits are displayed at malls, libraries, civic centers, or at other high-traffic locations.

Fan Clubs. Some products inspire fandom. Companies recognizing the public relations value of these superfans have organized fan clubs and provided financial support to spontaneously formed fan clubs.

Examples: The Barbie Fan Club has played a significant role in maintaining high visibility for the best-selling toy of all time. Collectors of Swatches, Hummel figures, and Royal Doulton Character Jugs are so important that the companies produce special limited editions for fan club members. Fan clubs for the Ford Mustang and Harley motorcycles (HOG) are described elsewhere in the book.

Festivals. Companies in some fields regularly sponsor or participate in festivals celebrating various food and beverage items. Some even sponsor their own— Hershey's Chocolate Festival, for example. One company created its own traveling festival to celebrate its corporate culture—Ben & Jerry's One World, One Heart Festival.

Fun Facts. Collection of trivia that feature writers can have fun with in telling your company story.

Examples: The average man spends 3,350 hours—or 140 days of his life—shaving and he grows twenty-seven feet of facial hair in a lifetime (courtesy of Gillette). The number of Sucrets sore throat lozenges produced in the past twenty-nine years would circle the world around the poles almost five-and-one-quarter times.

Grand Openings. Grand openings have been used to focus attention on new stores, hotels, plants, and corporate headquarters. In highly competitive markets, department stores are staging ever more elaborate events, including black-tie vip charity benefits featuring big-name entertainers and celebrities. Customer and other databases are used to identify best customers and community movers and shakers to invite. Less elaborate grand opening events are routinely staged at supermarkets, mass merchandisers, and restaurants featuring bands, balloons, spokescharacters, giveaways, and special prices.

Graphs and Charts. These elements are increasingly being used by the print media and on television to present marketing-related information such as market share, audience share, and consumer research findings. The use of charts and graphs has been accelerated by computer graphics and the trend to make newspapers more user-friendly.

Green Marketing. Environmental initiatives can enhance corporate reputation and win support from activists, environmentally conscious consumers, and the media. A distinction should be made between environmentally safe product claims and proactive programs that benefit the environment such as the use of recycled and biodegradable packaging materials.

Examples: McDonald's replaces polystyrene packaging with paper; dolphin-free tuna.

Guideline Kits. Comprehensive how-to-do-it informational packages prepared by organizations to help branch offices, dealers, distributors, franchisees, volunteers, etc., adapt national public relations programs to their markets.

Examples: Glad Bag-A-Thon; Midas Project Safe Baby; McDonald's All-American Basketball.

Hot Lines. Free telephone connection for consumers to call companies to receive information and advice on product use or to discuss product problems. Calls are personally handled in most cases, but advances in technology have made it possible to provide answers to a variety of frequently asked questions via recorded messages. Many companies enter caller information in their database so that customers can be informed about future products and developments.

Example: The Butterball Turkey Talk-Line that dispenses advice on how to cook a turkey is described in this book.

Interviews. One-on-one interviews with the media enable companies to communicate with stakeholders. Many proactive public relations programs aggressively schedule interviews for company spokespersons with editors, reporters, commentators, and talk-show hosts. When the media initiates the interview, public relations advice, in most cases, is to be accessible to the media and to present the company position positively and accurately and to attempt to control damage in negative or crisis situations.

Junkets. Used when there is an advantage to taking the reporter to the story rather than the story to the reporter. Junkets are free trips to out-of-town locations. Often used in the travel industry, by other industries whose operations are in remote locations, and to maximize media coverage of special events. Some media do not accept junkets and pay their own way to cover the story.

Largest, Longest, Most. Tried-and-true tactic to gain media attention. If you build it, they will come and cover it, especially if it's a candidate for *The Guinness Book of Records.*

Examples: World's largest cheesecake served at the opening of Eli's cheesecake factory; world's largest (inflatable) hamburger unveiled at the introduction of McDonald's Arch Deluxe in Los Angeles; world's largest greeting card; longest kiss; most wonderful pet.

Mat Releases. Material for newspapers delivered in camera-ready format. Mats are used for new-product news stories, feature stories, pictorial features, byline columns, and editorials. The material is particularly suitable for weekly and community newspapers. Mat release services now distribute material on compact discs and have Web sites from which reporters can download mat material.

Media Tours. Company spokesperson tours of major markets for the purpose of obtaining publicity in local media. The spokesperson may be a company expert, an outside authority, or a celebrity. Typically, the spokesperson is booked on various local radio shows, and local television news and talk shows, and is interviewed by newspapers and other local or regional publications. The spokesperson may also make local personal appearances that are covered by the media; for example, book signings or appearances at local events. In recent years, many marketers have supplemented or replaced traditional media tours with satellite media tours where the spokesperson is interviewed from one location on a prearranged schedule by television reporters in a number of key markets. Celebrity or executive interviews can also be offered online.

Milestones. Like birthdays and anniversaries, company occasions—such as the production of the ten-billionth can of Campbell's tomato soup, the 100-billionth Crayola crayon, the 100th birthday of Jell-O—offer opportunities for special events and promotions and updating the company's success story.

News Conferences. Used to announce significant information about the company to the news media. In marketing public relations, used most frequently to announce important new products, event sponsorships, or ad campaigns. Venue may be company headquarters, news centers such as New York City and Washington, D.C., or cities where important trade shows are held. News conference implies both print and broadcast media. "Press conferences" applies primarily to print media.

Newsgroups. Newsgroups, chat groups, and chat rooms all describe Internet forums where people discuss subjects of common interest. There are newsgroups devoted to virtually every subject under the sun. They are used by companies to monitor what consumers are saying about their products and services and those of their competitors. They can also be used to participate directly in dialogue with consumers, answer their product questions, and respond to criticism.

Newsletters. Companies and trade groups have adapted the newsletter format to keep their products top-of-mind and communicate news and views to customers on a regular basis. Trade newsletters contain information about products, advertising, promotional and public relations support, and available point-of-sale material. Newsletters are also used to maintain contact directly with consumers identified by database as heavy users. They may combine useful information with coupons and response devices offering products directly to consumers.

News Releases. Remain the basic vehicle for transmitting news to the media. The news release (or press release) is written in journalistic news style covering who, what, when, where, and why, with the most important news at the top of the story. News releases are distributed at news conferences or transmitted to the media directly (delivered, mailed, faxed, e-mailed) or by commercial news wire services. Many companies now post their news releases on their Web sites.

Official Endorsements. Official recognition of a company or company-sponsored event by mayors, governors, city councils, or members of Congress. Often involves official proclamations. An official endorsement can attract media coverage and photo opportunities. When U.S. senators and representatives commend companies in the *Congressional Record*, reprints can be merchandised to customers and influencers.

Example: Mayors greet Dancing California Raisins in town to entertain handicapped children.

Online Services. Computer information service companies such as America Online make available text from a variety of traditional news sources such as online editions of newspapers, news magazines, and those created for computer publications and Internet sites. All these are outlets for communicating product and service information, features, and pictorials. The commercial online services look for "news you can use" angles to attract browsers.

Online Forums. Forums in which top management, marketing executives, and celebrity spokespersons and consumers can communicate with each other directly via a computer bulletin board system.

Parades. Parades offer companies a chance to gain positive exposure in an upbeat noncommercial environment. Company-sponsored floats and giant balloons featuring company advertising characters are popular ways to participate in nationally televised holiday parades.

Photographs. A picture may still be worth a thousand words when it comes to attracting reader attention. Editors know it and are always receptive to interesting photos of commercial subjects. The trend to make newspapers more reader-friendly extends opportunities for placing creative photos (and line art). While most magazine photos are shot by staff or contracted photographers, opportunities remain to place exceptional photos in a variety of consumer and trade publications. A good wire service photo may appear in hundreds of newspapers.

Photo Ops. The same applies to photo opportunities—situations set up to capture the attention of still photographers and TV camera operators looking for a visually interesting event or setting for a speech or personal appearance.

Plant Tours. Many companies have made their plants popular tourist destinations by designing special facilities for visitors to observe the manufacturing process. Plant tours are an excellent way to involve people and products. At the conclusion of most tours, there is usually an opportunity to sample or buy company products and branded merchandise.

Examples: Most brewery tours end with an opportunity to sample products in a taproom setting. Popular destination tourist attractions include the Ben & Jerry's ice cream plant in Waterbury, Vermont, and the Steuben tour at Corning Glassworks, Corning, New York.

Polls. A popular vote sponsored by a company or brand can involve the public and the media. Polls are promoted by publicity and ballots made available at the point of sale. Balloting also may be conducted by fax, phone, in malls, or online.

   Examples: Polling for which image of Elvis should be on a postage stamp, which color should be added to M&M's, and whether Betty should be a Flintstones vitamin are described in this book.

Press Kits. The basic package of publicity and promotional material that provides media with all the information they need to cover a story. Typically, the press kit includes news releases, fact sheets, feature stories, and photos. It might also include video news releases and B-roll, transparencies, sales literature, advertising proofs, audiotapes, diskettes, or CD-ROMs.

Press Parties. A variation of a news conference, the press party may be used to dramatize a product launch, company milestone, or event sponsorship. The announcement is made in a festive atmosphere over cocktails, lunch, or dinner in a favored or unusual location. Editors and reporters receive mementos of the occasion in addition to press kits and have the opportunity to meet company executives and celebrity endorsers.

Product Placement. Placement of products in movies and on television shows. Sometimes the product is used for authenticity. Sometimes it becomes integral to the plot, from E.T.'s following a trail of Reese's Pieces to using a Coca-Cola can in *Independence Day* to demonstrate how to deactivate an alien spaceship. Sometimes it's just for fun, like the arches of a Stone Age McDonald's that proclaim "Over 10 dozen sold" in *The Flintstones.* Some products such as cars are exchanged for exposure to millions of moviegoers. Other companies provide edibles and drinkables to the crew for months of shooting. Still others are exchanged for promotional consideration. Supporting a hit movie can benefit both the product and the film.

   Example: Disney and McDonald's have a long-term agreement to offer special merchandise featuring characters from new films and available only at McDonald's.

Public Service Announcements (PSAs). PSAs are television and radio messages that are run free of charge by stations in public service time. Some marketers find ways to tie in with nonprofit organizations to produce messages that serve the public interest. Others underwrite the production of PSAs for nonprofit organizations. For example, a pharmaceutical company may produce public service messages for professional medical societies in specialty practices in which its products are prescribed. PSAs may also be used to promote local events supporting local charities.

Radio Promotions. Radio offers trade-for-mention promotional opportunities in which the station trades free airtime for merchandise used for prizes in station promotions. This may be offered as part of a merchandising package to advertisers or because of the value or special interest of the promotional idea and merchandise offered in exchange for the product mention.

Reprints. Reprints of articles in respected trade publications or the general business press can be valuable door openers for salesmen. Case histories that include customer endorsements or byline articles that convey the implied endorsement of the publication are particularly valuable in marketing business-to-business products.

Road Shows. Some companies take their show on the road to major markets to introduce management and showcase current and future products to customers and other key stakeholders. Special events are held for audiences of dealers and wholesalers, shareholders, employees and retirees, and the press. Road shows offer management an opportunity to discuss the company's mission, vision, and plans. In addition to product displays and demonstrations, multimedia and interactive exhibits can be used to dramatize the company's research and development and operations.

Example: Chrysler's "Drive the Showroom" road shows introduce new models and enable journalists in major cities to drive the cars and interview the chairman and president.

Sampling. Public relations sampling differs from general sampling programs for it is intended to reach highly specialized target audiences of opinion leaders. Other PR sampling programs can be staged to gain positive exposure or publicity.

Examples: Quaker Oats CEO Bill Smithberg personally handed out bottles of Snapple in Chicago to bring attention to a national sampling program intended to revitalize interest in the brand. Distribution of Hall's Cough Lozenges to patrons of dozens of symphony orchestras to prevent coughing during performances.

School Programs. Many companies provide valuable supplemental classroom teaching materials to schools. A typical school package might include student activity books, a classroom poster, an educational video, a teacher's guide, and suggested lesson plans. The materials are often teacher-tested to assure usability and are sold at or below cost to teachers. Food company–sponsored programs may show how to shop for the best value; bank programs may explain money management; sewing machine company programs may explore making your own clothes. Many of these programs are designed to invite parental participation.

Searches. Searches that invite public participation can generate local as well as national media coverage. Talent and look-alike searches are old standbys.

Examples: Oshkosh B'Gosh celebrated its centennial with a well-publicized search for the oldest bib overall. Other examples include the search for a new Miss Chiquita Banana, Tide's search for America's Dirtiest Kids, the Purina Dog Chow Search for the Great American Dog, and the Combat Search and Rescue Mission to identify and treat America's worst cockroach-infested homes.

Seminars and Symposia. Company-sponsored events provide opportunities for consumers to obtain useful information on subjects of interest from recognized experts in their fields. Seminars on lifestyle management subjects such as health, exercise, nutrition, and money management have been particularly popular. Participants are given information kits from the sponsoring company and their names may be put on a database for future informational mailings and seminar announcements. Seminars also offer media relations opportunities such as interviews with company executives, authors, and expert panelists.

Signage. Advertisers, of course, buy space on scoreboards and elsewhere in sports arenas. Signage is also an important element in media events and video news releases. Signs, banners, and wearables assure video identification of the company sponsoring the event, for example, at the finish line of a marathon or on the T-shirts worn by million-dollar sports challenge contestants.

Speakers' Bureaus. Some companies, trade associations, and professional societies have formed speakers' bureaus that provide speakers for civic groups, service clubs, schools, clubs, and libraries. Telecommunication companies, public utilities, and others serving a broad cross section of the business community frequently appear at luncheon meetings, assemblies, and special events. At these appearances, they often distribute informational materials and branded mementos. These appearances offer good opportunities to collect names and addresses for database marketing uses.

Spokespersons. Public relations executives are often identified as company spokespersons in business news stories. Marketing executives and company experts such as designers, engineers, and researchers may also be made available to the media. The company may also employ celebrity and advertising spokespersons to participate in special events and go on media tours. Others frequently utilized as traveling spokespersons are experts and authorities such as doctors, psychologists, teachers, dietitians, nutritionists, fitness experts, journalists, and authors.

Sports Sponsorships. Sports together with pop music are the two most universally popular kinds of event sponsorships. They transcend language barriers and international borders. Title sponsorship has gone beyond golf, tennis, and

NASCAR sponsorships to football bowl games, horse racing, and yachting. Sponsors trying to reach the youth market look for opportunities to "own" newly emerging sports such as beach volleyball or extreme sports. Marathons and triathlons for charitable causes also provide an opportunity for relationship building and media coverage.

Example: The Advil Minimarathon enlists elite athletes and sports-medicine specialists as spokespersons and distributes hundreds of Advil caps, bags, and T-shirts, and Advil signs along the race course can be seen on national TV.

Stunts. The stock-in-trade of theatrical and movie press agents, stunts are still effectively used by companies to attract attention to their products. Television is particularly attracted to unusual, offbeat, or funny events for the lighter side of the news.

Examples: The Empire State Building is a favorite setting for stunts because it is universally known and because it is convenient to the TV networks and other national media. Hershey's dropped a giant Hershey's Kiss from it; M&M's lit it blue to announce its new candy color; Microsoft bathed it in the five colors of its Windows 95 logo. The building itself celebrated its own sixty-fifth birthday with a personal appearance of Faye Wray who was snatched by King Kong in the immortal 1930s film of the same name.

Surveys. Like polls, surveys are proven ways to achieve positive media exposure. Material may be derived from market research or may be generated exclusively for publicity purposes. Survey sponsorship conveys industry leadership to the consumer. Surveys have become a staple of *USA Today* and other reader-friendly newspapers. The results are often presented in color graphs and charts with credit to the company in both the article and the graphics.

Examples: Levi Strauss conducted a national lifestyle survey defining "the New American Man" to introduce its Slates brand of men's dress pants. Lands' End conducted a "Truth About Turtlenecks" survey on how and where turtlenecks are worn to introduce its new cotton turtleneck, and a survey on holiday shopping habits to introduce its Christmas catalog.

Tie-Ins. Picking the right partner may contribute to the success of a marketing public relations program. The right commercial partner may provide borrowed interest necessary to attract media attention. The right nonprofit partner can lend credibility to the company. For example, the endorsement of a company-sponsored public service program by a respected organization such as the National Safety Council, the American Dietetic Association, the American Cancer Society, the National Parent-Teachers Association, or the American Association of Retired People (AARP) can have a significant effect on marketing.

Example: The American Dental Association endorsement of Crest toothpaste propelled the brand to category leadership.

Trade Shows. Trade shows are often used as the launching pads for new products. They are covered extensively by the trade and business press and often by consumer news media. Companies compete to be the big news from big shows such as the Comdex, Toy Fair, and Food Marketing Association. They often stage preshow events and on-site stunts to capture the attention of buyers and the media. Their executives may also gain visibility and publicity for the company as convention speakers and panelists. Some shows, such as the major automotive shows in Detroit, Chicago, and Frankfurt, are open to the public and generate widespread media coverage. Fashion shows staged by the famous designers in Paris, Milan, and New York are covered extensively by television and the print media.

Vehicles. Some brands have maintained high brand awareness by sponsoring vehicles that visit key markets, compete in races, or appear at televised events.
   Examples: Oscar Mayer Weinermobile; Budweiser, Met Life, Fuji, and Goodyear blimps; and sponsored racing cars, sailing ships, and hot-air balloons.

Video. Videotapes are versatile public relations tools. In addition to video news releases, videos are used for information and educational purposes. Company-sponsored videos are frequently provided to schools and used to reach other target audiences. They are produced by automotive companies to introduce new models, by the travel industry to promote destinations, by athletic equipment manufacturers to demonstrate their products, and by pharmaceutical companies to reach doctors and their patients.

Videoconferences. Satellite transmission has facilitated the linking of sites by closed-circuit television. There is a multiplicity of public relations uses for videoconferences. They can be used to link special events in several markets for transmission to employees, dealers, distributors, franchisees, retailers, and the media. Microsoft used closed-circuit videoconferencing to transmit a TV special launching Windows 95 from company headquarters to customers of key retail chains. Videoconferencing and its audio equivalent, teleconferencing, can also be employed in crisis communications situations that critically impact marketing.
   Example: The effective use of teleconferencing was pioneered in 1982 by Johnson & Johnson at the outset of the Tylenol poisoning. The company's CEO answered questions from reporters in major markets openly and honestly, setting the course for an open-door media policy.

Video News Releases. Often described as the electronic equivalent of the news release, VNRs are news or feature stories produced on videotape for use on television newscasts. VNRs are frequently edited on the spot and transmitted immediately to networks and stations by satellite. Today ready-to-use VNRS are usually accompanied by B-roll from which networks or stations can create their own stories. Some stations localize VNRS with supplemental footage shot in their markets.

Websites. At this writing the hottest new medium for transmitting information, entertainment, and advertising is via the Internet. Most major companies today have one or more sites on the World Wide Web. The cost of entry is negligible so the Web is cluttered with text from organizations and individuals all over the world. This new medium can reach consumers, influencers, and the traditional media simultaneously with a variety of stories, pictures, and interactivities twenty-four hours a day. The Web can handle text, graphics, video, and sound. Many marketers include their Internet addresses in their advertising and update the information on their sites continuously. Special short-term sites are set up to support sports events, motion pictures, political conventions, and other events. Many public relations firms have their own Web sites that provide information about the firm and its clients.

Example: Miller Brewing Company pioneered public relations use of the Web with its MGD Tap Room, a virtual pub that identified Miller Genuine Draft with the music, fashion, nightlife, arts, and sports interests of its target-market consumers.

Days, Weeks, Months. Created by trade associations and companies to focus attention on their products, these special events offer promotional and publicity opportunities. They provide a news angle that gives the media a reason to feature a product. Special days, weeks, or months may also be supported by in-store events at retail and special newspaper and magazine advertising sections with story material provided by public relations sources.

Examples: Campbell Soup Company's National Soup Month, Purina Fit & Trim National Rib Check Day, Whirlpool Corporation's Clean Out Your Refrigerator Day.

CHAPTER 31

Step Five: Measuring and Evaluating MPR Programs

THE FINAL AND IN MANY WAYS THE MOST IMPORTANT ELEMENT OF THE PUBLIC relations plan is evaluation. It measures how well the plan did in meeting its objectives. The use of research to evaluate public relations programs has been growing as client management steps up its demand for accountability throughout its operations. This has accelerated the growth of research departments at major public relations firms that measure everything from media coverage to behavioral shifts. The new bottom-line focus among clients has also led to the creation of strategic alliances between public relations and research firms. Burson-Marsteller has an exclusive partnership with the Wirthlin Group. Hill & Knowlton has a partnership arrangement with Yankolovich Partners.

Wirthlin President Jim Granger told *Advertising Age* that unlike the advertising business, which banded together decades ago to create standards for research, public relations has no unified measurement standards. "The public relations community as a group did not embrace the idea of measurement or research for developing a strategy of communications," he said.[1]

It must be admitted that while the tools for measuring public relations effectiveness have been understood for years, evaluation has historically been underused. An important reason is cost. Marketing public relations budgets, especially those for consumer products, while growing, are still in most cases dwarfed by advertising and promotion. Ten percent of the budget recommended by public relations research experts can take a healthy bite out of the total MPR budget. When it comes time to take a sharp pencil to the budget, clients often opt to either use that ten percent to buy more PR or to cut it entirely as an expendable expense.

The advent of integrated marketing has simultaneously signaled the growing recognition of the value of public relations and has made that value more difficult to measure. If MPR is an integral piece of a multidimensional marketing program, it is more difficult to isolate the effectiveness of the individual pieces. IMC is at least theoretically seamless. If it works, it is because all the pieces fit harmoniously.

That said, it is possible, if sometimes costly, to design a sophisticated measurement model that measures the contribution of each of the major components in terms of how well their specified objectives were met.

MPR objectives, as we have seen, are generally stated in terms of creating awareness and changing attitudes. These are, in fact, also the goals of most advertising campaigns. Only in direct-response advertising can sales be directly attributable to specific pieces with any degree of accuracy, but there are a few instances where direct response is expected to carry the entire marketing load.

While it is difficult to assign awareness values to the various components of the marketing plan, an exception occurs when the announcement of a new product precedes the break of advertising. A number of companies have used this window of opportunity to measure awareness levels attributable exclusively to PR activity.

In their classic planning resource *How to Write a Successful Marketing Plan*, Roman Hiebing Jr., and Scott Cooper make it clear that "while increased sales is a very valuable indicator of the success of a marketing execution, it is not the only one. Many times while sales remain relatively flat, there is a significant movement in awareness and attitudes. As has been proven time and time again, with increase in awareness there is a good probability that there will be an increased level of purchases."

Three levels of measuring public relations effectiveness have been identified by Dr. Walter K. Lindenmann, Senior Vice President and Director of Research at Ketchum Public Relations. He labels the basic level "Outputs," the intermediate level "Outgrowths," and the advanced level "Outcomes."

- Outputs measures message transmission, i.e., the amount of exposure in the media, the number of placements and audience impressions, and the likelihood of having reached specific target audiences.

- Outgrowths measures message reception. It measures whether or not a target audience actually received the messages directed at them, and whether they paid attention to, understood, and retained those messages.

- Outcomes measures attitude and behavioral change, i.e., whether anyone changed his or her mind or went out and did something as a result of what was said or done through public relations.[2]

Let's examine each and how they can be measured.

Measuring Outputs

Level one measures how we did in getting the message out. Outputs measures media placements, impressions, and target audiences reached. Measurement of outputs has been the option most frequently used by public relations.

Outputs becomes a relevant measure if the MPR plan is media-driven. Results can be measured on how well publicity objectives were met. As we have seen, publicity objectives can be set in terms of total audience exposed to the message and/or specific media objectives, i.e., how successful the program was in placing stories in specified types of media, or in some cases, specific publications or broadcasts. Results can also be measured on how well specified target audiences were reached by all media. The least-difficult to measure target audiences are demographic, but compiling demographically segmented audience data for each program and publication reached is tedious and costly.

Publicity results can also be evaluated in terms of geographic audiences reached. The goal of some programs is to achieve a balance of coverage across the country or wherever the product is sold. On the other hand, coverage in certain key markets may be important enough to be spelled out in publicity objectives.

While these kinds of measures are available, the measurement of the number of stories and the accumulated circulation of print publications remains the most frequent method for measuring outputs. As broadcast media has gained in importance as a publicity outlet, clip count has been supplemented by audience count. Television measures assume that when sets are turned on, more than one person is watching. That, in turn, influenced the print media to the practice of adding a multiplier to account for the number of people that have the opportunity to read an ad or an article. A multiplier of from two to three is commonly used to compute "impressions" or more accurately "potential impressions." Many publications publish information on impressions based on their research measuring "pass-along" readership. Of course, there is no guarantee that a particular article, or ad for that matter, has been read even if it was passed along without conducting further story-specific readership studies.

To compile audience figures, many organizations use press-clipping and broadcast-monitoring services. The three major press-clipping services are Luce, Burrelle's, and Bacon's. Clipping services typically charge a monthly service fee and a cost per clipping. Some services clip everything about their clients, but orders can be brand- or story-specific to control costs. Some organizations also clip publicity of their competitors for informational and comparative purposes.

The advent of online networks and Nexis that carry text of articles in leading publications has led some organizations to shortcut the clipping services in favor of immediacy and success in achieving major placements in those publications that they identify as most important in reaching target audiences. Data Times offers same-day access to business news from the leading regional U.S. newspapers, national news and business magazines, and international wire services.

When broadcast coverage is important, clients can engage a broadcast-monitoring service. Services such as Radio/TV Reports and vms (Video Monitoring Services of America) scan national and local television broadcasts around the clock for company or brand mentions. As with clipping services, they can be alerted to breaking news stories or video news releases. They are able to provide radio and TV tapes and scripts to subscribers. Radio/TV Reports and Nielsen Media Research offer vnr tracking systems. Vnr producers and distributors also document usage as part of the package. Today many news programs sell tapes of their programs. Companies can easily obtain tapes of segments about their competitors and themselves from network newscasts and newsmagazines such as *Sunday Morning* and *60 Minutes* by fax, telephone, or e-mail.

The importance of "big news" as a marketing tool is emphasized by Joseph F. McCann, Senior Vice President of Pepsico, Inc. He told *Inside PR* editor Paul Holmes that he doesn't subscribe to any clipping services because "if my cousin's sister doesn't ask me about it, if my doorman doesn't ask me about it, if I'm not hearing about it at work, then it wasn't a success."[3]

It should be remembered that Pepsi is one of the world's great consumer products marketers and that its products have very high awareness. Still, Pepsico's disciplined approach to measuring publicity effectiveness can be scaled down to apply to any marketing public relations situation. It is based on a very demanding Product Publicity Grid that McCann says forces the entire marketing team to deal with the right things.

The horizontal axis answers the question "Does the message reach and impact the target audience?" by focusing on levels of publicity obtained. The lowest of the three levels encompass one-time newspaper clippings and occasional TV exposure, usually single placements and local news. The midlevel measures broad exposure, a huge number of press clippings, lots of local TV news shows, cnn, *Entertainment Tonight*, etc. The highest level is massive exposure that creates broad awareness. At this level the story takes on a life of its own. Coverage includes network evening news, multiple repeats on cnn, lots of talk radio coverage, half-hour radio bulletins. He points out that this scale is designed for a major consumer product: cola, fast foods, sneakers. The description of the boxes would be adjusted for a more targeted product, such as a book or golf equipment.

The vertical axis answers the question "How persuasive is the message?" The three levels in ascending order are corporate goodwill, product awareness, and product trial. McCann defines corporate goodwill as news about the producer of the product rather than of the product itself. This publicity creates a good feeling about the company but doesn't necessarily say anything about the product. At the next highest level, the news is product-related and publicity creates awareness of its existence. Frequently the news is "borrowed interest" like a celebrity sponsorship rather than the product itself. It may also be about the advertising of the product rather than the product. The highest level of publicity in McCann's scheme is directly about the merits of the product. By hearing the news, the listener wants to sample the product.

Any product or service can be plotted on this grid to determine the degree of effectiveness and scaled down to targeted yet realistic objectives set forth in the public relations plan.

In addition to raw numbers obtained, outputs can also be measured in terms of messages delivered—that is, how successful the program was in delivering key messages defined in the MPR plan. This requires content analysis of publicity.

Three-quarters of the 2,000 clients responding to my 1997 survey reported using content analysis to determine delivery of key messages. Outfits such as News Analysis Institute, The Delahaye Group, Inc., Burrelle's Performa System, and Medialink Public Relations Research all analyze the content of all clippings of broadcast reports. They can determine the percentage of coverage that was positive, negative, and neutral. They also screen stories for specific messages communicated. This kind of analysis may be required because unlike the advertising message that is controlled, the public relations message must pass through media gatekeepers. Content analysis may specifically examine copy headlines, subheads, pictures, captions, whether the news was reported completely or edited, and which spokespersons were quoted in the story (yours, competitor's, third-party experts).

Delahaye pioneered presenting qualitative and quantitative data in presentation-ready charts and tables and written analyses. A standard report reveals how effectively and accurately messages are being communicated, how the company is positioned by the media on key issues, which audiences are being reached, and what messages they are exposed to, what subjects the media are following most closely, and the overall tone of coverage. Medialink provides its clients with an individual message summary broken down by predetermined subjects related to objectives, for example, product, advertising and promotion news, quality, value, customer service. Another service provided by these organizations is comparative analysis of competitors' media coverage to determine overall effectiveness, identify specific messages, and determine in what media the competition communicates best and least effectively. Client and competitive results can be broken down by media type, i.e., daily and weekly newspapers, trade magazines, consumer magazines, business press, radio, and television. The Newlin Company has developed a Publicity Value Analysis formula that takes into account the equivalent of advertising costs, the credibility of the media, the perception of key messages delivered, the index of target audiences reached, and the geographical distribution of the product—all factors that determine a hypothetical value for each placement.

Ad equivalency is another popular way to measure outputs. Organizations that measure ad equivalencies place a premium on publicity that delivers all the right key messages to the right audiences in the right media at the right time.

This method of converting print and broadcast public relations coverage into what it would have cost to buy this space and time requires measuring column inches and seconds/minutes of airtime and applying published rates for each individual media vehicle where the story appeared. While the difficulty of equating controlled advertising messages with uncontrolled publicity presents obvious problems, in the absence of other standard measures, it is used by many companies.

A public relations story differs from an ad in several fundamental ways. Advertising is understood by consumers to be a selling message. No matter how intrusive, it will be received and processed by the consumer only if he or she is interested in the product and receptive to the message at the time it is delivered. Harvard Professor Theodore Levitt, one of the world's leading marketing authorities, contrasts the advertising message with the public relations message, which he believes has added credibility precisely because it is delivered in a noncommercial context by the media with no commercial ax to grind.

Philip Kotler says that in addition to high credibility, the special appeal of publicity is that it catches the consumer off guard and therefore can reach many prospects who might avoid salespeople and ads. The message gets to consumers as news rather than as sales-directed communication.

A publicity placement may have greater or lesser intrinsic value than an ad depending on where it appears (front page or back of the publication), when it appears, how effectively the salient message points are delivered, and whether editorial endorsement is explicit or merely implied. The importance of the media in reaching influencers, particularly other media, is another consideration. One column in the front section of the New York Times may be more valuable than a full-page story in a publication with a larger circulation because of the importance of the Times in setting the news agenda for others newspapers, magazines, and TV and radio networks and stations.

The real importance of a critically placed article in a key trade publication likewise cannot be measured in terms of circulation or ad equivalency. The numbers are irrelevant. The real value of these articles is that they are carefully monitored by the customers, industry analysts, and general business media. These factors should be pointed out when reporting publicity results to management.

It has been suggested that publicity is equal to two to three times the ad equivalent because the message appears in an editorial context. Others believe in a formula that applies a higher multiple for coverage that appears in a premium location such as the front page of a newspaper, A.M. or P.M. drivetime radio, or evening television news. Most public relations practitioners, however, dismiss these formulas as unprovable and believe there is no statistical basis for applying any multiple in assessing value.

The problem with such formulas is that unlike commercials, all publicity is not created equal. Some publicity is worth much more than its equivalent in advertising space and time and some much less. A five-minute interview/demonstration about a new product on *Good Morning America* is clearly more valuable than a fifteen-second commercial for the same product on the same show. Conversely, a VNR that is edited by the station to delete brand mentions is less valuable than a fifteen-second commercial on the same news show.

Some time and space measures may be misleading. A celebrity spokesperson may appear on a local talk show for twelve minutes but only briefly mention your product. A print article may be an industry roundup that mentions your product along with those of your competitors. For greater accuracy, publicity placements could be screened for content and adjusted accordingly prior to conversion to ad equivalency.

If evaluation is based on measuring outputs, it is possible to determine return on investment (ROI) in terms of the cost required to obtain publicity results. Again ROI can be calculated on the cost for reaching the total audience, specific consumers, and influencers. This is typically expressed in cost-per-thousand (CPM) terms used in advertising. The more successful the publicity effort, the lower the CPM. Typically, CPM for gross media impressions is in the pennies, while CPM for advertising is in the many dollars. Unlike advertising that has high production costs in addition to the cost of time and space, the largest public relations cost factor may be the staff time required in planning, preparing, and placing the publicity. A recent study conducted by the Delahaye Group shows that the cost per public relations impression is less than a penny per impression, a tiny fraction of the cost of advertising and promotion. The average cost per article for twenty-five top companies was about $1,080. Cost-efficiency plus credibility are the key reasons for making MPR an integral component in IMC programs.

In summary, outputs are most frequently measured in terms of:

- Circulation/audience
- Impressions
- Target media reach
- Target audience reach
- Delivery of message points
- Qualitative analysis
- Advertising equivalency
- Competitive analysis

Benchmarking studies enable companies to track their coverage in specific print and electronic media with that of their competitors over time. Typical criteria for judging coverage is based on the number of mentions, influence or tone, audiences reached, and messages communicated. Katherine Paine, CEO of the Delahaye Group, suggests that company performance be compared to that of three competitive companies: a stretch goal, a peer company, and an underdog. She believes that it is important to benchmark on a continuing basis by tracking how your company and its competitors are covered by target media every year to every other year.

Measuring Outgrowths

The next level of measuring PR effectiveness is concerned with whether the target audience groups received the messages directed to them and whether they understood and retained them. Walter Lindenmann labels this level outgrowths.

To measure outgrowths, PR practitioners usually rely on a mix of qualitative and quantitative data-collection techniques. These include focus groups, depth interviews, and polling of key target groups exposed to the message by telephone or in person. A frequently used technique involves face-to-face interviews with mall shoppers that researchers call mall intercept interviews.

Clipping companies and companies that analyze the content of publicity placements are moving into the area of attitude research. After collecting press clippings and TV and radio placements, Burrelle's Performa System can analyze how well messages were communicated by media type, how well the audience was reached, and what the advertising equivalent was. It then can conduct attitude research. Working with Bruskin/Goldring Research, Burrelle's can determine how the targeted audiences reacted to the public relations message in terms of what they received, how well it was remembered, and how it influenced their buying interest and brand loyalty. Likewise, Medialink Public Relations Research conducts attitudinal research that can determine if the messages are getting through; which messages are most impactful, credible, and compelling; which media are most effective in delivering the message; and which combination of media and messages works best.

A 1995 survey on public relations measurement and accountability conducted by Schenkein/Sherman Public Relations, Denver, Colorado, and PR News found that creating awareness was mentioned most frequently as the most important area to measure, followed by changing behavior and increasing sales. When asked about the specific methodologies they employ to measure public relations, the respondents were about evenly split between the preference of benchmarking, mail or telephone studies, and focus groups.

Some commonly used ways to measure outgrowths are:

- Focus groups
- Day-after recall
- Mall intercepts
- Write-fors
- Call-ins
- Contest entries
- Event participation

Measuring Outcomes

The most advanced level of public relations effectiveness research measures what Lindenmann calls outcomes. This measures opinion, attitude, and behavioral change. He says that to measure outcomes, the PR practitioner needs to rely on techniques such as:

- Before and after polls (pretests and posttests)
- Experimental and quasi-experimental research designs
- Data collection methods such as observation, participation, and role-playing
- Comprehensive, multifaceted communications audits
- Advanced data analysis such as psychographic analysis, factor and cluster analysis, and perceptual mapping.

Classic research design as applied to marketing public relations uses benchmark research to measure how much a group of target consumers knew about, felt about, and used a product before being exposed to the public relations message. The group is then divided into a test group that is exposed to the messages delivered by the public relations campaign and a control group that does not receive these messages. The posttest determines the differences between test group and control group in what they know, if their attitudes were changed, and how it affected their behavior.

Another technique that is used to measure outcomes is the matched-market test. In addition to measuring public relations effectiveness, it can be used to test the value that each of the major components of the marketing mix adds to the effectiveness of integrated programs. As with the classic design, a pretest is used to measure knowledge, attitude, and predisposition to buy a product. Then groups in each market are exposed to the major components of the marketing plan in isolation and combination. For example, in one market, consumers would be exposed to advertising alone; in a second, public relations only; in a third market, both advertising and public relations; and in a fourth, neither advertising nor public relations. Follow-up research would reveal how much effect each or the combination had on attitudes, predispositions to buy, or actual sales. This technique can be used in the test market to determine the best mix. It can also be used to fine-tune advertising and public relations messages, execution, and delivery systems.

Walter Lindenmann cites a matched-market test conducted by Ketchum for a food company that was introducing a new product in four communities. Public relations was used alone in the first market, advertising alone in the second, a combination of advertising and public relations in the third, and neither in the fourth. Interviews were conducted with 250 people in each community to determine their familiarity with the product, and the effect on attitude change and buying behavior. In this test, public relations alone was found to be most effective, followed by the combination of advertising and public relations.

Several years ago, I was involved in a similar test for Campbell soups where a combination of advertising and public relations outperformed either alone. In this case, an integrated advertising and public relations campaign effectively delivered the same message that "soup is good food."

It should be noted that every campaign must be evaluated on its own. Some products or messages are more newsworthy than others. News value enhances the opportunity for public relations success. Similarly, some ad campaigns register better with consumers than others do.

Another sophisticated market research technique that can be used to measure public relations effectiveness is regression analysis. This statistical technique is used to study relationships among variables, measured at the interval or ratio level. The Newlin Company, for example, has developed a regression formula that tracks public relations versus, and in tandem with, other promotional communications activities occurring simultaneously that are likely to impact sales.

Cohn & Wolfe, a major public relations firm, has created an interactive software program to help clients assess the effectiveness of event sponsorships. Called SponsorSoft™, the program considers and evaluates ten key categories, including brand positioning, marketing objectives, customer focus, execution, cost analysis, and employee support.

Measuring Return on Investment (ROI)

Some critics question the value of public relations because they don't believe it can be measured in terms of return on investment (ROI). I take issue with that argument. In the first place, ROI can be measured.

Take the case of business-to-business products that aren't advertised. The objective of many a business-to-business marketing public relations program is to generate sales leads. Let's say that publicity in a trade magazine offers a brochure about a high-end product. The company receiving requests for the brochure provides these leads to its sales reps who use the opportunity to make a sales call to a qualified customer. ROI can be calculated simply by dividing all sales resulting from inquiries from publicity in trade publications by the cost of generating that publicity. Publicity costs are normally negligible, in this case the cost of preparing and mailing a press release and an existing sales brochure.

This can work, however, only if public relations is the sole component of the marketing communications effort, which it rarely is. The validity of integration as a marketing concept is that marketing works best when the sum total of a number of components are working together.

Some components, such as those that require a direct response, are by their very nature more measurable than others. But I believe that begs the question. Does more measurable mean more valuable? Is a freestanding insert more valuable than a television commercial that excites consumers about a product? Is a direct-mail piece about a new product, no matter how personalized, able to convey the news as well as a favorable story on a network news show? Is that least interactive of all media, outdoor advertising, to be discounted because there is no immediate response mechanism? Ask Nike, one of the world's most successful marketers who pours millions of dollars into outdoor advertising. As a matter of fact, ask Nike how many shoes it sold because it is omnipresent on TV sports. Or how many caps and jackets they sold because the coach on the sidelines wears the swoosh.

It seems to me that we are talking about apples and oranges and that an effectively integrated program is a great fruit salad. To use another food analogy, PR serves up the steak. Advertising adds the sizzle. Direct marketing asks for the order.

How do you measure the specific impact of a single component if all of the components of an integrated marketing plan are working together?

The advocates of ROI or nothing assume that every element in the marketing process can be controlled and measured. The trouble is that it can't.

How do you measure the damage that was prevented because public relations counseled management against making a politically, socially, or culturally incorrect marketing decision?

How do you measure the impact on sales of successfully executing a crisis communication strategy that controls the damage? Conversely, how do you measure what might have happened to sales had action and communications been too little or too late?

How do you measure the effect on sales of an otherwise excellent product made by a company that pollutes the environment, commits fraud, or engages in discriminatory behavior?

How do you measure the negative impact of a rude or stupid salesperson who kills a sale?

How do you measure the brand damage of an unwanted phone call from an unseen telemarketer trying to sell you something you don't want? Or from an intrusive sender of unsolicited junk e-mail clogging your electronic mailbox?

The Pad That Failed

How do you measure the marketing effectiveness of a product that doesn't live up to its promise?

Many a lavish advertising budget has been wasted on products that didn't satisfy a consumer want or need. Many a direct-mail program didn't work despite the pinpoint accuracy of its database and the excellence of its copy because the product was lacking. And many a public relations program has failed because the product didn't live up to its publicity.

Apple Computer Company was particularly successful in generating publicity for its Newton message pad. It was touted in the consumer and business worlds a full year before consumers could get their hands on one. When Newton was ready to go to market, the Apple public relations people orchestrated a unique demonstration on ABC's *Good Morning America*, the top-rated morning network television show. After a gee-whiz demonstration of what Newton could do, then-CEO John Sculley faxed the first Newton transmission to the show's weatherman, Spencer Christian, who was in Des Moines covering the great Mississippi River flood of the century. I have shown that segment to marketing and public relations audiences for years and they are always fascinated.

The advanced publicity was so valuable that 10,000 Newtons were presold—before the media backlash began.

After playing with Newton, reporters and consumers soon discovered that it had a problem recognizing people's handwriting. *Business Week* interviewed a software engineer who said that Newton has interpreted his message "My name is Curtis" as "My Norse 15 critics." The product was also damaged by Mike Doonesbury's handwriting recognition problems with Newton in the popular Gary Trudeau comic strip.

Publicity was so extensive and effective that it raised expectations that the product couldn't deliver.

Immeasurables and Imponderables

The impact of some positive public relations activities may be difficult or too expensive to measure. But immeasurable should never be confused with invaluable.

How do you measure the value of a company's socially responsible activities on its marketing success?

How do you measure the marketing value of community relations programs in places where it employs people and does business?

How do you measure the direct impact of event sponsorships on sales?

How do you measure the value of public relations in maintaining customer loyalty?

How, in fact, do you measure the long-term brand-building benefits against short-term sales?

How can you quantify the value of "news"? Ad people know that "new" is the most valuable word in advertising. News is the stock and trade of public relations.

How can you quantify the value of a great idea versus a nonidea on sales?

How do you measure the value publicity adds to making a product that people just can't live without?

In late 1996, children and their moms and dads fell in love with a cuddly Sesame Street character named Elmo that shakes with laughter when you tickle him. Tyco Toys Tickle Me Elmo became to the 1990s what Cabbage Patch Kids were to the 1980s, a must-have toy that made headlines when moms fought to get their hands on one. Like Cabbage Patch Kids, Tickle Me Elmo got its initial impetus from public relations. Cabbage Patch Kids were put on the map in 1983 when a doll was given to the then-pregnant host of the *Today* show Jane Pauly. In 1996, Tyco's public relations firm, Freeman Public Relations, borrowed a page from PR history and sent talk-show host Rosie O'Donnell a Tickle Me Elmo for her one-year-old son Parker. What followed, according to the *Wall Street Journal* was a promoter's dream:

> One day on the show Ms. O'Donnell announced she was going to play an old Groucho Marx game. Each time her guests said the secret word "wall," an Elmo doll would be tossed into the audience. Her guests that day: actor Tom Hanks, comedian Dom DeLuise, singer Willie Nelson, and an eleven-year-old basketball star, Cliffy Clinkscales, proved charming, if unwitting, participants.
>
> Every time the cameras panned the audience, a crimson mass of Elmos filled the screen. "That got us started," recalls [Freeman Public Relations executive Bruce] Maguire. Ms. O'Donnell's core audience, he notes, is stay-at-home mothers of preschool-age children—just the kind of fan club Tyco would wish for Elmo, a plain-speaking muppet whose character on TV resembles a tagalong younger brother.
>
> Retail sales of the doll quickly jumped. The following month it sneaked onto the what's-hot list of *Toy Book*, a trade monthly, ranking thirteenth on a list of fifteen hottest toys. That caught the attention of newspaper reporters, who listed Elmo in their what's-hot holiday guides.
>
> Elmo's second wind came the second week in November, when Bryant Gumbel, co-host of the *Today* show, invited JoAnne

Oppenheim, an author and publisher of a consumer guide, to discuss holiday gifts for children. Ms. Oppenheim only got four minutes of airtime and mentioned Tickle Me Elmo in passing as a genderfree toy—but the doll sat on Mr. Gumbel's lap through most of the show.

Playing hard-to-get even generated a bidding war on the Internet with the $25 toys offered for $200 and up. Fueled by publicity, Elmo sales, originally projected at 400,000 units for the year, reached well over a million during the holiday scramble. The publicity worked so well that Tyco pulled its TV commercial, fearing that it would only generate ill will among those who couldn't get their hands on an Elmo during the holiday stampede.[4]

Are all things in marketing public relations measurable? Some are. Some aren't. Do we really need to measure them if they are working? Does it really matter?

The body of anecdotal evidence collected in this book presents incontrovertible evidence that MPR works and that it adds value to integrated marketing that is, at once, measurable and immeasurable.

APPENDIX I

MPR Planning Checklist

THE STEPS OF THE PLANNING PROCESS DESCRIBED IN THE PRECEDING CHAPTERS CAN be summarized as follows:

I. Executive Summary

II. Situation Analysis

A. *The Consumer*
    1. Demographics
    2. Lifestyle
    3. Awareness/Attitudes/Behaviors

B. *The Product*
    1. Life Cycle Stage
        a. New
        b. Mature/Sustaining
        c. Declining
    2. Benefits
    3. Pricing
    4. Distribution
        a. Channels
        b. Geography

C. The Business Environment
1. Competition
2. Trade
3. Issues

D. Marketing Communications: You/Your Competitors
1. Advertising
2. Direct Marketing
3. Promotion
4. Public Relations

E. Research Tools (used to develop situation analysis)
1. Secondary Research
   a. Research Studies
   b. Government Reports
   c. Databases
   d. Internet
2. Primary Research
   a. Surveys
   b. Interviews
   c. Focus Groups
   d. Perceptual Mapping
3. Media Research
   a. Media Audits
   b. Soft Soundings
   c. Media Options

F. SWOT Analysis (based on all of the above)
1. Strengths
2. Weaknesses
3. Opportunities
4. Threats

III. MPR Objectives

A. Awareness

B. Attitudes

C. Behavior

IV. MPR Audiences

A. Audiences
1. Primary

      2. Secondary

      3. Specialized

      4. Influencers

      5. Customers (Trade)

      6. Other Audiences

         a. Internal Audiences: Sales Managers, Reps, Employees

         b. External Channels: Wholesalers, Dealers, Distributors, Franchisees

         c. Shareholders

B. MPR Strategic Options

      1. News/Borrowed Interest

      2. Push/Pull/Pass

      3. Complementary/Supplementary

V. MPR Tactics

A. Message Development

      1. Positioning

      2. Key Messages/Audiences

B. Message Delivery

      1. Direct to Consumer

      2. Indirect (Influencers)

      3. Transmitted by Media

         a. Publicity Objectives

         b. Media Plan

VI. Execution

A. Plan

B. Timetable

C. Budget

D. Responsibilities

VII. Measurement and Evaluation

A. Outputs

B. Outgrowths

C. Outcomes

APPENDIX II

MPR Plan for the Introduction of Crest Gum Care

THE FORMAT SUGGESTED IN THIS BOOK FOR THE MARKETING PUBLIC RELATIONS PLAN is illustrated by the following plan for the introduction of Crest Gum Care. The author wishes to thank Procter & Gamble, and Manning, Selvage & Lee for use of this material.

Situation Analysis

- Procter & Gamble is introducing Crest Gum Care, the only toothpaste available in the United States that is clinically proven to fight gingivitis and bleeding gums.
- Eight out of ten adults experience gingivitis or its most common symptom, bleeding gums.

However, consumer research reveals that:

- Most people don't know they have gingivitis because they don't know the symptoms or think they are normal. ("Sure my gums bleed after I brush, that happens to everyone, right?")

- Most people don't take gingivitis seriously. ("It's nothing to worry about; after all, I'm not going to die from it.")
- This lack of awareness among all adults is even more prevalent in the Hispanic population according to a study published in the *Journal of the American Dental Association.*
- The challenge is to develop a program to get consumers to pay attention to a product that treats a condition they don't know about or don't care that they have.

Objectives

- Add value to the integrated marketing program introducing Crest Gum Care.
- Educate adults about the importance of gum health.
- Provide a leadership platform for Procter & Gamble to "own" gum health.
- Generate significant positive media coverage.

Strategies

- Create a public education program to focus consumer attention on the problem.
- Position Crest Gum Care as the solution to the problem.
- Leverage the support of dental leaders.
- Secure implied third-party endorsement of the media.

Messages

- Gingivitis is a prevalent disease that, left untreated, can lead to more severe forms of gum disease, a major cause of tooth loss in adults.
- Gingivitis is the only stage of gum disease that can be reversed.
- Bleeding gums are not normal; they are signs of gingivitis.
- Crest Gum Care is the only toothpaste clinically proven to fight gingivitis and bleeding gums.

Tactics

- Create National Gum Care Month as the cornerstone of Crest Gum Care launch.

- Hold news conference in New York to make the product and the month big-breaking news.
- Conduct twenty-market media tour featuring nationally known dentists trained to deliver key messages about the disease and the product.
- Create a self-test to help consumers evaluate their level of gum awareness and gum health.
- Produce comprehensive gingivitis brochure on the disease, its causes, and treatment.
- Set up a twenty-four-hour information line (1-800-GUMHEALTH).
- Design a comprehensive media kit to serve as a long-term educational resource for media on gum disease and to introduce the product.
- Implement a special media program to reach Hispanic consumers.

Evaluation Criteria

- Media exposure.
- Content analysis of media coverage to determine use of key messages.
- Number of requests for brochures.
- Number of consumer calls on information line.

Results of the Plan

This plan achieved the public relations objectives specified in the plan:

- Educate the public. The News Analysis Institute reported that 76 percent of the media coverage educated the public about gingivitis and 91 percent mentioned the need and product benefits.
- Ownership of Gum Health. The exposure for National Gum Health Month positioned Crest as a leader in the fight against gum disease. Using credible dentists to educate the public and serve as spokespersons for the product strengthened that ownership positioning.
- General Media Exposure. The program generated more than 120 million consumer impressions in print and broadcast media nationally and in media tour markets with extremely high-quality rating on message delivery.
- Other Outcomes. After three months, Crest Gum Care's share of the market was 19 percent higher than the twelve-month goal. The brand credited the public relations program for this dramatic increase. Crest Gum Care met its objectives for displays and retail distribution. Media coverage is credited for causing consumers to ask for the product and retailers to stock it.

APPENDIX III

MPR Works!

The following list of anecdotal evidence of the effectiveness of public relations in the marketplace was collected for this book, my newsletter, and my graduate course in marketing public relations at the Medill School of Journalism, Northwestern University.

- Goodyear sold 150,000 new Aquatred Tires as a result of the company's advance publicity before the first advertising appeared.

- Breathe Right sales for a single quarter were double those of the entire previous year when National Football League players wore the strip on nationally televised games.

- Every title recommended by Oprah Winfrey's Book Club has become an instant best-seller, many selling more than one million copies.

- Sales of Drake's Cakes increased by 11 percent over the previous year after Rosie O'Donnell began to talk about them on her TV talk show.

- Starbucks net revenues grew more than 500 percent in less than four years and the brand became a household word through the use of public relations before the company ran its first advertising campaign.

- The U.S. Postal Service turned a profit of $29 million on the sale of Elvis Presley stamps, after a public relations–driven campaign made it the best-selling U.S. postage stamp of all time.

- Wonderbra became the number one push-up bra in the United States with virtually no advertising by using public relations as the key marketing tool.

- Nintendo 64 sold 1.75 million units within three months of its U.S. introduction and became the bestselling video game of the year as a result of an integrated campaign led by a three-year public relations effort.

- Kodak had written orders for two million Advantix cameras, the total the company projected for the entire year, by the time the cameras were shipped to retailers.

- Windows 95 had achieved 99 percent awareness at its launch as a result of a massive public relations campaign and sold more than one million copies before advertising began.

- Procter & Gamble's Aleve reached third place in the highly competitive over-the-counter pain-killer market in three months as a result of an integrated marketing campaign in which public relations played a prominent role.

- Chrysler generated more than 3,000 calls and letters from interested consumers as a result of a preemptive publicity blitz for the Dodge Viper and 60 percent of the first year's production was ordered a year before the cars were built and advertised.

- Butterball Turkey Talk-Line, a public relations initiative, which answers more than 250,000 calls a year from consumers, has become the brand's principal marketing tool.

- Sales of red wine increased 44 percent in the United States when *60 Minutes* ran a report that advanced the theory that two glasses of red wine a day could reduce the risk of heart attack by as much as 50 percent.

- Ben & Jerry's became a well-known national brand and built a $150 million ice cream business with no national advertising by creating events and supporting causes that drew media and consumer attention.

- Crayola crayons had record sales of $23 million for its ninety-six-color box and a total sales increase of 12 percent during its ninetieth anniversary year using public relations as the primary marketing vehicle.

- Swanson frozen dinner sales rose 44 percent over the previous year and the brand increased its market share as a result of a public relations–driven fortieth anniversary campaign that was so effective that ad support was canceled.

- Sales of Pillsbury products used in winning recipes of the Pillsbury Bake-Off dramatically increase when the winning recipes are publicized.

- Ocean Spray set record weekly and monthly sales records when news that Cranberry Juice Cocktail can prevent urinary tract infections reached hundreds of millions of consumers.

- OshKosh B'Gosh saw an annual 18 percent increase in market share with no increase in ad levels as a result of publicity resulting from a centennial search for the oldest bib overall.

- M&M's Chocolate Candies Color Campaign produced strong and sustainable sales results for the entire year, growing its first place market share by 6.6 percent.

- Sucrets sales jumped 40 percent in the first week after the retirement of the old package and the introduction of a new one. Sales remained 20 percent above average for two months after the program.

- Flintstones vitamins market share increased from 31 percent to 34 percent because of an integrated public relations program that polled consumers on whether Betty should be a vitamin.

- Valvoline became the number-one choice of mechanics as a result of a concerted public relations campaign to provide them with more technical information about motor oil.

- Hyde Athletic Industries credited the power of the press when it doubled its sales, depleted inventories, and caused retail shortages after *Consumer Reports* awarded its Saucony shoes the magazine's top rating.

- California Raisins recorded sales increases of 7 percent to 20 percent in markets where the California Dancing Raisins made personal appearances during a summer advertising hiatus.

- Sales of Glad Bags increased more than 20 percent in participating markets following Glad Bag-A-Thons.

- The Sony Walkman, one of the most successful consumer electronics products ever introduced, was supported by a worldwide PR-driven marketing campaign and no consumer advertising.

- Gillette's Sensor Razor sold out within weeks of its introduction because of an integrated campaign led off by heavy worldwide prelaunch publicity.

- Ford achieved 50 percent brand awareness and had orders for 146,000 new Taurus and Sable automobiles before they were advertised or put on sale based solely on public relations.

- A single article on Cuisinart in *Gourmet* magazine virtually created the food processor category, a new generation of cooking classes, cookbooks, columns, and more orders than the company could fill.

- Reese's Pieces Candy sales increased 65 percent in the first month after the release of the film *E.T.*, in which the lovable space alien was shown following a trail of the candies.

- Cabbage Patch Kids achieved sales of $600 million as a result of a sophisticated public relations effort that saw the dolls featured in every major newspaper and general-interest magazine and on TV network.

- Pepperidge Farm received 3,000 letters and doubled its sales within three months after an article about its home-baked bread appeared in *Reader's Digest*.

APPENDIX IV

MPR Tactical Alphabet

Advertising
Anniversaries
Annual Reports
Arts Sponsorships
Audiocassettes
Awards

Birthdays
Booklets
Books
Brochures
B-roll
Byline Stories

Case Histories
Cause-Related Marketing
CD-ROM
Celebrity Endorsements
Charities
Chotchkes
Competitions
Conferences
Contests

Days, Weeks, Months
Demonstrations
Deskside Briefings
Direct Mail

E-mail
Environmental Initiatives
Event Support
Exhibits

Fan Clubs
Fax mail
Festivals
Fun Facts

Grand Openings
Graphs and Charts
Guidelines Kits

Hot Lines
Human Interest

Icons
Interactive Software

Interviews

Junkets

Key Issues
Kiosks
Kits

Largest, Longest, Most
Launches
Leadership Positioning
Letters to the Editor

Mall Programs
Mat Features
Media Tours
Milestones
Multimedia
Museums

News Conferences
Newsgroups
Newsletters
News Releases

Official Endorsements
Online Forums
Op-Ed
Open Houses

Parades
Personal Appearances
Photo Ops
Photos
Polls
Posters
Press Kits
Press Parties
Product Placement
Promotion Support
Publications
Public Service Announcements

Quizzes

Radio Promotions
Reprints
Road Shows

Sampling
School Programs
Searches
Seminars
Signage
Software
Speakers' Bureaus
Special Events
Speeches
Spokespersons
Sports Sponsorships
Stunts
Surveys
Symposiums

Teleconferences
Thons
Tie-Ins
Trade Show Support

Underwriting
Unveilings

Vehicles
Video Conferences
Video News Releases
Videos
Voicemail

Wearables
World Wide Web

eXperts

Youth Programs

Zone/Regional Programs

©Thomas L. Harris & Company

Bibliography

Caywood, Clarke L., ed. *The Handbook of Strategic Public Relations and Integrated Marketing*. New York: McGraw-Hill, 1997.

Cohen, Ben, and Jerry Greenfield. *Ben & Jerry's Double-Dip*. New York: Simon & Schuster, 1997.

Dilenschneider, Robert, L., ed. *Dartnell's Public Relations Handbook*. 4th ed. Chicago: The Dartnell Corporation, 1996.

Duncan, Tom, and Sandra Moriarty. *Driving Brand Value*. New York: McGraw-Hill, 1997.

Gates, Bill. *The Road Ahead*. New York: Penguin U.S.A., 1996.

Harris, Thomas L. *The Marketer's Guide to Public Relations*. New York: John Wiley & Son, 1991.

Henry, Rene A., Jr. *Marketing Public Relations: The How That Makes It Work*. Ames, Ia.: Iowa State University Press, 1995.

Hiebing, Roman G., Jr., and Scott W. Cooper. *How To Write a Successful Marketing Plan*. Lincolnwood, Ill.: NTC Business Books, 1994.

Hiebing, Roman G., Jr., and Scott W. Cooper. *The 1-Day Marketing Plan*. Lincolnwood, Ill: NTC Business Books, 1996.

Kaatz, Ron. *Advertising & Marketing Checklists*. Lincolnwood, Ill.: NTC Business Books, 1995.

Kotler, Philip. *Marketing Management: Analysis, Planning, Implementation, and Control*. 6th ed. Englewood Cliffs, N.J.: Prentice Hall, 1988.

Kotler, Philip. *Marketing Places*. New York: The Free Press, 1993.

Lager, Fred "Chico." *Ben & Jerry's: The Inside Scoop*. New York: Crown Trade Books, 1994.

Love, John F. *McDonald's: Behind the Arches*. Toronto: Bantam Books, 1986.

Marconi, Joe. *Beyond Branding*. Chicago: Probus, 1993.

Marconi, Joe. *Image Marketing*. Lincolnwood, Ill.: NTC Business Books, 1996.

McKenna, Regis. *Relationship Marketing*. Reading, Mass.: Addison-Wesley Publishing, 1991.

Ogilvy, David. *Ogilvy on Advertising*. New York: Crown Publishing, 1983.

Popcorn, Faith. *The Popcorn Report*. New York: HarperCollins, 1992.

Rein, Irving, Philip Kotler, and Martin Stoller. *High Visibility*. New York: Dodd, Mead & Company, 1987.

Ries, Al, and Jack Trout. *Positioning: The Battle for Your Mind*. New York: Warner Books, 1993.

Schultz, Don E. *Strategic Advertising Campaigns*. Lincolnwood, Ill.: NTC Business Books, 1990.

Schultz, Don E., Stanley Tannenbaum, and Robert R. Lauterborn. *Integrated Marketing Communications: Pulling It Together & Making It Work*. Lincolnwood, Ill.: NTC Business Books, 1993.

Scott, Mary, and Howard Rothman. *Companies with a Conscience*. New York: Carol Publishing Group, 1992.

Seitel, Fraser P. *The Practice of Public Relations*. Englewood Cliffs, N.J.: Prentice-Hall, 1995.

Steckel, Dr. Richard, and Robin Simons. *Doing Best by Doing Good*. New York: Dutton Books, 1992.

Trout, Jack, with Steve Rivkin. *The New Positioning*. New York: McGraw-Hill, 1996.

Weiner, Richard. *Webster's New World Dictionary of Media and Communications*. New York: McMillan General Reference, 1996.

Wells, William, John Burnett, and Sandra Moriarty. *Advertising Principles and Practice*. 2nd ed. Englewood Cliffs, N.J.: Prentice-Hall, 1992.

Young, Davis. *Building Your Company's Good Name*. New York: AMACOM, 1996.

Endnotes

Part I

Chapter 1

1. Announcement for American Management Association forum May 8–9, 1996, The Drake Hotel, Chicago.
2. Tom Duncan, "The Concept and Process of Integrated Marketing Communication," *Integrated Marketing Research Journal*, University of Colorado, vol.1, issue 1, spring 1995, 5.
3. Adrienne Ward Fawett, "Marketers Convinced: Its Time Has Arrived," *Advertising Age*, November 8, 1993, 1.
4. *Ibid.*
5. Regis McKenna, *Relationship Marketing* (Reading, Mass.: Addison-Wesley Publishing, 1991), 5.
6. Integrated Marketing Communications Graduate Study Brochure, Medill School of Journalism, Northwestern University, 1996, 1.
7. Don E. Schultz, "The IMC Process," Integrated Marketing Communications Symposium, the transcript of the talks at Northwestern University's Third Annual Symposium, April 16, 1994 (Lincolnwood, Ill.: NTC Business Books, 1996), 7.
8. *Ibid.*

Chapter 2

1. Kevin Goldman, "Winemakers Look for More Free Publicity," *Wall Street Journal*, September 29, 1994, 353.
2. Anne Raver, "Behind a Boom in Blooms: Safety, Drama and TV," *New York Times*, October 2, 1994, 15.
3. Elizabeth Jensen, "Rosie and 'Friends' Make Drake's Cakes a Star," *Wall Street Journal*, February 10, 1997, B117.
4. Doreen Carvajal, "Marriage of Interests Binds Publishers, TV Shows," *New York Times,* November 10, 1996, 12.
5. Golin/Harris Communications, news release, "Marketers See Long-Term Trend as Consumers Reach for Store Brands, Generics," October 14, 1993, 1.
6. DDB Needham Study, 1994.
7. Thomas L Harris, *The Marketer's Guide to Public Relations.* (New York: John Wiley & Son, 1991), v.

8. Don E. Schultz, Stanley Tannenbaum, and Robert R. Lauterborn, *Integrated Marketing Communications: Pulling It Together & Making It Work* (Lincolnwood, Ill.: NTC Books, 1993), 84–85.

9. Judann Pollack, "New Marketing Spin: The PR 'Experience,'" *Advertising Age*, August 5, 1996, 3.

10. Robert L. Dilenschneider, ed., *Dartnell's Public Relations Handbook*, 4th ed. (Chicago, Ill., 1996), xxvii.

11. Susan Henderson, "Public Relations' Contribution to the Marketing Bottom Line," speech given to the Public Relations and Marketing: Integrated Communications for the 21st Century Seminar, September 26, 1996, at the Madison, Greater O'Hare, and Wisconsin Chapters of PRSA.

Chapter 3

1. Larry Light and Jim Mullen, *Your Brand Is Your Future: A Client's Guide* (American Association of Advertising Agencies, 1996), 33.

2. *Ibid.*, 27.

3. David Drobis, "Building Brand Equity with Public Relations," *Management Review*, May 1993, 52.

4. "PR Playing Larger Role in Creating, Communicating a Company's Brand," *Phillips Public Relations News*, V. 52; 45, November 11, 1996, 2.

5. Thomas L Harris, *The Marketer's Guide to Public Relations* (New York: John Wiley & Son, 1991), 12.

6. Rene A. Henry Jr., *Marketing Public Relations: The How That Makes It Work* (Ames, Ia.: Iowa State University Press, 1995), 3.

7. Richard Weiner, *Webster's New World Dictionary of Media and Communications* (New York: McMillan General Reference, 1996), 362.

8. Faith Popcorn, *The Popcorn Report* (New York: HarperCollins, 1992), 159.

9. Thomas Mosser, "Building Corporate Brands and Reputations with Public Relations, *A.N.A./The Advertiser*, summer 1993, 68.

10. Light and Mullen, *Your Brand Is Your Future: A Client's Guide*, 13.

11. Alvin Golin, speech given to Public Relations Society of America, November 19, 1996, Chicago Chapter.

12. Davis Young, *Building Your Company's Good Name* (New York: AMACOM, 1996), book jacket.

13. Edwin M. Reingold, "America's Hamburger Helper," *Time*, June 1992.

Chapter 4

1. Richard Weiner, *Webster's New World Dictionary of Media and Communications* (New York: McMillan General Reference, 1996), 460.

2. Jack Trout with Steve Rivkin, *The New Positioning* (New York: McGraw-Hill, 1996), book jacket.

3. Regis McKenna, *Relationship Marketing* (Reading, Mass.: Addison-Wesley Publishing, 1991), 46–48.

4. Trout and Rivkin, *The New Positioning*, 147.

5. *Ibid.*, 149.

6. *Ibid.*

Chapter 5

1. Patricia Lee Brown, "2 Kings: The Postal War Over Elvis's Image," *New York Times*, March 15, 1992, 1 and 12.

2. Mary B. Tabor, "People Say Don't Be Cruel to Image: They Like Younger Elvis," *New York Times*, June 4, 1992.

3. *Stamps: A Direct Mail Catalog*, U.S. Postal Service, 1.

Chapter 6

1. Jack Trout with Steve Rivkin, *The New Positioning* (New York: McGraw-Hill, 1996), 147.

2. Kendall Hamilton, "The Sharper Image?" *Newsweek*, February 12, 1996, 46.

3. "For Kodak's Advantrix, Double Exposure as Company Relaunches Camera System," *Wall Street Journal*, April 23, 1997, B2.

4. Michael Kranatz, "Super Mario's Dazzling Comeback," *Time*, May 20, 1996, 53.

5. "Nintendo's Hot Box," *Newsweek*, October 14, 1996, 12.

6. Neil Gross, "Infinitely Cool in 64 Bits," *Business Week*, October 14, 1996, 134.

7. "Nintendo's Hot Box," *Newsweek*, October 14, 1996, 12.

8. Genevieve Buck, "Nintendo 64 Star of the Season," *Chicago Tribune*, November 25, 1996, Business section, 1.

9. *People* (December 1996).

10. Michael Krantz, "64 Bits of Magic," *Time*, November 25, 1996, 74.

11. Nancy Millman and Mike Dorning, "Making McSlash in News Media," *Chicago Tribune*, May 10, 1996, Business section, 1.

12. "He Put Deluxe in the Arch," *Newsweek,* October 7, 1996.

13. "Chief Financial Officer Answers Shareholders Questions," McDonald's 1996 Annual Report, 12.

Chapter 7

1. Bill Gates, *The Road Ahead* (New York: Penguin U.S.A. 1996), xiv.

2. Regis McKenna, *Relationship Marketing* (Reading, Mass.: Addison-Wesley Publishing, 1991), 129.

3. Paul Holmes, "The Mainstreaming of Technology," *Reputation Management,* July/August 1996, 14.

4. *Ibid.*

5. "Grandmaster Sat at the Chessboard, but the Real Opponent Was Gates," *New York Times,* Monday, May 12, 1997, A14.

6. "Checkmate! Deep Blue Is IBM Publicity Coup," *Wall Street Journal,* May 9, 1997, B1.

7. Paul Holmes, "Salute to the 1996 CIPRA Winners," *Inside PR*, June, 1996, 7.

8. "For Microsoft, Nothing Succeeds Like Excess," *Wall Street Journal,* August 25, 1995, B1.

9. Bill Barnhart, Market Report column, *Chicago Tribune*, November 15, 1996, sec. 3, 4.

10. "Inside Microsoft: The untold story of how the Internet forced Bill Gates to reverse course," *Business Week*, December 10, 1996, 78.

11. Karl Von Clausewitz, "Whose Web Will It Be?" *Time,* December 10, 1996, 55.

12. Karl Von Clausewitz, "Winner Take All," *Time,* September 16, 1996, 59.

13. Steven Levy, "The Microsoft Century," *Newsweek*, December 2, 1996, 58.

14. Trip Gabriel, "Filling In the Potholes in the 'Road Ahead,'" *New York Times*, November 28, 1996, The Living Arts section.

15. "Rogaine PR Blitz Planned Using Satisfied Customers," *Advertising Age,* April 28, 1997, 12.

16. "Health, Consumer PR Combine to Reach Sophisticated Audiences," *O'Dwyer's PR Services Report*, October 1996, 18.

17. "Zinc Lozenges in Demand," *Tampa Tribune*, February 27, 1997, 1.

Chapter 8

1. "Jerry Rice Breathes a Little Easier," *Reputation Management*, March/April 1996, 6.
2. Nancy Millman, "Success Doesn't Let Firm Breathe Easy," *Chicago Tribune,* January 30, 1997, Business section, 1.
3. "How Crayola Used Marketing That's Almost Totally PR," *PR Reporter*, September 12, 1994, 1.
4. Paul Holmes, "When Product Tampering Pays Off," *Inside PR*, March 1991, 72.
5. "Celebrating a Milestone," *Promo Magazine*, April 1997, R7.

Chapter 9

1. "Hipping Up Hush Puppies," *Newsweek*, November 6, 1995, 10.
2. Amy Spindler, "Famous Feet Pick Old Favorites," *New York Times*, November 14, 1995, B12.
3. Jack O'Dwyer, "JWT PR Mixes Diamonds with Hush Puppies," *Jack O'Dwyer's Newsletter*, December 1995, 5.
4. Joan Hamilton, "Miracle Drug: Aspirin," *Business Week*, August 29, 1988, 56–61.
5. Sheryl Stolberg, "The Little White Pill That Could," *Los Angeles Times,* September 29, 1994, 1.

Chapter 11

1. Stuart Elliot, "A Magazine Offers Its List of the 50 Best TV Commercials Ever," *New York Times*, March 28, 1997, C2.
2. Randall Rothenberg, "Commercials Become News and the Airtime Is Free," *New York Times*, January 8, 1990.
3. "Drive Happy," *Reputation Management*, November–December 1996, 45.
4. Melanie Wells, "The Quest for Free Ink, Free Air," *USA Today*, May 19, 1997, 3B.
5. "Nissan's Ad Campaign Was a Hit Everywhere but in the Showrooms," *Wall Street Journal*, April 8, 1997, A1.
6. Mary Ellen Kuhn, "More Winning Coffee Talk from Taster's Choice," *ASAP,* September 1994.

Chapter 13

1. George Lazarus, "Kids Offer Heinz Some Tasty Labels," *Chicago Tribune*, June 9, 1997.
2. Michelle Healy, "Sucrets Tin Yields to Age of Plastics," *USA Today*, July 19, 1994.
3. Glenn Collins, "New Looks for 2 Staples of the Medicine Cabinet," *New York Times*, July 19, 1994.
4. Jonathan Welsh, "If You Like to Secrete Treasures in Sucrets Tins, Better Stock Up," *Wall Street Journal,* July 19, 1994, B1.

Chapter 14

1. Thomas L. Harris, "PR Gets Personal," *Direct Marketing*, April 1994, 29.

Chapter 15

1. Larry Light and Jim Mullen, "Your Brand Is Your Future: A Client's Guide," *American Association of Advertising Agencies*, 1996, 39.

2. Terry Thompson, speech at IABC-Ragan Communications, "The 1996 Strategic Public Relations Conference," October 7, 1996.

Chapter 16
1. Erin Flynn, "Campbell's: If the Legacy Fits . . . ," *Brandweek*, October 10, 1994, 24.
2. "Betty to Join Friends in Flintstones Bottle," *Chicago Tribune*, October 23, 1995.

Chapter 17
1. Sue Jordan, speech at IABC-Ragan Communications, "The 1996 Strategic Public Relations Conference," October 7, 1996.
2. "Hog Wild," *Reputation Management,* May/June 1996, 57.

Chapter 20
1. Dirk Johnson, "15,000-Mile Olympic Torch Route Gives Lots of People Reasons to Feel Good," *New York Times*, May 23, 1996.
2. Adam Shell, "Media Runs with Torch Relay Story," *Public Relations Tactics,* August 1996.
3. The Coca-Cola Company 1995 Interim Report, 8.
4. The Coca-Cola Company 1996 Interim Report, 2.
5. *IEG Sponsorship Report*, 1996.
6. *USA Today,* August 1996.
7. Richard Roper, "Maybe the Box Is the Best Thing About Wheaties," *Chicago Sun-Times*, August 6, 1996, 11.
8. "Old-Fashioned PR Gives General Mills Advertising Bargains," *Wall Street Journal*, March 20, 1997, A1–6.

Chapter 21
1. Jennifer Mangan, "Heaping Helpings," *Chicago Tribune*, June 22, 1995, sec. 5, 3.
2. Gary Dretzka, "Disney Not Playing Around with *Toy Story* Marketing," *Chicago Tribune*, November 24, 1995, N.
3. Lindsay Chappell, "PR Makes Impressions, Sales," *Advertising Age*, March 22, 1993, S–16.
4. *Ibid.*
5. Leah Rickard and Raymond Serafin, "Neon Is Scoring 'Hi' in College Carriculum (sic)," *Advertising Age*, March 1995.

Chapter 22
1. Ocean Spray Annual Report, 1995.

Chapter 23
1. "The Future of Spending," *American Demographics*, January 1995, 14.

Chapter 24
1. Carol Cone, *The 1997 Cone/Roper Cause Related Marketing Trends Report.*
2. *Ibid.*
3. *Ibid.*
4. Robin Simons and Dr. Richard Stechel, *Doing Best by Doing Good* (New York: Dalton Books, 1992), 13.

5. Jonathan Alter, "Powell's New War," *Newsweek*, April 28, 1997, 32.

6. Ben Cohen and Jerry Greenfield, *Ben & Jerry's Double-Dip* (New York: Simon & Schuster, 1997), 30–31.

7. *Ibid.*

8. Ben & Jerry's 1994 Annual Report, 4.

9. Claudia Dreifus, "Passing the Scoop: Ben & Jerry's," *New York Times,* December 18, 1996, 38.

10. Fred "Chico" Lager, *Ben & Jerry's: The Inside Scoop* (New York: Crown Trade Books, 1994), 219–220.

11. Nancy Haas, "Squares Need Not Apply," *Newsweek,* June 27, 1994, 44.

12. Charles Siler, "Body Shop Marches to Its Own Drummer," *Advertising Age,* October 10, 1994, 4.

13. Valerie Reitman, "Success of Body Shop Natural Cosmetics Attracts Imitators to the Scent of Profits," *New York Times*, September 4, 1992, B4.

14. Joe Marconi, *Image Marketing.* (Lincolnwood, Ill.: NTC Business Books, 1996), 187.

15. "PR, Not Advertising, Spurs Body Shop's Growth in U.S.," *O'Dwyer's PR Services Report*, September 1992, 45.

16. Siler, 4.

17. American Express Advertisement in *The New Yorker*, August 1992.

Chapter 26

1. Adam Shell, "Pepsi's Big Scare," *Public Relations Journal*, August 1993, 6.

2. *Ibid.*, 7.

3. Michael Janofsky, "Under Siege Pepsi Mounts a TV Counteroffensive," *New York Times,* June 17, 1993.

4. Gary Strauss, "Scare Fails to Flatten Pepsi Sales," *USA Today*, June 24, 1993.

5. Marcy Magiera, "The Pepsi Crisis," *Advertising Age*, July 19, 1993, 14.

Part II

Chapter 27

1. Ron Kaatz, "Strategic Technique to Assess Media Possibilities," paper for Integrated Marketing Communications Department, Medill School of Journalism, Northwestern University, 1995.

2. "The Future of Spending," *American Demographics*, January 1995, 14.

Chapter 28

1. Roman G. Hiebing Jr., and Scott W. Cooper, *How To Write a Successful Marketing Plan* (Lincolnwood, Ill., NTC Business Books, 1994), 184.

Chapter 29

1. Ron Kaatz, "Strategic Technique to Assess Media Possibilities," paper for Integrated Marketing Communications Department, Medill School of Journalism, Northwestern University, 1995.

Chapter 30

1. Julian Dibbell, "Nielsen Rates the Net," *Time*, November 13, 1995, 121.

2. "Public Relations Will Play a Major Role in Interactive Media, Say Big PR Firms," *Interactive PR*, June 6–18, 1995, 3.

3. "Media in Cyperspace," study by Middleberg & Associates and Columbia University School of Journalism, 1995.
4. Elizabeth Gleick, "Read All About It," *Time,* October 21, 1996, 70.
5. "Internet Boom to Revamp Way PR Pros Deal with Reporters," *O'Dwyer's PR Services Report*, November 1996, 16.
6. *Ibid.*
7. John Markoff, "If Medium Is the Message the Message Is the Web," *New York Times*, November 2, 1995, c 5.

Chapter 31
1. Gary Levin, "Global PR Efforts on the Wane," *Advertising Age,* May 16, 1994.
2. Dr. Walter K. Lindenman, Ketchum Public Relations, "It's the Hottest Thing These Days in PR," a presentation at PRSA Counselors Academy, Key West, Florida, April 25, 1995.
3. Paul Holmes, "Old Fashioned Publicity Is the Priority at Pepsi," *Inside PR,* April 28, 1995, 4.
4. Joseph Pereira, "Toy Story: How Shrewd Marketing Made Elmo a Hit," *New York Times*, November 18, 1996.

Index

About the Author

THOMAS L. HARRIS IS MANAGING PARTNER OF THOMAS L. HARRIS & COMPANY, A Highland Park, Illinois, marketing and public relations management consultancy. He is also an adjunct professor in the Integrated Marketing Communications Division of the Medill School of Journalism, Northwestern University. He is the author of two other books, *The Marketer's Guide to Public Relations* (1991) and *Choosing & Working with Your Public Relations Firm* (1992).

Harris was formerly principal, president, and vice chairman of Golin/Harris Communications, one of the largest public relations firms in North America. Previously, he was president of the public relations division of Foote, Cone & Belding; executive vice president of Edelman Public Relations Worldwide; and vice president public relations of Needham, Harper & Steers. He holds a bachelor of arts degree from the University of Michigan and a master's degree in communications from the University of Chicago.